BARBECUE

BARBECUE

THE HISTORY OF AN AMERICAN INSTITUTION

REVISED AND EXPANDED SECOND EDITION

ROBERT F. MOSS

THE UNIVERSITY OF ALABAMA PRESS   TUSCALOOSA

The University of Alabama Press
Tuscaloosa, Alabama 35487-0380
uapress.ua.edu

Hardcover edition published 2020.
Paperback edition published 2025.
eBook edition published 2020.

Typeface: Adobe Caslon

Cover design: Michele Myatt Quinn

Paperback ISBN: 978-0-8173-6224-9

A previous edition of this book has been cataloged by the Library of
Congress.
ISBN: 978-0-8173-2065-2 (cloth)
E-ISBN: 978-0-8173-9312-0

For my father

CONTENTS

PREFACE TO THE SECOND EDITION

When I wrote the introduction to the first edition of this book almost a decade ago, I opened by observing that barbecue had long been a beloved American food and a popular topic for food writers, but very little had been written about its history. Indeed, most writing about barbecue to that point had focused on recipes, restaurants, and cooks. Few authors gave more than passing attention to how this great American tradition came to be. In particular, apart from a few pages of vague, speculative material in the midst of larger works, almost nothing had been written about the history of barbecue before 1900.

And little wonder, for—at the time, at least—the details of barbecue's history were not easily found. Barbecue men did not leave their personal papers to archives. The first recipes for pit-cooked barbecue did not appear in print until after the Civil War, and the first cookbooks devoted to the subject were not published until the 1940s. The history of barbecue before 1900 could be found only as fragments scattered lightly through newspapers, letters, private journals, and travel narratives. Reconstructing this history required sifting through reams of material to find the many disparate scraps and arranging them into a coherent story.

Fortunately, since the first edition was published, more and more writers have decided to take their own journeys into the food's history. Daniel Vaughn of *Texas Monthly* has studied the roots of Texas's barbecue tradition, identifying the first meat markets to sell barbecue on a regular basis in the Lone Star State and tracing the evolution of Texas's restaurants over the course of the twentieth century. Writers like Michael Twitty, author of *The Cooking Gene* (2017), have explored the role of barbecue in the lives of enslaved African Americans and traced its connections to African culinary traditions.

Others, like Robb Walsh and Rien Fertel, have taken personal journeys through America's great barbecue regions, talking to the men and women who practice the old art and pondering what it means for themselves and for the culture at large.

Arcadia Publishing, under its History Press imprint, launched a series of books devoted to the history of barbecue in specific American states or cities. In *Memphis Barbecue: A Succulent History of Smoke, Sauce & Soul* (2014), Craig Meek documents that city's long, rich restaurant tradition, while Mark Johnson tells the story from an Alabama perspective in *An Irresistible History of Alabama Barbecue: From Wood Pit to White Sauce* (2017). Joe Haynes, author of *Virginia Barbecue: A History* (2016), dug deep into the Virginia tradition and its roots in the Caribbean, and he turned up a trove of details from the early colonial era. (He also uncovered the story of the "barbecue trees" on the Capitol Grounds in Washington, DC, which I discuss in chapter 2.)

I've continued to dig further into the history, too, and the tools of the trade—online newspaper archives, digitized books, genealogical databases—get better with each passing year. The efforts of my fellow researchers and my own subsequent diggings have not dramatically reshaped the overall narrative that I laid out in the original edition of this book. They have, instead, added much more color, nuance, and detail to the story—put a lot more meat on the bones, if you will—and they've helped fill in a number of previous gaps or ambiguities in the story.

So what's new? In the original edition, I brushed lightly over the early roots of barbecue in the Caribbean and South America, starting the story proper with the arrival of barbecue in the British colonies in North America. But how it got to the American colonies has been the topic of much debate in recent years, and this time around I go into much more depth on barbecue's Native American roots, drawing on information uncovered by other authors as well as my own reexamination of the period. I filled in a lot of gaps and smoothed out the story in the nineteenth century, too, adding more information about the creation of Brunswick stew (including a recipe from 1870) while streamlining the discussion of the cultural context for the evolving food tradition.

More names and faces appear in this expanded edition. In the original one, I identified Levi and Katie Nunn, who briefly operated a barbecue stand in downtown Charlotte, North Carolina, as the first barbecue restaurateurs whose names were captured in the historical record. The Nunns opened their stand in 1899, but we can take commercial barbecue operations back further now, and this edition includes a lot more material on early barbecue stands and other commercial operations. It includes new profiles of the individuals who pioneered the craft of barbecue, too, like A. M. Verner of Atlanta and John Mills, Memphis's first famous rib cook.

Not coincidentally, many of these pioneers—John Mills among them—were people of color, and for too long their names have been excluded from culinary histories. In many cases these omissions are due to outright bias and fallacies about how American food (and southern food in particular) originated and evolved. They have been compounded by the simple fact that the names of the people who helped create and transmit America's barbecue traditions—enslaved workers tending the pits in the plantation era, early commercial pioneers during the Jim Crow days—were rarely captured in newspaper and magazine accounts. The increased availability of digitized, searchable texts and online genealogical records has allowed us to start piecing together more of the story. This edition includes a more detailed and nuanced account of the career of John W. Callaway, the famous (white) barbecuing sheriff of Wilkes County, Georgia, and that account includes a name that did not appear in the original edition: Henry Pettus, the African American man who actually managed the barbecue cooking that earned Callaway national fame. This edition also offers new profiles of two of Pettus's contemporaries, Pickens Wells and Gus Ferguson, two notable barbecue men from Augusta, Georgia, whose stories were almost lost to history.

Since the original edition was published, a few (but fortunately just a few) of America's classic barbecue restaurants have closed their doors. A great many still remain, and since signing on as the contributing barbecue editor for *Southern Living* magazine, I've had the opportunity to visit a whole lot more of them and talk with the families who operate them. As a result, I've expanded the discussion of early restaurants in chapter 6 and added more "classic examples" where readers can sample the distinctive style of each region. The original version inexplicably skipped the state of Kentucky and the origins of the mutton-centric barbecue that lives on today in and around Owensboro. That sin of omission has been rectified. The sections on other states have been expanded, incorporating additional restaurants and adding biographical details about early restaurateurs. The original book addressed the late nineteenth and early twentieth century wave of African American migration that shaped the early barbecue scene in cities like Houston and Kansas City, but it omitted a later movement—the Second Great Migration—that took southern-style barbecue even farther to places like

Chicago, Oakland, and Los Angeles. The new edition adds the story of South Side Chicago barbecue and its signature glass-walled aquarium smokers.

As I was revising the manuscript, it struck me that the original title of chapter 8, "The Golden Age of Barbecue," needed to be amended. Back in 2008, when I was completing the first edition, it was clear that barbecue had rebounded from near extinction in the low years of the 1970s and 1980s. But it had not returned to anything approaching its former prominence on the American culinary scene during the years right after World War II. From the vantage point of 2019, though, things look very different, for we are indeed in the midst of a full-on barbecue renaissance. So, chapter 8 became "The First Golden Age of Barbecue," and I added a new afterword to make the case that we are now living in the Second Golden Age.

In 2008, it appeared that high-tech "gas-assist" cookers had won the field and that traditional wood-cooked barbecue would soon be a relic of the twentieth century. Barbecue competitions, chain restaurants, and commercial sauces were blurring old regional lines and carrying us relentlessly toward the single homogenized style that sociologist and wood-cooked barbecue evangelist John Shelton Reed has termed the "International House of Barbecue." Like many writers, I accepted without skepticism the much-repeated explanation for why so many barbecue restaurateurs had switched to electric- or gas-powered cookers: that they had been forced to by health departments and other meddling bureaucrats. Since the first edition of this book was published, though, I've become increasingly suspicious of that claim.

One reason for that suspicion was the outcome (or lack thereof) of the True 'Cue Challenge, which was laid forth by Reed and his collaborator Dan Levine. In 2014, their Campaign for Real Barbecue publicly announced a prize to anyone who could identify a statute or regulation that forbade barbecue restaurants from cooking with wood or could name a single governmental official who had actually forced a restaurant to switch to gas. The prize was an apron embroidered with a "No Faux 'Cue" logo. When no one stepped forth to take the challenge, they threw in first a ball cap and then a free barbecue sandwich at the legendary Allen & Son in Chapel Hill. To date there have still been no takers, and I delve further into the claim of governmental antiwood bias in chapter 9.

But we don't need unclaimed aprons to prove that someone can open a twenty-first-century restaurant with wood-fired pits, for so many people have gone out and done it. In the space of just a few short years, dozens of aspiring restaurateurs have launched traditional wood-cooked barbecue operations in towns and cities across the country. They've been looking back to the past, studying the techniques of the old brisket masters in Lockhart, Texas, and whole hog cooks in the Carolinas while carrying the tradition forward, merging it with the sensibilities of contemporary fine dining and adding flavors and elements borrowed from food cultures around the globe.

Today, barbecue is riding high again, and for me that's a very encouraging development.

ACKNOWLEDGMENTS

First Edition

This project began almost ten years ago when I went to the University of South Carolina library to read about the history of barbecue. I discovered, to my surprise, that not only had no one written a full book on the subject but there really wasn't much historical research published on barbecue at all. For several years I haphazardly collected old newspaper stories and diary entries about barbecue and slowly began piecing together the story. This research eventually evolved into a book. During that time, I had two children, changed jobs three times, and moved cities and houses three times, too.

As with any project with this long a gestation, there are dozens of people who helped along the way, and I am sure I will forget more than a few of those who deserve thanks. John Shelton Reed shared valuable research, encouragement, and much-needed advice as I was finishing this book and trying to figure out how to get it published. I owe him and Dale Vosberg Reed a big blowout at Hominy Grill. Jeff Allen and John T. Edge read chapters from the manuscript, and their comments helped make it better.

By the time I'd gotten seriously under way on this project, Robert W. Trogdon had already been exiled to the barbecue-less backwoods of Ohio, but he and I ate a lot of mustard-sauced pork together in Columbia, South Carolina, and he helped fuel my early passion for the subject.

The interlibrary loan staff at the Charleston County Public Library were invaluable in helping me complete my work far from the walls of a research library, and Ray Quiel of San Bernardino, California, was very generous in providing material on the early McDonald's restaurants back before they gave up barbecue in favor of hamburgers.

The whole team at the University of Alabama Press has done a remarkable job of taking an unwieldy manuscript and turning it into a finished book, and I thank them all for their efforts.

And finally, I owe a tremendous debt to my wife, Jennifer, who has always been my strongest supporter and has patiently endured countless side trips down country roads seeking out obscure barbecue joints in the days before GPS. I'm not contesting her claim that this whole project was just a big ruse to allow me to eat barbecue every weekend in the name of "research," but at least I have a book to show for it.

—Mount Pleasant, South Carolina, December 2009

Second Edition

This new edition of *Barbecue: The History of an American Institution* is better and more complete thanks to the contributions of many kind and passionate individuals. Over the past nine years, I have learned much and have been greatly inspired—both through reading and in conversations—by my fellow barbecue writers, especially John Shelton Reed, Jim Shahin, Daniel Vaughn, Kathleen Purvis, Adrian Miller, Robb Walsh, Jim Auchmutey, and Rien Fertel. Joe Haynes generously shared the new material he turned up while working on his history of Virginia barbecue, which helped fill in important gaps in the original narrative.

Sid Evans and Krissy Tiglias at *Southern Living* have been generous in supporting my long-running project to explore and celebrate the vibrant diversity of barbecue restaurants across the South—and kudos to Hunter Lewis for helping conceive the whole project in the first place. I am grateful as well to the talented pitmasters who have tolerated my hanging out around their pits and asking naive questions over the years.

A big thanks to Dan Waterman at the University of Alabama Press for seeing the value in a second edition of this history, and to the whole team at the press for pulling it together.

And once again, I must acknowledge the forbearance of my wife, Jennifer, who thought all this barbecue nonsense was finished when the first edition came out. This time around, I must also thank my sons, Bobby and Charlie, who are now old enough to protest endless barbecue detours during family trips but only occasionally do. I promise the next book will be about mac 'n' cheese.

—Mount Pleasant, South Carolina, November 2019

INTRODUCTION

THE STORY OF BARBECUE involves much more than explaining how people came to roast whole pigs or beef briskets over open pits. It is the story of a vital institution in American life. The specific term "barbecue" originated among the various Native American tribes in the Caribbean and along the eastern coast of North America, and it was adopted by English colonists and enslaved Africans in the seventeenth and eighteenth centuries. The word was used throughout the American colonies to refer to the cooking technique as well as the social event, but the institution took root most firmly in Virginia and became an essential part of Tidewater plantation culture. From there it spread southward through the Carolinas and into Georgia and across the Appalachians into Tennessee and Kentucky, following the main pattern of southern settlement. In the early nineteenth century, the barbecue tradition moved westward with American settlers across the Gulf states and into Texas, and later through the Southwest all the way to the Pacific coast.

Barbecue has always been more than just something to eat. For three centuries it has been a vital part of American social and political life. Entire communities would come together at barbecues for celebration and recreation and to express their shared values. In the early years of the republic, Fourth of July barbecues were not just a time to celebrate the nation's independence but also a means of reinforcing the democratic values of the community. The tradition has evolved over time, following the larger evolution of American society. In colonial days, barbecues were rough, rowdy festivals accompanied—like much of frontier life—by drunkenness and fistfights. In the early nineteenth century, the reform movements that transformed American society—most notably the temperance movement—also changed the character of barbecues. The events became more staid and ritualized, evolving into respectable affairs that bound communities together. They also became an essential part of the political life of the nation, as events staged by politicians to woo potential voters and as expressions of community support for leaders and causes. For decades, barbecues were the traditional way to honor local politicians for their service, and they played a prominent role in the sectionalist controversies that led to the Civil War. Such events rallied support for secession, honored troops as they were sent off to battle, and survived the war as the standard form of large-scale civic celebration in the South and West.

Before the Civil War and after, barbecue was a tradition shared by white and black Americans alike, and the issues of race are intertwined with the food's history. Enslaved African Americans did most of the cooking at the large barbecues hosted and attended by whites, and they played a formative role in developing the techniques and recipes of southern barbecue. Barbecues were a popular form of recreation for enslaved people, too, at events they staged for themselves and also as a form of paternalistic entertainment granted by slaveholders as a means of reward and control. After emancipation, barbecue continued to play a key role in the lives of African Americans, serving as the center of a wide range of community celebrations and becoming a core part of African American foodways.

One of the most significant changes in barbecue culture occurred around the turn of the twentieth century, when it became a product of commerce. Before the 1890s, barbecue was almost never sold but instead given away at public festivals, which were generally hosted by organizations or prominent citizens and open to all members of the community. This began to change when itinerant barbecue men started selling their services for events such as school commencements and other celebrations. These cooks would set up tents on special occasions such as the Fourth of July, Labor Day, and court days in county seats and on street corners in cities. The tents evolved into more permanent structures, and the modern barbecue restaurant was born.

The restaurant trade helped create today's distinctive regional variations of barbecue. Cooks settled on a few types of meat based on local tastes and availability. In the Southeast, pork was the standard, but goat and mutton were common in Kentucky, and in Texas and the West beef was king. Regional variations became more pronounced over the decades, with cooking styles, sauces, and side dishes becoming distinctive to each region. Business was boosted by the rise of the automobile, and barbecue stands became an iconic feature of the roadside not just in the South but across the country. Some but not many of these establishments survive today as legendary barbecue restaurants, such as Sprayberry's in Newnan, Georgia, and McClard's in Hot Springs, Arkansas. Most did not last, their slow-cooking methods and diverse regional variations ill suited to the standardized demands of the fast-food industry.

But the very qualities that kept barbecue from becoming a fast-food staple are what make it a classic American dish today. No one travels from town to town sampling cheeseburgers, and no one has heated debates over which state serves the best chicken fingers. A newspaper article on tomatoes or fried chicken is unlikely to generate much controversy, but one on barbecue is almost guaranteed to provoke dozens of angry letters to the editor (or, in 2020, a flood of abuse on Twitter). Something about barbecue brings out the passion in both cooks and eaters. Few American dishes can boast of the sheer variety of barbecue, whose ingredients and cooking styles can differ completely in restaurants separated by only a few hundred miles, creating strong geographic preferences and loyalties. Barbecue as an event remains an important form of celebration and gathering, be it for family reunions, campaign fundraisers, or outdoor festivals; and the art and science of cooking barbecue is enjoying a remarkable resurgence throughout the country.

Most of all, barbecue has shown an enduring power to bring people together. From the very beginning, the eating of barbecue was a powerful social magnet, drawing people from a wide range of classes and geographic backgrounds. Because of this, it has played an important role in three centuries of American history, reflecting and influencing the direction of an evolving society. As Americans founded a nation, defined their civic values, expanded democracy, built canals and railroads, and threw themselves westward, barbecue was there. The same forces that shaped the larger contours of American life influenced barbecue, too, and over time the institution evolved to reflect the country's progression from a rural, agricultural society to an industrialized, commercial world power. To trace the story of barbecue is to trace the very thread of American history.

This is that story.

1

BARBECUE IN COLONIAL AMERICA

IN THE SUMMER OF 1707, a group of Englishmen gathered in the town of Peckham, just south of London, for a most un-British feast. Drunk on "the American tipple"—that is, rum—they built a rack of sticks and started a fire beneath it. Once the fire had burned down to coals, they laid long wooden spits across the range and hoisted three whole pigs on top. As the swine roasted, the cook basted them with a combination of green Virginia pepper and Madeira wine, using a fox's tail tied to a long stick. After many hours of cooking, the pigs were removed from the fire, laid upon a log, and divided into quarters with an ax. They were then distributed to the gathered revelers, who delighted in what writer Ned Ward described as "Incomparable Food, fit for the Table of a Sagamoor."

The details of this feast were captured by Ward, a London satirist, in his pamphlet *The Barbacue Feast: or, the Three Pigs of Peckham, Broiled under an Apple-Tree* (1707). Roasting meat over flames was nothing new to Englishmen, of course, but the event Ward witnessed struck him as decidedly foreign to British tastes and traditions. The feast, he explained, was staged because the organizers had "their English appetites so deprav'd and vitiated" by "the American tipple" that they craved "a Litter of Pigs most nicely cook'd after the West Indian manner." The hogs were cooked whole "with their Heads, Tails, Pettitoes, and Hoofs on . . . according to the Indian Fashion."[1]

Ironically, this description of a Caribbean-inspired barbecue staged in England is the most detailed account we have of a barbecue from the early colonial period. The feast displayed many of the features that we would find today at a community barbecue in the Carolinas: whole hogs cooked slowly over a pit of coals and basted with a spicy sauce. Then, as now, barbecue was more than just a type of food or a method of cooking. It was also an event, a form of social gathering that brought people together from across the community. Indeed, the attendees at the feast Ward witnessed included "the best Part of the town of Peckham" as well as those "of lower Rank and Quality." The festivities began long before the food was served, for the cooking itself was part of the experience. The citizens watched with fascination as the range was constructed and the fire stoked. Once the pigs were laid upon the spits, the crowd gathered around, "expressing as much Joy in the Looks and Actions, as a Gang of wild Canibals who, when they have taken a Stranger, first dance round him, and afterwards devour him."

Like many a barbecue writer to follow, Ned Ward was prone to purple prose, but his descriptions capture the ritualistic nature of barbecue that was present from the very beginning. Those rituals quickly became ingrained in the culture of the British colonies, and later they would become an integral part of the social life of the young United States.

But what is barbecue, this American practice that so intrigued Englishmen like Ward? In the broadest sense, the word today can simply mean food cooked over a fire—usually meat, like hamburgers or shrimp kebabs, or even vegetables, like corn on the cob. For many Americans, though, the word has a more precise definition. It is, for starters, a particular kind of food, though its nature might vary greatly from one part of the country to another. When eastern North Carolinians say, "Let's go get some barbecue," they are referring to finely chopped bits of smoked pork mixed with a vinegar-based sauce. Texans saying the same thing usually mean sliced beef brisket and sausage, while someone from Memphis may be talking about a tray of pork ribs. As different as these definitions are, there are a few common qualities to what Americans call barbecue: meat cooked slowly over wood coals and served (usually) with a sweet or spicy sauce.

But barbecue has always been more than just something to eat. It is also a social event—the occasion when barbecue is cooked and served. This may be something small and informal—a handful of friends grilling out in the backyard for a weekend barbecue—or it might be a major production. When a southern church holds a barbecue, its organizers arrange rows of folding tables on the grounds and let people park their cars on the grass once they overflow the parking lot. In many parts of the country, a barbecue is the standard way to celebrate a wedding, kick off a political campaign, or pass the hat for a charitable cause. If you want to get a lot of people together, a barbecue is the way to do it. And it has been this way for a very long time.

A Native American Technique

By the time Ned Ward wrote his pamphlet in 1707, the cooking of pigs and other whole animals over open pits was a popular pastime in the English colonies in the Caribbean and also up and down the Atlantic coast of North America. How those colonists came to cook those animals over glowing coals is the subject of some debate among historians and food writers. Almost every account has it emerging from the intersection of European, Native American, and African foodways in the early colonial era. The proportion in which each culture contributed is where the disagreement lies.[2]

What we know for sure is that by the time the first European explorers arrived in the Western Hemisphere, Native Americans on the Caribbean islands and on the mainland of Central and South America shared a common cooking technique and used a similar word to describe it. The first known account of this word and technique appears in the writing of Gonzalo Fernández de Oviedo y Valdés, who was part of two Spanish expeditions to the New World that took him to modern-day Antigua, Colombia, and Panama. After returning to Spain, he captured his experiences in *A Natural History of the West Indies* (1526), which included a chapter on the customs, rites, and ceremonies of the "Indians of Terra Firma"—meaning Native Americans on the Isthmus of Panama instead of the Caribbean islands. Fish were the natives' primary source of food, but Oviedo noted the presence of "wild pigs and deer, which they also kill and eat." These they would trap with nets or hunt with arrows and spears. Because they had no knives to skin or dress the animals, they would instead "cut them to pieces with stones and flints" and then "roast the flesh on sticks which they place in the ground, like a grating or trivet, over a pit. They call these barbacoas, and place fire beneath, and in this manner they roast fish also."[3]

Several decades later, a Frenchman named Jean de Léry encountered a similar cooking technique near the Bay of Rio de Janeiro in Brazil. In his *Histoire d'un voyage fait en la terre du Bresil* (1578), de Léry described how the Tupinambá constructed an apparatus "which in their language they call Boucan." They started out by placing in the earth "four forks of wood, each as big as their arm, in squares of about three feet in width and two and a half feet in height." Upon this frame they would lay sticks, "one

The broyling of their fish ouer the flame of fier

Native Americans barbecuing fish in North Carolina, watercolor by English artist John White, who sailed with Richard Grenville in 1588 to explore the coast of present-day North Carolina.

or two fingers close to each other, making in this manner a large wooden grate." Upon this Boucan the Americans cooked fish as well as tapir, which de Léry noted had "almost the same taste as that of beef." They put the carcasses on the grate with "a slow fire under . . . turning it every half an hour." In 1585, Thomas Hariot, a member of Sir Walter Raleigh's failed colony on Roanoke Island, observed the Americans there broiling their fish in the exact same manner as the Tupinambá in Brazil. Hariot describes four stakes placed in the ground "in a square roome" and four poles laid upon them, "and others over thwart the same like unto an hurdle." Another of the Roanoke colonists, John White, depicted this cooking process in a series of watercolor paintings, and from these the Belgian artist Theodor de Bry created engravings that were published in Hariot's travelogue *A Briefe and True Report of the New Found Land of Virginia* (1589). These are the first pictorial representations we have of the American practice of barbecuing.[4]

The cooking technique that Hariot described was widespread along the eastern coast of North America. In *The History of Virginia* (1705), Robert Beverley noted about the local tribes: "They have two ways of broiling, vis. one by laying the Meat itself upon the

Ein höltzern Roost/darauff sie die XIIII.
Fische besengen.

[Gothic German text within the engraving]

1590 engraving by Theodor de Bry based on John White's watercolor. The image is from the German edition of Thomas Hariot's *A Brief and True Report of the New Found Land of Virginia.* (Courtesy Library of Congress, Prints and Photographs Division)

coals, the other by laying it upon sticks raised upon forks at some distance above the live coals, which heats more gently, and dries up the gravy; this they, and we also from them, call barbecuing." John Brickell's *Natural History of North-Carolina* (1737) indicates that the Native Americans in this area, like those in the Caribbean, used barbecue racks for dual purposes. The first was to dry meat for preservation: "They commonly barbecu or dry their Venison on Mats or Hurdles in the Sun, first salting it with their Salt, which is made of the Ashes of the Hickory Wood." The second, more common usage was for cooking meat, particularly wild turkeys, which "they Barbecue and eat

Early Florida barbecue. Engraving by Theodor de Bry after a painting by Jacques le Moyne de Morgues, a French artist who traveled through North Florida in 1564 and documented the Timucua culture.

with Bears's grease, this is accounted amongst them a good Dish." The technique was also used for fish and shellfish, which they would "open and dry upon Hurdles, keeping a constant Fire under them; these Hurdles are made of Reeds or Hollow Canes, in shape of a Grid-iron." Barbecuing several bushels at a time, the Native Americans would preserve skates, oysters, and cockles for times of scarcity.[5]

Neither Beverley nor Brickell was a fan of Native American cooking. Beverley claimed that it had "nothing commendable in it, but that it is performed with little trouble." Their fellow colonists must have disagreed, for barbecuing was soon adopted by British settlers in an area spanning from the Carolinas all the way to New England. But how did this Native American word and the cooking technique it described cross over to become commonly used by the Europeans and Africans within the early American colonies? The short answer is that we don't really know.

Ned Ward's account of the barbecue in Peckham, England, is notable because of the characteristics he identifies as being "the West Indian manner" or "the Indian

Fashion." These include the wooden range on which the pigs were roasted and the fact that they were cooked whole "with their Heads, Tails, Pettitoes, and Hoofs on"—a method quite different from roasting joints of meat on a spit, as the English did. Prior to Ward's travelogue, all the known accounts describe a cooking apparatus and technique used by Native Americans, not by Europeans or Africans. The *Three Pigs of Peckham*, which was published in 1707, is the first known depiction of a barbecue cook who was not Native American—though Ward makes clear that his English cooks were following "the West Indian manner." Sometime in the late seventeenth century, it seems, newcomers to the Western Hemisphere began adopting a Native American cooking technique, and they soon made it their own. I say "newcomers" here, because the practice of slavery was present in the English and Spanish colonies long before we have any record of colonists cooking meat in the Native American barbecue style. Both European and African foodways have long traditions of roasting meats over fire, and the Native American technique seems likely to have held equal appeal for all the cultures that intersected in the North American colonies.

We do know, however, that by the early eighteenth century barbecue had been adopted not only as a method of cooking but also as an event in all the British North American colonies, including those in New England. This may seem surprising considering how rare barbecue is in that region today, but some of the earliest written records of American barbecues are for events in Massachusetts and Maine. In 1733, Benjamin Lynde Jr. of Salem wrote a cryptic diary entry for August 31: "Fair and hot; Browne, Barbacue; hack overset." Lexicographers have interpreted this to mean that Lynde went to a barbecue with Mr. Browne and had an unfortunate carriage accident along the way. If they're right, it's the first written usage of "barbecue" in the sense of a gathering or an event. Other Massachusetts diaries from the period show a similar usage. The Reverend Ebenezer Bridge of Chelmsford recorded "a Barbacue in Dracut" in 1752, while the diary of Mary Holyoke of Salem references three "barbeques" between May 1761 and June 1762. Barbecues were held as far north as Falmouth, Maine, where in 1759, following the fall of Quebec City during the French and Indian War, the citizens celebrated with a "festal barbecue" on an island in the harbor. This island would later become known as "Hog Island" because of the event.[6]

The popularity of barbecues as a form of entertainment continued to grow in Massachusetts through the eve of the American Revolution. In 1767, seventy gentlemen were invited to a barbecue to celebrate the launching of the brigantine *Barnard* at Braintree. Two years later, Thomas Carnes announced in a newspaper advertisement that he was opening a tea and coffee house about four miles outside Boston where, he promised, "If any select Company at any Time should incline to have a Barbecue, either Turtle or Pigg, they may depend having it done in the best Manner." This flourishing of barbecue in New England proved short-lived, though. The events faded from the region following the Revolution and were rarely seen thereafter. It took almost two centuries before barbecue—in the form of Texas-inspired restaurants—returned to New England's culinary landscape.[7]

Barbecue Takes Root in Virginia

It was farther south, in Virginia, that the institution of barbecue took its strongest root in colonial America. Both as a food and as a social event, barbecue was more consistent with the tastes of Virginians than with those of New Englanders, for reasons deeply rooted in the cultural backgrounds of the colonists. The English who colonized America are often portrayed as if they all came from a single, homogeneous British culture, but there were significant differences in the customs and tastes of the various American colonies. Their residents came from different parts of Britain and therefore had different regional habits and preferences, including how they cooked and entertained and what they liked to eat.

In New England, baking was the favored method, while boiling predominated in the Delaware Valley and Southern Highlands. Tidewater Virginians inherited a culture of roasting and broiling from their forebears, who came mostly from southern and western England, so the wood fires of the barbecue pit were a natural fit. Feasting was also a more vital part of the culture of Virginia than of Massachusetts. New Englanders might eat and drink heavily every now and then (such as at annual Thanksgiving celebrations or to commemorate the death of a neighbor), but almost any event was occasion for feasting in Virginia: a marriage, a christening, Christmas, Easter, and visits from family members—or from anyone else, for that matter.[8]

Another reason that barbecue was so popular in Virginia is that the colony had a lot of pigs. Swine first arrived in the New World in 1493 on the second voyage of Christopher Columbus, who brought eight hogs to the island of Hispaniola. Descendants of these pigs were brought to the North American mainland by Hernando de

The Derivation of the Word

MOST LEXICOGRAPHERS HAVE concluded that the English word "barbecue" and its Spanish equivalent, *barbacoa*, were adopted from Taino, one of the Arawakan languages spoken in the Caribbean and on the northern coast of South America. It was the term for a frame of green sticks that was used both as a sleeping platform and for smoking or drying meat. Initially, the word had the dual meaning of a physical piece of equipment and a method of cooking. Gonzalo Fernández de Oviedo y Valdés recoded it as "barbacoa" in *A Natural History of the West Indies* (1526). The English form first appeared in print over a century later in Edmund Hickeringill's travel narrative *Jamaica Viewed* (1661), which described the hunting of animals: "Some are slain, And their flesh forthwith Barbacu'd and eat." Other explorers recorded the term (often spelled "borbecue" or "barbecu"), as well as the similar-sounding "boucan," to describe the cooking technique being used by Native Americans from New England all the way to Brazil. ("Boucan," incidentally, spawned the word "buccaneer," the anglicized version of the French *boucanier*, a term that originally described French hunters on the island of Hispaniola who cooked feral pigs on boucans and was later applied to privateers in the Caribbean.)

By the end of the seventeenth century the word "barbecue" had moved into common English usage as a synonym for roasting or grilling, even outside the context of food. In Aphra Behn's play *The Widow Ranter* (1690), a riotous crowd seizes a rebel

Soto in 1539, and many escaped and turned feral. These Spanish pigs are believed by some scholars to be the ancestors of the Arkansas razorback and other wild southern pigs, and many barbecue writers have tried to link them to the birth of the American barbecue tradition. The pigs cooked at Virginia barbecues, however, had British, not Spanish, roots. Many were brought to Jamestown on the first three ships of the Virginia Company in 1607. Just two years after they landed, the colonists possessed only seven horses and a few goats and sheep, but they had between five hundred and six hundred swine.[9]

Pigs were the ideal livestock for the Virginia colonists. They are prolific animals, with a four-month gestation time and an average litter size of ten or more. Being and demands, "Let's barbicu this fat Rogue." Cotton Mather used the term to describe the burning deaths of Native Americans in Massachusetts: "When they came to see the bodies of so many of their countrymen terribly barbikew'd." (From the very beginning, no one could agree on the proper spelling. We still argue over it today.)

Lexicographers have pretty well established the word's origins, but that hasn't prevented people from coming up with their own, more fanciful derivations. The most common of these is from the French *barbe-a-queue*, or beard-to-tail, referring to the cooking of whole hogs over the pit. This hoary explanation has been bandied around for almost two centuries, appearing in print as early as 1829 and frequently listed in general reference works as a legitimate alternative derivation to the Native American origins. The editors of the *Oxford English Dictionary*, however, dismiss "barbe-a-queue" as "an absurd conjecture suggested merely by the sound of the word." Other oft-repeated stories are that the word originated from a restaurant offering whiskey, beer, and pool along with its roasted pork (bar-beer-cue), or from a rancher with the initials B. Q. who branded his cattle with the two letters topped by a bar, or Bar-B-Q Ranch. These come from the school of popular etymology known as "just making stuff up," for the word "barbecue" is clearly much older than such explanations would allow.

Source: *The Oxford English Dictionary*, 2nd ed. (Oxford University Press, 1989); *OED Online*, http://dictionary.oed.com/cgi/entry/00181778.

omnivores, they are easy to feed and, left to their own devices, are adept at rooting out food. Of all the domesticated animals they are the most efficient in terms of translating energy intake into pounds of meat. Virginians were notoriously lax at animal husbandry and tended to let their livestock roam free in the woods rather than erecting fences or sties. The pigs flourished in the forests, with their plentiful acorns and chestnuts, and Virginians hunted them like wild game at slaughter time, earning a substantial return of meat with minimal care and feeding. This allowed Virginians to focus on more pressing pursuits, like trying to get rich growing tobacco.[10]

Grazing pigs in the woods required a lot of forestland, and Virginia had plenty of it. After the colonists settled on tobacco as their primary cash crop, the colony grew rapidly. By the 1670s settlements stretched out from Jamestown along the shores of Chesapeake Bay and pushed their way up the banks of the James, Rappahannock, and Potomac Rivers. A Virginia planter needed lots of land with nearby water for transport and plenty of forest in which his livestock could roam, and the number of pigs owned by these planters grew by leaps and bounds. At the time of his death in 1651, Ralph Wormeley of "Rosegill" plantation on the Rappahannock had 439 head of cattle, 86 sheep, and "too many pigs to count." Inventories of estates regularly excluded swine because no one knew where to find the pigs to count them.[11]

Thanks to its residents' inherent love of feasting and the easy availability of pork, Virginia was perfectly positioned to become the cradle of American barbecue. A final factor was the value that the emerging plantation society placed on home and hospitality. Once the agricultural economy had developed sufficiently to support large plantations and the building of "great houses," the dinner table became the central focus of elite Virginia society, and it was common for planters to throw open their homes to dozens of guests for dinners and dancing. As these entertainments grew, they moved outdoors, allowing planters to extend their hospitality widely without encroaching on the formalities of the household.[12]

By the 1750s, outdoor barbecues were one of the chief forms of entertainment in the Tidewater colony. On July 21, 1758, John Kirkpatrick wrote to George Washington and complained about life in Alexandria during the French and Indian War: "To tell you our Domestick occurrences would look silly—& ill sute your time to peruse—We have dull Barbecues—and yet Duller Dances—An Election causes a Hubub for a Week or so—& then we are dead a While." Washington himself was a frequent barbecue guest. In his diary he recorded attending six such events between 1769 and 1774—including, on September 18, 1773, "a Barbicue of my own giving at Accotinck."[13]

Barbecues had evolved from casual gatherings of families and friends into a more formal social institution. A "barbecue day" was spent feasting and celebrating from morning until late into the evening and drew attendees from all levels of society. Most accounts of barbecues from this period can be found in brief journal entries or newspaper items, and their authors spend little time describing the type of meat that was served, how it was prepared, or how it was served to guests. In 1784, however, Lawrence Butler, who had recently arrived in Westmorland County from London, wrote to a family member back home in England that he was very happy since arriving in

Virginia and enjoying the frequent balls and barbecue. "The latter I don't suppose you know what I mean," he wrote, and then offered a description: "It's a shoat & sometimes a Lamb or Mutton & indeed sometimes a large Beef split into & stuck on spits & then they have a large Hole dugg in the ground where they have a number of Coals made of the Bark of Trees." They cooked the meat six inches from coals, basting it with "butter & Salt & water" and turning it occasionally until it was done. "We then dine under a large shady Tree or an harbour made of green bushes," Butler reported, "under which we have benches & seats to sit on when we dine sumptuously." Horse racing occupied the rest of the afternoon, and then the party would retire to one of the local gentry's houses where they would dance the rest of the evening before retiring to the guest rooms.[14]

Over time, the barbecue became part of the political sphere as well, and it was in Virginia that the first campaign barbecues were held. Election days in colonial Virginia were infrequent, occurring whenever the governor dissolved the Assembly or a member quit or died. Each county was allotted two seats in the House of Burgesses, the only real elected body in the colony. To choose their representatives, eligible voters would gather at the county courthouse, coming into town in wagons and on horseback from miles around. Elections were usually held on court days, when many men would already be traveling to the county seat to conduct business such as buying and selling land, slaves, and supplies. These gatherings were rowdy events, with lots of liquor and fistfights, and the candidates didn't need exit polling to know how their constituents voted. The casting of ballots occurred publicly in the courthouse in front of the sheriff and the competing candidates, which only added to the drama of the day.[15]

According to the unwritten code of political conduct, candidates in Virginia were supposed to compete on their natural virtues and abilities, staying aloof from voters and not stooping to active campaigning. But doing so was a surefire way to lose, and office seekers knew they needed to go out among the voters and drum up support. The practice of "treating"—plying voters with liquor and food—was widespread, and though practiced discreetly, it became an indispensable component of a campaign. Election treats always included copious quantities of rum punch and other liquors, and often sweets such as cookies and ginger cakes. Some candidates took the practice a step further, hosting outdoor picnics for the public and providing barbecued bullocks and pigs—the first instances of American campaign barbecues.[16]

Three Views of Virginia Barbecues

ONE OF THE more detailed early descriptions of Virginia barbecue appears in the journals of Nicholas Cresswell, a young Englishman who came to the colony in 1774 to tour the Tidewater region and the frontier lands to its west. In July 1774, as Cresswell was taking passage on a boat down the Potomac River, he attended a barbecue, which he described in his journal: "About noon a Pilot Boat came along side to invite the Captn. to a Barbecue. I went with him and have been highly diverted. These Barbecues are Hogs, roasted whole. This was under a large Tree. A great number of young people met together with a Fiddler and Banjo played by two Negroes, with Plenty of Toddy, which both Men and Women seem to be fond of. I believe they have danced and drunk till there are few sober people amongst them." Philip Vickers Fithian, another visitor to Virginia, recorded a similar account in a September 1774 journal entry: "I was invited this morning by Captain Fibbs [Gibbs] to a Barbecue: this differs but little from the Fish Feasts, instead of Fish the Dinner is roasted Pig, with the proper appendages, but the Diversion & exercise are the very same at both—I declined going and pleaded in ex[c]use unusual & unexpected Business for the School." Fithian was a Princeton seminarian from New Jersey who spent a year tutoring the children at Nomini Hall, the Northern Neck plantation seat of Robert Carter III. Though Fithian recorded no judgment on the dish itself, his journals make clear that the "Diversion & exercise" of the barbecues offended his austere Presbyterian sensibilities.

Assembling the necessary food and drink for barbecues required funds and

Treating was expensive, but most Virginian officeholders were drawn from the upper classes and could pay out of their own pockets. In his 1758 run for the House of Burgesses, for example, George Washington spent £39.6s to purchase "28 gallons of rum, 50 gallons and one hogshead of rum punch, 34 gallons of wine, 46 gallons of 'strong beer,' and 2 gallons of cider royal"—a generous outlay for a district that contained only 391 voters. But candidates had to be subtle in their treating, for any suggestion that the food and drink were being explicitly traded for votes was considered dishonorable and could disqualify a candidate. In 1758, Matthew Marrable of Lunenburg County got a little carried away and provided seven barbecued lambs and logistics, and that meant either sponsorship by a wealthy individual or a coordinated subscription effort to finance the entertainment. Colonel Landon Carter, uncle of Robert Carter III, discussed the evolving tradition in his diary on September 5, 1772:

> It is our third Barbacue day [this year]. I think it an expensive thing; but submit to the opinions of others.
>
> I went to the barbacue and cou[ld not help] observing that [original torn] many on the credit of their Su[bsc]ription brought eaters enough there, some 5 and 6 for one Subscription. So that they all eat at about the price of 15d a head, when others paid at least 7/ for themselves alone which I think is a very unequal disposal of money. But as others submit to it I will not be the first to alter it: I confess I like to meet my friends now and then; but certainly the old method of every family carrying its own dish was both cheaper and better because then nobody intruded, but now everyone comes in and raises the club; and really many do so only for the sake of getting a good dinner and a belly full of drink.

Carter was particularly wary of the drinking and dancing that went on at these events, fearing that "barbecues and what not deprived some of their senses" and were a form of "treachery to decoy young people off from Duty."

Sources: Nicholas Cresswell, *The Journal of Nicholas Cresswell, 1774–1777* (London: Dial, 1924), 16; Philip Vickers Fithian, *Journals and Letters of Philip Vickers Fithian, 1773–1774: A Plantation Tutor of the Old Dominion*, ed. Hunter Dickinson Farish (Williamsburg, VA: Colonial Williamsburg, 1957), 183; Landon Carter, *The Diary of Colonel Landon Carter of Sabine Hall, 1752–1778*, ed. Jack P. Greene (Charlottesville: University Press of Virginia, 1965), 2:722, 900.

thirty gallons of rum to a militia company on election day. It also came to light that he had written a letter to an influential citizen offering support for specific pieces of legislation in exchange for an endorsement in the upcoming election. The Burgesses' Committee on Privileges and Elections declared Marrable's actions to be improper and voided his election.[17]

Done right, treating was supposed to demonstrate the candidate's generosity and hospitality—the defining traits of a gentleman—and not buy off voters. George Washington recognized this distinction, writing to one of his allies, "I hope no exception were taken to any that voted against me but that all were alike treated and all had enough; it is what I much desird—my only fear is that you spent with too sparing a hand." It was a curious mix of aristocracy and democracy. Because the gentry presented themselves for approval before the common citizenry, they could claim the consent of those they governed and declare that their natural fitness to rule had been recognized by the people. But each Virginian had to cast his vote aloud before a table at which the candidates were seated, and the chosen candidate generally thanked each person as his vote was cast. Officeholders knew full well who had given support and who had not.[18]

Barbecue in the Carolinas

Though barbecue was firmly entrenched in the daily life of Virginia planters, it does not seem to have played a significant part in the Lowcountry plantation culture of Charleston, South Carolina. Early diaries and other accounts of Charleston life make no reference to barbecue, and even descriptions of the city's horse races—occasions that were almost always accompanied by barbecues in Virginia—do not mention any sort of pit-cooked meats. The only trace of a barbecue in colonial Charleston can be found in verse—specifically in an imitation of Horace published in the *Gentleman's Magazine* of London in 1753. It's written by one "C. W.," who is "now residing in Charles Town, South Carolina," and he is reveling in the spring, which marked the end of Charleston's social season. The planters were wrapping up their business in town and preparing to head back to their rice plantations for the next growing year, but the poet implored that before leaving they should enjoy themselves a little: "Let's each hold a gen'rous *barbicu* feast / And with toddy and punch drink rich wine of the best." If any planters heeded C. W.'s advice, they left no trace of it. Charleston society tended toward more formal entertainment such as banquets and balls. Its cookery was characterized by shrimp, wild game, rice dishes, and rich desserts such as syllabubs, not roasted meats such as pork and mutton.[19]

Fifty miles down the coast in Beaufort, though, a barbecue tradition did flourish around the time of the Revolutionary War. It was different from the Virginia style in that it was not an institution for the entire community—male and female, upper and lower classes—but rather a form of entertainment for an exclusively male and mostly well-to-do group. In his autobiography, William J. Grayson, a prominent lawyer and man of letters born in Beaufort in 1788, recalled growing up among the older men who had participated in the Revolution. He remembers them as "a jovial and some-what rough race, liberal, social, warm-hearted, hospitable, addicted to deep drinking, hard-swearing, and practical-joking and not a little given to loose language and in-delicate allusions. . . . They were fond of dinner, barbacues, and hunting clubs." These barbecues were hard-drinking, all-male events. Each guest was expected to match his fellow drink for drink; refusing to continue was a breach of what Grayson termed "barbacue-law" and would result in harsh punishment for the offender. Grayson re-membered one violator, a young man newly arrived from Scotland, who declined fur-ther drink and was sentenced to a one-mile footrace. He was given a five-yard head start and had to outrun the entire "barbacue posse." If caught, he had to go back to drinking; if he won, he could do as he pleased. The Scotsman "outran his pursuers without trouble," Grayson reported, presumably because he was the only sober one in the bunch.[20]

The Beaufort hunting club had a barbecue house located about a mile outside of town. It's not clear when the structure was built, but it was destroyed by a hurricane in 1804. The event was recorded by a schoolteacher named Findlay, who had recently arrived from the north. His mock-heroic poem "On the Fall of the Barbacue-House at Beaufort, S.C. during the Late Tremendous Storm" was published in the *Charleston Courier* on November 1, 1804. It describes the "sacred temple—where, in mirthful glee, the jovial sons of Pleasure oft convene." As expected, there was plenty of drink-ing and practical joking:

> Grog's mellow radiance set their souls on fire,
> Till kindling into generous rage, the group
> Caught inspiration from each other's eye;
> Then, bright witticisms flash—the merry tale—
> Satirical description—*jeu de wel*—
> Song—and conundrum—in their turn succeed.

This poem gives us a peek at the ingredients used at early barbecues. In his introduc-tion to *The Confederate Housewife*, John Hammond Moore speculates that early South Carolina barbecues were likely "little more than alfresco animal roasts, without the to-mato, ketchup, mustard, and pepper-vinegar concoctions now associated with a good plate of barbecue" and that it wasn't until the Mexican-American War (1846–1848), when South Carolinians discovered new, hotter varieties of peppers, that barbecue became heavily seasoned. Findlay's poem, however, makes clear that the South Carolina version of the dish was highly spiced long before the influence of Mexican peppers, and the meat wasn't limited to pork. The poet describes the "famed SIRLOIN" and "Turkey-cock" that were regularly consumed at the barbecue house and notes:

> These roasted—bak'd—grill'd—devil'd—barbacu'd—
> Like Heretic or Jew beneath the claws
> Of Spain's dread Inquisition, feel the pangs
> Of pungent Cayenne, Mustard's biting power,
> And many a stimulant to me unknown,
> Judiciously applied, exhale their sweets,
> Grateful to hungry Poet and his Muse.

The remainder of the poem describes the hurricane and the destruction of the barbecue house where, in the words of William J. Grayson, "generations had feasted and made merry." The structure was apparently never rebuilt.[21]

The barbecue house in Beaufort seems to have been an anomaly for Lowcountry South Carolina. The barbecue tradition that developed in the nineteenth century did not move from the coast inland; instead, it spread down into the Carolinas from Virginia, following the main migration patterns of backwoods settlers. In the 1740s, frontier families began moving south from Virginia and Pennsylvania, following the eastern edge of the Appalachian Mountains and seeking new lands to farm. Through the 1750s the backcountry was unstable and unorganized, and the outbreak of the Cherokee War in 1760 and the lawlessness that followed created further chaos. It was not until the 1770s that the region became stable enough for a reliable agricultural economy to develop. Barbecue as an institution—that is, large social gatherings where whole hogs, cows, and sheep were cooked and eaten—was not feasible on the frontier, for it required not only large amounts of food but also a concentrated enough population to gather for a feast. Once farms and plantations began to prosper in the Carolina backcountry, the residents resumed many of the social traditions they had enjoyed in Virginia. In many cases, these settlers had moved southward with ambitions of founding their own plantations and becoming landed gentry themselves. Their adoption of barbecue was not just a continuation of the food preferences they had learned in their native Virginia but also an attempt to re-create Tidewater society in the newly settled backcountry.

One common occasion for a backcountry barbecue was a militia muster, which brought together the white men from all over a county for a day of drilling followed by socializing. A barbecue feast was usually prepared for the occasion. One such muster in 1766 in New Hanover, North Carolina, occurred at a time of high tensions over the recently passed Stamp Act. A few weeks before the muster, the militia companies from several counties had marched to the town of Brunswick and refused to let a cargo of stamped paper be brought ashore. Alarmed by the unrest, Governor William Tryon—who was widely regarded as a tyrant—chose a conciliatory path. At the next militia muster in New Hanover, he prepared a feast for the troops that included a whole barbecued ox and several barrels of beer. When called to the feast, the soldiers mocked Tryon's hospitality, poured the beer onto the ground, and pitched the ox, untasted, into the Cape Fear River. This happened a good seven years before a bunch of irate Bostonians donned Mohawk warrior garb and dumped three shiploads of tea into their harbor to protest British taxation, and yet the Boston Tea Party—and not the New Hanover Barbecue—is the event that everyone remembers.[22]

Barbecues were fairly common throughout the upstate region of South Carolina. Charles Woodmason, an itinerant Anglican minister assigned to the western parishes of the colony, described one in his journals in the late 1760s: "I had last Week Experience of the Velocity and force of the Air—By smelling a Barbicu dressing in the Woods upwards of six Miles." In 1775, William Henry Drayton was sent to South Carolina's Upper District (near present-day Spartanburg) to enlist the support of backcountry residents for the cause of independence. That August he held a meeting at Wofford's Iron Works and barbecued a beef for the event.[23]

By most accounts, these backwoods events were pretty crude affairs. They took place in clearings in the woods or in dusty open fields, with improvised tables and furnishings and whatever dishes and utensils the settlers had on hand. The meat might be pork, beef, or mutton, depending on what was available, and accounts of stifling heat, undercooked meat, and other unappetizing conditions are common. Carolina barbecues still had a way to go before they would match the elegance of their Virginia predecessors. The institution had been established, however, and was beginning to spread southward and westward through the frontier states.

An Early South Carolina Barbecue

ONE OF THE most detailed accounts of a colonial South Carolina barbecue can be found in the letters of William Richardson, a Charleston merchant who left the city in the early 1770s to become a planter in South Carolina's Camden District. Richardson attended a local horse race in March 1773 and described it in a letter to his wife, who was still living in Charleston:

> First then suppose us in the midst of a new ploughed field, the Wind blowing excessively hard, clouds of dust arising every [original torn] & [a] Quarter of Beef Barbacuing in this dust and nicely browned indeed, but not with the fire, Three planks laid a Cross some sticks for a Table, this elegant table covered, not with damask or diaper, I would not have you think, [original illegible] to your self two superb Oznabrigs sheets (not white) no! they scornd to have any thing so formal as to be clean) that had perhaps been laid in a month at least & the couler of a dishclout that had served the uses of the kitchen, for a month at least without washing . . . well then this Table coverd, the pewter arranged, a knife to some plates & half a one to others, Enter two Hogs & a Quarter of Beef of the couler of a piece of Beef Tied to a string & dragged thro' Chs Town streets on a very dry dusty day & then smoke dried, a Dish of Bacon & Turnip Tops & a Dish of Beef, plenty of Brown loaves their looks not inviting & in taste resembling Saw dust.

Richardson found the meal appalling, but his fellow diners seemed to enjoy it:

> I absolutely saw one lady devour a whole Hog head except the bones, don't tell this to any of your squeemish C Town ladies for they will not believe you, had some of them been near our feast & their appetites Gorged with what you in town call delicases (but what we Crackers dispise) they perhaps might think us cannibals & with some propiety they might think, if they could suppose a half rosted hog, with the blood running out at every cut of the Knife, any thing like human flesh but ye squeemish C Town ladies I would not have ye think our buxom Cracker wenches so degenerate! no they can eat when hungry a piece of the devil roasted, in the shape of a Hog & to wash down this [superb e]legant repast, we did not gulp down necter, no, that would [original torn] liquor of life mingled with the dust of the field whole pails we Quaf'd, not quite so transparent indeed as the Kennell water that runs thro' your streets after a shower of rain.

Source: Emma B. Richardson, ed., "Letters of William Richardson, 1765–1784," *South Carolina Historical and Genealogical Magazine* 47 (January 1946): 6–7.

2

"REPUBLICAN PLENTY"

Fourth of July and Campaign Barbecues

Barbecue restaurants today do a brisk business on the Fourth of July. Customers are warned to place orders several days in advance to ensure they can secure enough pulled pork, brisket, or ribs for their family celebrations. The meat and the accompanying sides—coleslaw, baked beans, banana pudding—are carried home in foil-covered aluminum pans and served on paper plates on front porches and in backyards at gatherings of families and friends.

These gatherings have a long history in the American South, a history that stretches back to the very first Independence Day celebrations. In the years just after the Revolution, community barbecues became the standard way to celebrate the country's independence and its egalitarian principles. At the same time, barbecue was expanding beyond its early foothold in Virginia and the Carolinas and starting to make its way across the rest of the South. As settlers headed west into Tennessee and through the Cumberland Gap into Kentucky, they carried the barbecue tradition with them. So did the planters who pushed southwestward through Georgia and into Alabama, seeking new land for farming. Both on the frontier and in more established communities back East, the events took on increased social importance. Barbecues became the quintessential form of democratic public celebration, bringing together citizens from all stations to express and reaffirm their shared civic values.

The surprising thing about early Fourth of July celebrations is how formal and standardized they became. Town after town celebrated the Fourth with an almost identical set of ceremonies that featured a barbecue at their center. As settlers moved west into the frontier territories, they took these holiday customs with them, making July Fourth barbecues not just a southern tradition but an American one. And, of course, it was only a matter of time before the politicians showed up.

"For the Common Benefit": Early July Fourth Barbecues

From the very beginning, Americans chose to celebrate their independence from Britain with public dinners, and these gatherings quickly grew from small affairs hosted by prominent citizens to large outdoor events attended by entire communities and featuring whole animals barbecued over pits in the ground. On July 9, 1808, *Miller's Weekly Messenger* of Pendleton, South Carolina, reported the July Fourth celebration at Occoney Station in the mountainous western part of the state. Following a parade by the local militia, "a short address suited to the occasion was delivered by the Rev. Mr. ANDREW BROWN; after which they marched to an agreeable and natural arbor, where, in the company with a number of others, they partook of an elegant barbecue." Occoney (now spelled Oconee) was a newly settled frontier district, and the *Messenger* correspondent wrote, "It was a sight highly pleasing, to see such respectable members meet for the first time in this remote place, to celebrate the anniversary of our national existence."[1]

The naturalist John James Audubon, traveling in Kentucky in the early part of the century, was a guest at a similar event, which he described at length in *Delineations of American Scenery and Character* (see pages 26–27). Audubon's account links the frontier barbecue to its Virginia roots, noting, "The free, single-hearted Kentuckian, bold, erect, and proud of his Virginia descent, had, as usual, made arrangements for celebrating the day of his country's Independence." Unlike the tradition in colonial Virginia, where society's elite hosted barbecues as part of their duties of hospitality, the frontier celebration Audubon attended was organized and prepared by the entire community. Local residents donated the provisions "for the common benefit"—including ox, ham, venison, turkeys, and other fowls—and cleared a large area in the woods for the barbecue grounds. The day began with a cannon salute and a patriotic oration delivered by "the most learned" of the community. The company then proceeded to the tables for the feast, which was followed by a series of toasts and dancing that continued until sundown.[2]

Most frontier barbecues were free to all comers, with the provisions donated by various members of the community. A few, however, were for-profit events staged by entrepreneurs who charged for admittance. The following advertisement, for example, appeared in a Lexington, Kentucky, newspaper in June 1815.

BARBACUE

The subscriber respectfully informs the citizens of Fayette and the adjoining counties, that he will prepare an elegant Barbacue Dinner, on the Fourth of July, at his own house, on the Limestone road, nine miles from Lexington. . . . The subscriber furnishes foreign liquors of the best quality for the LADIES—the gentlemen will have free access to the use of domestic liquors. Tickets of admittance, two dollars—there will be no expense nor personal trouble omitted to render his entertainment brilliant and interesting.

Commercial events such as this one seem to have been the exception, not the rule. It took another century for barbecue to become a regular commercial enterprise.[3]

The elements captured in these early descriptions—free communal gatherings with lots of drinking, orations, toasts, and dancing—were typical of frontier barbecues, and they soon became part of the ritual in settled towns, too. By the 1820s, Independence Day celebrations had become standardized throughout the Carolinas, Kentucky, and Tennessee. Newspaper accounts of these events read almost like boilerplate. The day began with the citizens of the surrounding region gathering to form a procession. Led by local militia units in uniform, the community would march to a central location—usually the county courthouse or a church—for the day's ceremonies. These opened with a prayer, and then the Declaration of Independence would be read aloud. In many communities, local musicians would play and the crowd would sing patriotic songs. The ceremonies always concluded with an oration delivered by a prominent citizen that served as a sort of community civics lesson, with the speaker expounding on topics such as the principles of the Revolution or the importance of the Constitution to civic life. After the florid oratory, the citizens would retire to a shady grove for a large dinner, which usually featured barbecued pigs, sheep, and goats.

These early barbecues were by no means sober affairs. Dinner was followed by round after round of toasts made in celebration of Independence Day, the United States, and its leaders. These began with a series of "regular" toasts, usually thirteen (to celebrate the thirteen original states), given by prominent persons who had been chosen in advance for the honor. The subjects for the toasts varied from celebration to

Audubon's "Kentucky Barbecue on the Fourth of July"

JOHN JAMES AUDUBON, the great American naturalist and painter, recorded the following account of a Fourth of July barbecue in Kentucky during the early part of the nineteenth century as part of a sketch in *Delineations of American Scenery and Character*:

> The free, single-hearted Kentuckian, bold, erect, and proud of his Virginia descent, had, as usual, made arrangements for celebrating the day of his country's Independence. The whole neighborhood joined with one consent. No personal invitation was required where everyone was welcomed by his neighbor, and from the governor to the guider of the plough all met with light hearts and merry faces. It was indeed a beautiful day; the bright sun rode in the clear blue heavens; the gentle breezes wafted around the odours of the gorgeous flowers; the little birds sang their sweetest songs in the woods, and the fluttering insects danced in the sunbeams. Columbia's sons and daughters seemed to have grown younger that morning. For a whole week or more, many servants and some masters had been busily engaged in clearing an area. The undergrowth had been carefully cut down, the low boughs lopped off, and the grass alone, verdant and gay, remained to carpet the sylvan pavilion. Now the waggons were seen slowly moving along under their load of provisions, which had been prepared for the common benefit. Each denizen had freely given his ox, his ham, his venison, his turkeys, and other fowls. Here were to be seen flagons of every beverage used in the country; "La belle Riviere" had opened her finny stores; the melons of all sorts, peaches, plums and pears, would have been sufficient to stock a market. In a word, Kentucky, the land of abundance, had supplied a feast for her children.
>
> A purling stream gave its water freely, while the grateful breezes cooled the air. Columns of smoke from the newly kindled fires rose above the trees; fifty cooks or more moved to and fro as they plied their trade; waiters of all qualities were disposing the dishes, the glasses, and the punch-bowls, amid vases filled with rich wines. "Old Monongahela" [that is, aged rye whiskey from Pennsylvania's Monongahela Valley] filled many a barrel for the crowd. And now, the roasted viands perfume the air, and all appearances conspire to predict the speedy commencement of a banquet such as may suit the vigorous appetite of American woodsmen. Every steward is at his post, ready to receive the joyous groups that at this moment begin to emerge from the dark recesses of the woods.

Each comely fair one, clad in pure white, is seen advancing under the protection of her sturdy lover, the neighing of their prancing steeds proclaiming how proud they are of their burdens. The youthful riders leap from their seats, and the horses are speedily secured by twisting their bridles round a branch. As the youth of Kentucky lightly and gaily advanced towards the Barbecue, they resembled a procession of nymphs and disguised divinities. Fathers and mothers smiled upon them, as they followed the brilliant cortége. In a short time the ground was alive with merriment. A great wooden cannon, bound with iron hoops, was now crammed with home-made powder; fire was conveyed to it by means of a train, and as the explosion burst forth, thousands of hearty huzzas mingled with its echoes.

From the most learned a good oration fell in proud and gladdening words on every ear, and although it probably did not equal the eloquence of a Clay, an Everett, a Webster, or a Preston, it served to remind every Kentuckian present of the glorious name, the patriotism, the courage, and the virtue, of our immortal Washington. Fifes and drums sounded the march which had ever led him to glory; and as they changed to our celebrated "Yankee Doodle," the air again rang with acclamations.

Now the stewards invited the assembled throng to the feast. The fair led the van, and were first placed around the tables, which groaned under the profusion of the best productions of the country that had been heaped upon them. On each lovely nymph attended her gay beau, who in her chance or sidelong glances ever watched an opportunity of reading his happiness. How the viands diminished under the action of so many agents of destruction I need not say, nor is it necessary that you should listen to the long recital. Many a national toast was offered and accepted, many speeches were delivered, and many essayed in amicable reply. The ladies then retired to booths that had been erected at a little distance, to which they were conducted by their partners, who returned to the table, and having thus cleared for action, recommenced a series of hearty rounds. However, as Kentuckians are neither slow nor long at their meals, all were in a few minutes replenished, and after a few more draughts from the bowl, they rejoined the ladies, and prepared for the dance.

Source: John James Audubon, *Delineations of American Scenery and Character* (New York: G. A. Baker, 1926), 241–43.

celebration, but they almost always saluted the US Constitution, prominent political leaders, and abstract patriotic principles such as "Political Liberty" and "The Right to Fight" (see page 29). The thirteenth toast was almost always devoted to honoring American women (or "The American Fair," as it was usually phrased). As each toast was made, the crowd would respond, in the words of the Camden, South Carolina, *Journal* in 1831, with "loud huzzas and the firing of guns."[4]

Once the prepared set of regular toasts were drunk, "volunteer toasts" followed—often thirty or more. In addition to celebrating war heroes and democratic ideals, these toasts routinely addressed the vital political issues of the day. At the 1824 celebration in Jackson, Tennessee, for example, the volunteer toasts included support for the country of Greece ("May it be sustained by the Eagle of America") and a call for the navigation of the Mississippi to remain free to the citizens of the United States and unencumbered by foreign partnerships. In 1834, in the wake of the Nullification Crisis, the thirty-six volunteer toasts made at the Sherman's Store celebration in South Carolina's Greenville District were staunchly pro-Union, pro–Andrew Jackson, and anti–John C. Calhoun, for the region was a hotbed of Unionist sentiment. Such toasts may seem obscure today, but they were of considerable interest to the community at the time, and most newspaper accounts of July Fourth celebrations published transcripts of the regular toasts and, in many cases, the volunteer ones as well. One feels sorry for the poor newspaper correspondent frantically scribbling in his notebook while the rest of the gathering polished off their whiskey and beer.[5]

Not surprisingly, considering the sheer number of toasts drunk at the typical Fourth of July gathering, early nineteenth-century barbecues became notorious for drunkenness and the violence that came along with it. Recalling the Fourth of July barbecues of his childhood in antebellum South Carolina, Dr. Samuel B. Latham noted that the various local militia companies would let loose at the annual celebration at Caldwell Cross Roads. Once the drills, oration, and dinner were complete, "hard liquor would flow; and each section would present its 'bully of the woods' in a contest for champion in a fist and skull fight. Butting, biting, eye gouging, kicking, and blows below the belt were barred. It was primitive prize fighting."[6]

Nothing goes together like booze and firearms, and there was no shortage of unfortunate accidents at early barbecues. In 1834 at the celebration in South Carolina's Union District, Washington Sample had his right hand blown off and his left arm

Fourth of July Toasts

THE FOLLOWING REGULAR toasts were delivered at the 1824 Fourth of July barbecue in Madison County, Tennessee:

1. "The Day we celebrate"—The birthday of American Independence; duly appreciated, and held sacred by its votaries.

2. "The memory of George Washington"—Encomium would be fulsome: Let expressive silence muse his praise.

3. "Thomas Jefferson and James Madison"—Ex-Presidents of the United States.

4. "James Monroe, President of the U. S."—The voice of an independent people will award him an escutcheon worthy of his services.

5. "The American Revolution"—Founded upon principle; its origin the source of lasting happiness of millions yet unborn.

6. "The memory of our fellow citizens who fell in the late war"—Their services are still fresh in our recollections.

7. "General Andrew Jackson"—Our Chief in War; our Ruler in Peace.

8. "The 8th of January, 1815"—A day on which Britain's Invincibles crouched to American valor.

9. "Grecian Emancipation"—In a cause so glorious, she has our best wishes.

10. "The Western District of Tennessee"—The most desirable part of our state.

11. "Internal Improvements"—The surest basis of National Wealth.

12. "Our Country"—Breathes there a man with soul so dead, Who never to himself hath said, "This is my own, my native land."

13. "Woman"—Her smiles our richest reward, her protection our solemn duty.

Source: *Jackson (TN) Gazette*, July 10, 1824.

broken when an old cannon, taken from the British during the Revolution, discharged while he was reloading it. In his hurry, he had "neglected to swab out the gun, and a burning cinder still inside came into contact with the new gunpowder being loaded." There were only "some faint hopes of his life."[7]

Rough as they were, Fourth of July barbecues contributed more to the community than mere merrymaking. The entire populace would come together at these events and—through the reading of the Declaration and the patriotic orations—reaffirm the guiding principles of the early republic. The toasts were a celebration of the new country's history and, in their commentary on current events, a form of political discourse. Barbecues also embodied the evolving notion of American democratic values. In colonial Virginia, the events had been part of an aristocratic social structure, in which wealthy planters demonstrated their kindness and hospitality by hosting barbecues for those on the lower rungs of the hierarchy. After the Revolution, though, the gatherings became increasingly egalitarian. This change can be seen in the *North-Carolina Gazette*'s account of an armistice celebration in New Bern, North Carolina, in June 1778, which featured "a barbecue (a roast pig) and a barrel of rum, from which the leading officials and citizens of the region promiscuously ate and drank with the meanest and lowest kind of people." The correspondent declared it impossible to imagine a more purely democratic gathering, adding that "there were some drunks, some friendly fisticuffs, and one man was injured. With that and the burning of some empty barrels as a feu de joie at nightfall, the party ended and everyone retired to sleep." Such portrayals of barbecues as fundamentally democratic gatherings—what the *Camden Journal* termed "the enjoyment of republican plenty, with republican care and hospitality"—can be found again and again in newspaper accounts from the early nineteenth century.[8]

In keeping with this republican spirit, most Fourth of July celebrations were organized by a "Committee of Arrangements," which generally consisted of three to five men elected at a public gathering. In 1824, the citizens of Jackson, Tennessee, met on Saturday, June 12, "to make arrangements preparatory to a celebration of the approaching anniversary of American Independence." In other communities the committee was chosen as much as a year in advance. An advertisement in the July 2, 1831, *Camden Journal*, for example, announced, "The citizens of Camden and its vicinity are requested to meet at the Court House on Monday the fourth day of July next; at 9 o'clock AM . . . to elect an orator and appoint a Committee of Arrangements for the succeeding Anniversary." As was typical for elected offices in the early nineteenth century, the members of the committee were usually prominent local citizens such as planters, lawyers, and doctors.[9]

To this point most of the barbecues we've discussed were organized by white southerners, but from the earliest days barbecue was eaten by African Americans as well as European Americans, sometimes in the same venues but frequently in separate ones. Most accounts of eighteenth-century barbecues are sparse on detail, so it isn't clear how frequently enslaved African Americans attended early Fourth of July or other community barbecues and in what capacity they might have participated in the events. In the slaveholding South, it is safe to assume that much of the labor at early barbecues—from digging the pits to basting the meat—was performed by enslaved workers. (In 1774, as we have seen, Nicholas Cresswell had noted "a Fiddler and Banjo played by two Negroes" in his description of a Virginia barbecue.)

We know for sure, however, that African Americans in the South staged barbecues on their own. In the colonial era and for the first few decades of the new republic, enslaved people in Virginia and the Carolinas were allowed to travel and assemble outside appointed work hours. Many—particularly skilled artisans—regularly traveled between plantations and cities as well as to church meetings, funerals, and barbecues. For enslaved southerners, barbecues were a common form of recreation, particularly on Sundays, when they were usually released from labor. Few descriptions of these gatherings survive, but we can surmise that the cooking techniques and styles were essentially the same as those used when enslaved cooks prepared the barbecue for larger gatherings attended by whites.

Barbecues provided a convenient and yet inconspicuous way for enslaved people to gather and interact with one another, so the events played prominent roles in several slave revolts during the early years of the republic, most notably Gabriel's Rebellion in Virginia. In 1800, an enslaved blacksmith named Gabriel mapped out a plan for a massive revolt in the Richmond area. His plan was to kill the two men who owned him, seize their arms, and then murder all the neighboring whites. From there he would raise an army and proceed to Richmond to seize the arms and ammunition from the city's magazine. To enlist supporters, Gabriel and a coconspirator named Solomon invited slaves to attend several barbecues, using the occasions as cover to plan the uprising. Before the plot could get under way, it was unraveled by informants, who notified authorities in Richmond of the plan. Gabriel and twenty other conspirators were arrested and executed.[10]

The Politicians Arrive

The volunteers who helped stage Fourth of July barbecues—the committee members who made the arrangements, the prominent men who delivered the orations—did so in part out of a sense of civic responsibility. Many had an eye on commercial and political advancement, too. In his memoirs, Robert B. McAfee of Mercer County, Kentucky, recalled that during his early days as a young lawyer, he drummed up a fair amount of business by making orations at any and all occasions, speaking on political issues and other topics of public interest. His first public speech was made at a July Fourth barbecue at William Adams Spring in 1801, and as a result he "soon obtained more business than I expected." The experience convinced him to try to make his way to Harrodsburg, which at the time was the state capital. "I was ardently ambitious," he explained, "and determined to rise before the public as soon as I could." Though McAfee was only seventeen years old when he gave his first barbecue speech, it put him on the path to political success, and he went on to become a state senator and lieutenant governor of Kentucky.[11]

Plenty of other ambitious men found barbecues to be a promising springboard for a political career. In addition to speechifying and glad-handing at Fourth of July and other community events, politicians soon began hosting their own barbecues for the sole purpose of attracting the stomachs and the ears of potential voters. In part, this was a matter of simple expedience. In an era with limited forms of mass communication, such gatherings were one of the few ways for campaigners to reach a large number of voters. But the popularity of the campaign barbecue also reflected a fundamental shift that was under way in the American political scene, as the rise of populist politics reshaped electoral standards and established for the first time a permanent political party system.

American politics was evolving away from the old aristocratic model to a more inclusive, rough-and-tumble democracy. In the colonial days, the ruling gentry had mouthed classical Republican ideals, casting themselves as a disinterested elite who governed with the deferential consent of the rabble. Even in Tidewater Virginia, though, barbecues and similar forms of treating offered early signs that voters held a certain amount of political power. If this trend was noticeable in older communities where the social structure was relatively stable and defined, it was even more evident

David Crockett. (Courtesy Tennessee State Library and Archives)

on the frontier, where the social order was still being sorted out. In such communities, ordinary citizens were more likely to demand that their representatives cater to their personal interests, and public gatherings such as barbecues took on increased importance as venues where ambitious men could establish themselves politically.

In old Virginia, education, good breeding, and family connections were the essential qualifications for political office. On the frontier, the rules were still being sorted out. Military service was one route to distinction, as was success in farming and business. In his autobiography, David Crockett recalled that a candidate for colonel in the Tennessee militia, whose members elected their officers by popular vote, was considered particularly qualified because "he was an early settler in that country, and made rather more corn than the rest of us." Equally important were hunting skill, joviality, and the ability to uncork a rousing stump speech—a talent that would be demonstrated in the weeks before an election at public barbecues. In his first campaign for the Tennessee legislature in 1821, Crockett himself made up for his lack of political experience by making a series of folksy speeches at events such as a squirrel hunt barbecue (see below). He credited those speeches with winning him his first seat in public office.[12]

By the 1820s, campaign barbecues were common throughout the settled portions of the South, which at the time included Virginia, the Carolinas, Tennessee, Kentucky, Georgia, and northern Alabama. Some local newspapers advertised three or four barbecues a week during the election season. Many of these, like the squirrel hunt attended by Crockett, were community amusements that the politicians horned in on to get themselves in front of likely voters. Others, though, were organized specifically for electioneering. A newspaper ad for a barbecue at Byrd's Big Spring in northern Alabama, for example, announced that "voters and candidates 'two by two in couples

Davy Crockett's First Barbecue Stump Speech

THE FOLLOWING PASSAGE is taken from Davy Crockett's *A Narrative of the Life of David Crockett of the State of Tennessee* (1834):

About this time there was a great squirrel hunt on Duck river, which was among my people. They were to hunt two days: then to meet and count the scalps, and have a big barbecue, and what might be called a tip-top country frolic. The dinner, and a general treat, was all to be paid for by the party having taken the fewest scalps. I joined one side, taking the place of one of the hunters, and got a gun ready for the hunt. I killed a great many squirrels, and when we counted scalps, my party was victorious.

The company had every thing to eat and drink that could be furnished in so new a country, and much fun and good humor prevailed. But before the regular frolic commenced, I mean the dancing, I was called on to make a speech as a candidate; which was a business I was as ignorant of as an outlandish negro.

A public document I had never seen, nor did I know there were such things; and how to begin I couldn't tell. I made many apologies, and tried to get off, for I know'd I had a man to run against who could speak prim, and I know'd, too, that I wa'n'y able to shuffle and cut with him. He was there, and knowing my ignorance as well as I did myself, he also urged me to make a speech. The truth is, he thought my being a candidate was a mere matter of sport; and didn't think, for a moment, that he was in any danger from an ignorant backwoods bear hunter. But I found I couldn't gert off, and so I determined just to go ahead, and leave it to chance what I should say. I got up and told the one after another' are respectfully invited to attend . . . and partake of whatever may be found to regale the soul and the senses." An 1825 notice in the *Huntsville Democrat* promised "a greater collection of people than has ever been seen at a barbecue in any of the southern states," with no less than "ONE THOUSAND weight of meat put upon the pitt, besides other necessaries to give zest to the entertainment. All this will be like God's blessing, 'without money and without price.'" As campaign barbecues grew larger and became more frequent, they were increasingly hosted not by the candidates themselves but by groups of their supporters, who arranged the entertainment, paid for the food and drink, and placed advertisements in local newspapers. Such actions were some of the first examples of political party organization in the southern states.[13]

people, I reckoned they know'd what I come for, but if not, I could tell them. I had come for their votes, and if they didn't watch mighty close, I'd get them, too. But the worst of all was, that I couldn't tell them any thing about government. I tried to speak about something, and I cared very little what, until I choked up as bad as if my mouth had been jam'd and cram'd chock full of dry mush. There the people stood, listening all the while, with their eyes, mouths and ears all open, to catch every word I would speak. At last I told them I was like a fellow I had heard of not long before. He was beating on the head of an empty barrel near the roadside, when a traveler, who was passing along, asked him what he was doing that for? The fellow replied, that there was some cider in that barrel a few days before, and he was trying to see if there was any then, but if there was he couldn't get at it. I told them that there had been a little bit of a speech in me a while ago, but I believed I couldn't get it out. They all roared out in a mighty laugh, and I told some other anecdotes, equally amusing to them, and believing I had them in a first-rate way, I quit and got down, thanking the people for their attention. But I took care to remark that I was as dry as a powder horn, and that I thought it was time for us all to wet our whistles a little; and so I put off to the liquor stand, and I was followed by the greater part of the crowd.

Crockett's maneuver left few people to hear his opponent's speech. Crockett won the election with twice the votes of his competitor.

Source: David Crockett, *A Narrative of the Life of David Crockett of the State of Tennessee* (Philadelphia: Carey and Hart, 1834), 138–42.

The Antibarbecue Backlash

Not everyone was thrilled by the rise of campaign barbecues, and those of more elitist sentiments began to chafe at the new ritual of barbecue stump speaking. In Frederick County, Maryland, in 1818, a commentator identifying himself only as "AN INDEPENDENT VOTER" published a broadside that compared the qualifications of two candidates for the state House of Delegates. "They are both amiable men," he admitted, but "the modest unassuming manner in which Mr. Worthington has gone through the drudgery of public speaker at your barbecues, sets him, in my estimation, above the common democratic seekers for fame or office." Such veiled disapproval gave way to more explicit condemnation as the political practices established on the frontier began making their way back East to the older, more established states. In 1825, the editor of the *Norwich Courier* fretted that New Yorkers were starting to adopt "the modest custom of their Southern neighbors." Candidates first started announcing publicly that they were running for office, and then they began buying newspaper ads that laid out their qualifications for the general public to read. "We shall doubtless next hear," the *Courier*'s editor harrumphed, "of stump orations, barbecues, and prime bang up knock me down whiskee frolicks."[14]

The resistance wasn't just among grumpy Yankees. In the late 1820s, as historian Daniel Dupre has documented, a remarkable backlash against campaign barbecues erupted in Madison County, Alabama. This movement began in July 1827 when the *Southern Advocate* published the first of a series of letters from a correspondent calling himself "Barbecuensis." The letter attacked election barbecues as licentious and corrupt, and it opened with a poem condemning the rowdiness of the gatherings:

> Did you ever see a Barbecue? For fear
> You should not, I'll describe it you exactly:—
> A gander-pulling mob that's common here,
> of candidates and sovereigns stowed compactly,—
> Of harlequins and clowns, with feats gymnastical
> In hunting-shirts and shirt-sleeves—things fantastical;—
> with fiddling, feasting, dancing, drinking, masquing
> And other things which may be had for asking.

Barbecuensis complained that barbecues were where "sobriety is exchanged for intemperance . . . and liberty chastened to licentiousness," but he was even more worried that they were debasing the standards for choosing leaders. "The question now," he wrote, "is not, what is his mental capacity? But, what are the dimensions of his stomach? Not, does he read and think? But, does he eat and digest? Not, if he will enact wholesome laws and promote and preserve the peace, happiness, and prosperity of the State, but if he will drink raw whiskey, eat rawer shote, dance bare foot on a puncheon floor . . . and pull at a gander's neck?"[15]

The editors of the two local newspapers picked up Barbecuensis's refrain, and within a few months a full-fledged antibarbecue movement was under way. The *Southern Advocate* condemned events for degrading the health and morals of the community, conjuring specters of poor victims "shattered and shipwrecked, driven helpless and nerveless before the slightest blast . . . and which encountered their first and fatal gales on the stormy seas of barbacue politics." Undercooked pork and bad whiskey must have been common at these events, for the editor echoed Barbecuensis in his condemnation of "the "gorging upon raw shote, and of a swilling of a species of liquor little less pernicious than liquid fire is worse than actual and immediate death." The *Huntsville Democrat* struck a similar chord, arguing that because of electioneering, "many a man who would otherwise remain employed on his farm is induced to forsake his business and his family by the temptation" until "the sober industrious citizen becomes a sot."[16]

What these critics feared most about barbecues was not that they would spread intemperance or overeating but rather that they would lead to disorder and mob rule—a common anxiety during the age of Jacksonian democracy. Madison County's antibarbecue movement culminated in a petition drive in July 1829 that gathered more than a thousand signatures from citizens opposed to the campaign practice. At the next election, a handful of candidates for state and local offices took a bold stand and pledged to shun all barbecues and other public gatherings organized for electioneering purposes. They paid the price on election day, for democratic politics required campaigning, and barbecues were one of the most effective ways of doing so. Josef Leftwich, who publicly announced his refusal to attend barbecues while running for county tax collector, finished seventh out of nine candidates. Campaign barbecues remained controversial, but they had become permanent features of the southern political scene and would only grow in size and popularity over the succeeding decades.[17]

"Tippecanoe and Tyler, Too": The Political Barbecue Comes of Age

The tradition of the political barbecue in the 1830s and 1840s emerged alongside organized party politics in the United States. Having competing factions was hardly a new thing in American politics. The Federalists and the Democratic Republicans had locked horns bitterly in the early years of the republic, but these were not formal political parties but loose coalitions of politicians and voters who shared similar interests. By 1816 the Federalists were effectively extinct, and the 1820s witnessed a brief period of virtual one-party rule known as the "Era of Good Feelings." But good feelings seldom last long in politics, and by the end of the decade the Democrats had become split by ideological differences and personal rivalries. These divisions culminated in the contentious 1828 presidential race between Andrew Jackson and John Quincy Adams, a race that Jackson won by a 178 to 83 margin in the electoral college. A new political

An 1834 political cartoon showing President Andrew Jackson being barbecued over the fires of public opinion after his removal of the deposits from the Bank of the United States. (Courtesy Library of Congress, Prints and Photographs Division)

party called the Whigs began to coalesce in the mid-1830s, united primarily by opposition to Jackson's policies, particularly his attack on the Bank of the United States and his forceful response to the Nullification movement. Their name was a nod to the English political party that tried to limit the power of the king, for the members of the new party considered it their first duty to rein in the excesses of "King Andrew."

The Whigs' founding coincided with a dramatic expansion in the American electorate. States began loosening or abolishing requirements like property ownership or tax payments that had previously limited the vote to only a small minority of white males. These electoral reforms began in the West and spread to the older states on the East Coast, which were forced to follow suit to slow the out-migration of residents to the frontier. In 1800, only four out of the then sixteen states chose their presidential electors by popular vote rather than legislative appointment; by 1824, eighteen out of twenty-four had instituted the popular vote. Between 1824 and 1828 alone, the number of voters casting ballots in the presidential election almost tripled, from 400,000 to 1.1 million. By the time Andrew Jackson was elected president, almost all white male Americans were eligible to vote.[18]

To appeal to this newly expanded electorate, candidates had to adopt much broader electioneering tactics, and barbecues were the perfect fit. Of course, staging barbecues and other campaign events for hundreds or even thousands of people required more formal organizations to plan and pay for campaigns. Political parties, which the Founding Fathers had condemned for putting partisanship ahead of principle, gradually gained acceptance in the United States as formal groups were established within the individual states and soon developed into national organizations.[19]

As the events became more organized, the conventions for staging a barbecue, such as distributing published invitations, also became more formal. Compare, for example, the earlier-cited advertisements from the 1820s, which touted the sheer quantities of meat and liquor to be served, with the following notice from the *Pendleton Messenger* in 1838: "As a Committee of Invitation on behalf of the citizens of Pickens district," it read, "we do most respectfully invite to attend a Barbecue to be given to the Hon. John C. Calhoun at this place, on Wednesday the 12th inst. all the revolutionary soldiers of Pickens, Anderson, and the adjoining districts, the Candidates for both branches of the State Legislature, and the citizens generally." Barbecues were becoming downright respectable affairs—serious venues for public discourse over the ideas and issues of the day.[20]

They also grew larger. In September 1836, the Whigs in Kentucky staged a massive barbecue on Lafayette Green on the outskirts of Versailles to welcome home their leader, Henry Clay, after the adjournment of the US Senate. Clay brought along several other national Whig leaders, including Daniel Webster and John J. Crittenden. In their addresses before an "immense throng," these noted statesmen railed against the excesses of the Jackson administration. The following spring, Daniel Webster embarked on a tour of the western states, making his way down the Ohio River by steamboat. The Whig diarist Philip Hone recorded that Webster was greeted with great enthusiasm at one town after another, and "public dinners and barbecues have been tendered to him in great profusion." In St. Louis, over five thousand people turned out to welcome Webster at a barbecue in a grove owned by Judge J. B. C. Lucas. Webster, apparently well fortified with smoked pork and perhaps a little whiskey, delivered a two-hour oration for the occasion.[21]

A year later, another prominent southern statesman, John C. Calhoun, threw himself headlong into barbecue speeches, too. Though his own Senate seat was not up for reelection, he took to the stump to campaign in favor of Martin Van Buren's plan for a subtreasury system and against the reelection of any officeholders who opposed his position. The first barbecue Calhoun attended was on August 28, 1838, at Sandy Spring Church in South Carolina's Greenville District, where he spoke before a crowd of 1,500. Representative Waddy Thompson Jr., one of the rival politicians Calhoun was trying to unseat, had also been invited, and after Calhoun finished his oration, Thompson arose in response to attack the subtreasury system and what he characterized as Calhoun's flip-flopping on the issue. The two men sparred at several other barbecues that fall, signs that the political barbecue had progressed beyond one-sided partisan logrolling and, in many cases, had become a public forum for political discourse.[22]

By the time Andrew Jackson took office, the barbecue was an inseparable part of the American political routine. Jackson celebrated the first Fourth of July of his presidency by hosting a barbecue on the grounds of the White House—the first recorded instance of a White House barbecue. Not long after, barbecue gained a more physical presence in Washington, DC, when James Maher, manager of the Capitol Grounds, planted two circular groups of trees on the large grassy area just east of the Capitol

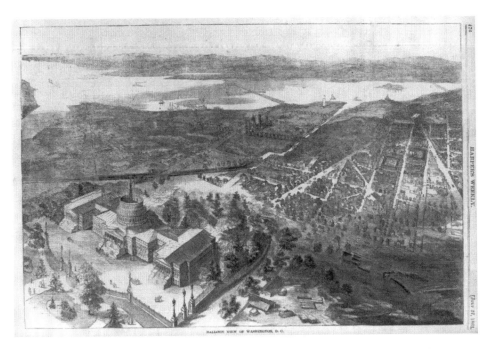

An aerial "balloon view" of the US Capitol from *Harper's Weekly*, July 27, 1861. The Capitol's dome was still being completed, and the barbecue groves are visible in the lower left corner of the picture. (Courtesy Library of Congress, Prints and Photographs Division)

building. These trees, the great landscape architect Frederick Law Olmsted later wrote, served as "barbecue groves," with one "intended for Democratic, the other for Whig jollifications." The "barbecue trees," as they were commonly known, remained visible on the grounds until the early twentieth century.[23]

The antebellum political barbecue only grew in popularity in the years after Jackson, reaching its full flowering in the presidential election of 1840. It was the second national contest between the Democrats and the newly organized Whigs. Four years earlier, Democrat Martin Van Buren, Jackson's vice president and handpicked successor, had trounced the Whigs in a landslide. Still stinging from the loss, the Whigs in 1840 united behind the ticket of William Henry Harrison and John Tyler, and they adopted an entirely new message and strategy. Harrison was basically an empty suit,

Woodcut emblem from William Henry Harrison's 1840 "Log Cabin" presidential campaign, showing the candidate sharing hard cider with soldiers in front of his log cabin. (Courtesy Library of Congress, Prints and Photographs Division)

with little political philosophy and a campaign based mostly on his military record, especially his victory over the Shawnee leader Tecumseh at the Battle of Tippecanoe in 1811. The result, as historian Samuel Eliot Morison phrased it, was "the jolliest and most idiotic presidential contest in our history. . . . [The Whigs] adopted no platform, nominated a military hero, ignored real issues, and appealed to the emotions rather than the brains of voters." Determined to "agitate the people," the Whigs assembled strong local organizations and insisted on using "every lawful means" to lure voters to the polls. Those means included extensive treating, picnics, processions, and, of course, lots of barbecue, all accompanied by catchy campaign songs and slogans like "Tippecanoe and Tyler, Too."[24]

The Whigs stumbled onto their favorite slogan thanks to the scorn of a Democratic journalist, who sneered that, given a barrel of hard cider and a $2,000 pension, Harrison would prefer his log cabin to the White House. The Whigs immediately flipped the insult around and declared they were running a "Log Cabin, Hard Cider" campaign, portraying Harrison as a humble farmer/soldier and Van Buren as a decadent politician addicted to luxury. Soon, Whigs were bedecking themselves in log-cabin badges, bellowing log-cabin songs, and lubricating their throats with plenty of hard

Questioning the Campaign Barbecues

ELECTION BARBECUES DREW huge crowds during the 1830s and 1840s, but not everyone was convinced that they were effective means of winning votes—especially if they were being held by a rival party. In November 1842, Henry Clay addressed a crowd of three thousand at a Whig barbecue in Frankfort, Kentucky. The solidly Democratic *Brooklyn Eagle* delightedly reported an incident that allegedly brought the event to a rapid close: "In the midst of [Clay's] speech, Nichol's circus company entered the town; whereupon nine-tenths of his auditory scampered off to look at the circus cavalcade and monkeys that accompanied it. We are informed that 'that same old coon' was exceedingly enraged at the ill-manners of the flint pickers, and broke off in the midst of his harangue, and started off in double-quick time for the 'peaceful shades of Ashland' [Clay's Kentucky estate]."

Source: *Brooklyn (NY) Eagle*, November 18, 1842, 2.

cider. In Bowling Green, Kentucky, James Murrell constructed an eight-by-twelve-foot log cabin for the Harrison barbecue on the Fourth of July. The structure was drawn to the barbecue grounds on a wagon by six white horses decorated with flags and banners, and some four thousand attendees listened while speeches were made from the cabin's front door. A hundred miles west in Henderson County, the female attendees at a Harrison barbecue wore white aprons with log cabins painted on them and dined at long tables decorated with log cabins built out of stick candy. Similar events were staged across the South and Midwest, ranging as far west as Mendon, Illinois, where hundreds of Whigs came from miles around to "consume the roasted carcasses of oxen, sheep, and hogs."[25]

The popular vote was close, but Harrison beat Van Buren handily in the electoral college, 234 to 60. The Whigs' successful tactics would be repeated by both parties in the presidential elections of 1844 and 1848 as well as the congressional elections in intervening years, establishing the barbecue as the premier form of political campaigning in mid-nineteenth-century America.

Whig Election Chant

Democrats—
They eat rats!
But Whigs
Eat pigs!

Source: Marion Harland, *Marion Harland's Autobiography: The Story of a Long Life* (New York: Harper & Brothers, 1910), 122.

A Visit to an Antebellum Barbecue

By the 1840s enough descriptions of barbecues had been published for us to piece together a composite picture of a typical event. The setting was almost always outdoors, usually in a wooded grove near a running spring. The shade was essential during the heat of summer and early fall, and the spring was not only cooling but also provided drinking water for the dinner—for those who were interested in water, at least.

The preparations typically began several days before the actual event, as animals had to be procured, brought to the site, and slaughtered and dressed. Barbecue fans today debate whether pork or beef or even mutton is the proper meat for "real barbecue," but in the early days there were few regional preferences. Members of the community donated whatever livestock they had on hand, and it is quite common in early descriptions to see a long list of animals including beef cattle, oxen, hogs, sheep, goats, and chickens. In frontier areas, game such as deer, wild turkeys, and squirrels were often donated for the cause, too.

To create the pit, workers dug a long, shallow trench in the earth, four to six feet wide and anywhere from six to several hundred feet long, depending on the size of the gathering and the amount of meat to be cooked. Piles of hardwood such as oak or hickory were set ablaze in the pits and allowed to burn until reduced to coals, which were then spread throughout the trenches to prepare for the cooking. Once the pits were ready, the animal carcasses, which generally were kept whole or split lengthwise, were run through with either green sticks or iron bars and laid across the pit.

THE BARBECUE.

Basting the whole hogs at an antebellum Virginia barbecue. From *My Ride to the Barbecue: or, Revolutionary Reminiscences of the Old Dominion.* (New York, S. A. Rollo, 1860)

Tending the pit was a difficult job. In the South, as had been the case in the co-lonial era, the actual work was usually performed by enslaved persons. In some cases white men might have supervised the pits, but frequently an older African American man would be recognized as the area's top barbecuer, and he would oversee the entire cooking operation. Pots of basting liquid—usually melted butter, vinegar, and/or water along with salt and pepper—were kept along the trench, and the cooks would move up and down either side, basting the meat with long-handled brushes. The whole carcasses had to be lifted periodically and turned over, and a small pit of hardwood was kept burning off to the side to supply fresh coals, which were shoveled into the trenches to ensure a constant source of slow, steady heat. This procedure lasted many hours—frequently beginning early in the morning or even the night before—so that the meat would be finished and ready for the crowds by early afternoon.

The grove in which the barbecue was held would be temporarily transformed from an ordinary stand of woods into an outdoor auditorium and banquet hall. Stakes were driven into the ground, crosspieces attached, and boards laid along the top to form long if somewhat rude tables. Puncheons—large logs hewn in half—were used for benches, and they were sometimes buried into the dirt, too, flat sides up, to form a floor for dancing. A platform was generally erected at one end of the grove, where the politicians would make their speeches. These typically began before noon and lasted well into the afternoon before the crowds were finally released to go to the tables and begin feasting.

By most accounts, barbecues were boisterous events and—through the early decades of the nineteenth century, at least—whiskey flowed freely alongside the pit-cooked meats. Once the meal was over, toasts were drunk, and the celebration generally lasted through the afternoon and sometimes into the early evening. The combination of alcohol with political passions was sometimes a dangerous one, and campaign barbecues were occasionally marred by violence. At a barbecue at Bynum's Spring in Alabama, for example, an altercation erupted between "Squire" Maury, a Whig partisan, and a Jacksonian Democrat silversmith named Murdock. Maury drew a spear hidden within his walking cane and ran Murdock through three times in his abdomen. Maury seems to have gotten his point across, but fortunately for Murdock, the spear was not particularly sharp. The Democrat survived, and "in a short time he was out again hurrahing for Jackson."[26]

The ongoing presence of whiskey and violence aside, by the 1840s the campaign barbecue had evolved, both in the older eastern states and on the western frontier, from a rustic celebration into a more organized venue for political discourse. Its significance to American public life only continued to grow in the decades that followed.

A Democratic Barbecue, 1844

As a young woman, the author Marion Harland (born Mary Virginia Hawes) attended a Democratic campaign barbecue in 1844 near her home in Powhatan, Virginia. She recorded a detailed remembrance of the event in her autobiography. It was held in a field on the outskirts of the village, and though the Hawes family were the staunchest of Whigs, they showed up for the festivities along with most of the other area residents. Harland's account offers the first recorded appearance of Brunswick stew at a barbecue. A dish that generally includes chicken or squirrel meat, corn, lima beans, and tomatoes, Brunswick stew is a traditional accompaniment to barbecue in Virginia and eastern North Carolina.

We crossed the stream upon a shaking plank laid from bank to bank, and strolled down the slope to the scene of operations. An immense kettle was swung over a fire of logs that were so many living coals. The smell of Brunswick stew had been wafted to us while we leaned on the fence. A young man, who had the reputation of being an epicure, to the best of his knowledge and ability, superintended the manufacture of the famous delicacy.

"Two dozen chickens went into it!" he assured us. "They wanted to make me think it couldn't be made without green corn and fresh tomatoes. I knew a trick worth two of that. I have worked it before with dried tomatoes and dried sweet corn soaked overnight."

He smacked his lips and winked fatuously.

"I've great confidence in your culinary skill," was the good-natured rejoinder.

I recollected that I had heard my father say of this very youth: "I am never hard upon a fellow who is a fool because he can't help it!" But I wondered at his gentleness when the epicure prattled on: "Yes, sir! a stew like this is fit for Democrats to eat. I wouldn't give a Whig so much as a smell of the pot!"

"You ought to have a tighter lid, then," with the same good-humored intonation, and we passed on to see the roasts. Shallow pits, six or seven feet long and four feet wide, were half filled with clear coals of hard hickory billets. Iron bars were laid across these, gridiron-like, and half-bullocks and whole sheep were cooking over the scarlet embers. There were six pits, each with its roast. The spot for the speakers' rostrum and the seats of the audience was well

continued on next page

continued from previous page

selected. A deep spring welled up in a grove of maples. The fallen red blossoms carpeted the ground, and the young leaves supplied grateful shade. The meadows sloped gradually toward the spring; rude benches of what we called "puncheon dogs"—that is, the trunks of trees hewed in half, and the flat sides laid uppermost—were ranged in the form of an amphitheatre.

"You have a fine day for the meeting," observed my father to the master of ceremonies, a planter from the Genito neighborhood, who greeted the visitors cordially.

"Yes, sir! The Lord is on our side, and no mistake!" returned the other, emphatically. "Don't you see that yourself, Mr. Hawes!"

"I should not venture to base my faith upon the weather," his eyes twinkling while he affected gravity, "for we read that He sends His rain and sunshine upon the evil and the good. Good-morning! I hope the affair will be as pleasant as the day."

Source: Marion Harland, *Marion Harland's Autobiography: The Story of a Long Life* (New York: Harper & Brothers, 1910), 24–26.

3

≡

THE BARBECUE COMES OF AGE

THE PRESIDENTIAL ELECTIONS OF the 1840s cemented the status of the barbecue as a political institution not only in the American South but in the Midwest, too. Over the next two decades, the barbecue continued to mature, becoming the preeminent form of public celebration in America. Propelled by the expansionist aims of Manifest Destiny, the barbecue moved west, becoming a regular part of frontier life everywhere from Texas all the way to the Pacific coast. Along the way, it became more civilized, too.

This change was, in part, a reflection that America was transitioning from a frontier nation to a settled society. The rough trappings of the early days—especially the hard drinking and fighting—were increasingly found unacceptable by many citizens. The growing presence of women at barbecues—particularly at political ones—also helped make the events more sedate. Even though women were denied the vote, the Whigs made a special effort to welcome them to their campaign events, believing they would influence the views of the male voters in their families. On August 5, 1844, Missouri Riddick of Suffolk, Virginia, wrote to her husband and described the preparations for a Democratic gathering at Cowling's Landings, to be held on August 10. Mrs. Riddick predicted that it would be "a poor affair" because "the ladies are not invited. I believe all of the ladies will attend the Whig Barbecue, as they are particularly invited, and tables and seats are to be provided for them."[1]

Barbecues remained predominantly male affairs, with the female attendees greatly outnumbered by males and treated as special guests. At a barbecue in Ninety Six, South Carolina, in 1856, some ten thousand people turned out to welcome Senator Preston Brooks home from Washington (more about that event in a moment). Only a thousand—one-tenth of the crowd—were women, and they sat in special temporary seating constructed on either side of the speakers' platform.[2]

The presence of women was not the only force driving change. The barbecue came of age amid the welter of reform movements spawned by the Second Great Awakening of the 1830s, most notably the temperance movement. Barbecues—especially Fourth of July barbecues—soon became a target for religious and civic reformers. The Old Salt River Primitive Baptist Church, one of the oldest organized churches in Anderson County, Kentucky, kept a tight rein on its congregation's moral conduct. In August 1815, several members were chastised for attending a July Fourth barbecue, and the following question was put before the church: "Is it right or wrong to attend a barbecue?" The congregation answered succinctly: "It is wrong." In July 1837, the editor of the *Cheraw Gazette* urged the town to cancel its annual Independence Day feast. "A people whose patriotism needs to be forced," he argued, "by the stimulants of alcoholic liquors and rich dinners may make good subjects, but not good citizens." Those sentiments were echoed by temperance advocate Frederic Lees, who complained that "drunkenness is so invariably a concomitant of great political excitement, that a vast concourse of men at a Presidential barbecue, without a single case of intoxication in it, is not merely a striking curiosity, but a subject worthy of profound study for the statesman."[3]

Most early temperance advocates were drawn from the ranks of the well-to-do and the clergy, and most were lifelong abstainers from alcohol. Portrayed as nagging scolds opposed to fun and sociability in all forms, some received rough treatment at the hands of prodrinking crowds. One unfortunate Methodist minister in Key West fell victim to "washing" by a crowd of sailors and local tavern goers, who tied a rope around his waist and shoulders, cast him from a wharf into the water, then reeled him in and cast him back again. In 1839 Josiah Flourney, a Methodist planter from Georgia, launched a statewide campaign to elect protemperance candidates to the legislature. His meetings were broken up by angry crowds, who threatened Flourney, destroyed his buggy, and shaved and painted his mule.[4]

No one likes a killjoy, and reformers quickly realized that they were unlikely to succeed if, in their zeal to stamp out drunkenness, they attacked the amusement and social interaction that came along with the drinking. After all, it wasn't the cooking or eating of barbecue that the temperance advocates found objectionable; it was the excessive boozing that took place at the events. Instead of condemning barbecues, why not enlist them in the cause? So, temperance organizations started staging competing events to draw crowds away from the whiskey-soaked affairs. In 1846, the Salubrity Temperance Society staged a July Fourth Temperance barbecue near Liberty, South Carolina. Allen Fuller, the society's secretary, contrasted his organization's event with the dissipated Fourth of July barbecue at nearby Wolf Creek. At the latter, "the lovers of strong drink assembled in multitudes. The candidates for office were there, and dealt out the liquor in profusion, and profanity, drunkenness and quarrelling were the order of the day. One of its advocates admitted that it was the most disorderly company he had ever seen." In contrast, the Salubrity Temperance Society's event, held "on cold-water principles," was calm and pleasant, and Fuller believed it to be "the means of advancing the temperance cause in this vicinity."[5]

"Cold water barbecues" were warmly embraced by the Washingtonian Temperance Society, an organization of "dry drunks" who sought to convert other drinkers to the life of temperance. Rather than pursuing prohibition through legislation, the Washingtonians focused on the individual drinker, with the goal of getting converts to sign the "teetotal" pledge of total abstinence. To do so, they embraced public meetings, parades, and—especially in the southern states—barbecues. A Washingtonian cold water barbecue held in July 1842 in Quincy, Florida, illustrates the evangelical and ritual aspects of the temperance gatherings that made the Washingtonian events such a draw. Dressed in their finest clothes, the participants created a grand procession, with the women in carriages flanked by the men on horseback, "with badges on their left breast and the banner of Temperance unfurled to the breeze." They paraded to the Methodist church, where a series of speeches encouraged attendees to come forward and sign the pledge. Lee Willis, who studied the temperance and prohibition movement in Florida for his doctoral dissertation, concluded that the Washingtonian revivals flourished because "they substituted for masculine drinking rituals and provided an alternative form of intoxication." Which is to say they offered the holy spirit instead of the more earthly variety.[6]

Before long the influence of the temperance movement began to shape mainstream public barbecues, too. In 1837, Mary Morangé, the daughter of a planter in the

Abbeville District of South Carolina, attended the local Fourth of July barbecue and noted that after the barbecue was served, "some cold water toasts were drunk which nearly froze on the lips." In 1843, the *Greenville Mountaineer* noted that in Pickens, South Carolina, the Independence Day barbecue had been served "with nothing to wash it down but cold water." Though the newspapers still published the text of the toasts made at these events, many, like the *Greenville Mountaineer* in 1844, noted "the drink part, as is usual, being dispensed with."[7]

Now barbecues were no longer frowned on as dangerous or dissolute by the more respectable members of the community, and they only grew in popularity. By the 1840s newspaper stories and advertisements were referring to "old-fashioned" barbecues, for the rituals and characteristics of the events had long become part of society's traditions, and the largest gatherings grew to tens of thousands of guests. When a barbecue was held, virtually everyone in the surrounding county would turn out to eat roasted pork and listen to campaign speeches and, above all, to meet their friends and see what everyone else was doing. Barbecue had become an essential American social institution.

"Nat Joined the Temperance Society"

Nat Monteith was a good-natured free and easy individual from boyhood up. He was a great lover of "pot-liquor," and whenever cabbage would be prepared for dinner, the cook would invariably call to him, when she'd hear his well known footsteps, to come and get some of the homely beverage. There had been quite a revival among the advocates of temperance, and a "Cold Water Army," for the benefit of the boys, had been organized—backed by a barbecue in the Court House grounds, northeast corner Main and Washington streets. Next day the cook called to him that she had his "pot-liquor" ready. "No, Aunt Jane, can't take it: joined the temperance society."

Source: Julian A. Selby, *Memorabilia and Anecdotal Reminiscences of Columbia, S.C. and Incidents Connected Therewith* (Columbia, SC: R. L. Bryan, 1905), 34.

Tending the pits at a Georgia barbecue, late nineteenth century. (Author's collection)

Brunswick Stew

As barbecue spread, new elements were incorporated into the tradition, including new dishes that started to be served alongside the roasted meat. One of the earliest barbecue side dishes was Brunswick stew. The origins of this now-famous concoction have been hotly debated, with two different Brunswicks—one a city in Georgia and the other a county in Virginia—claiming to be its original home. The Georgia contingent offers a very tangible piece of evidence to support its claim: a twenty-five-gallon iron pot. It's affixed to a stone base in a park in downtown Brunswick, with an inscription reading, "In this pot the first Brunswick Stew was made on St. Simon Isle July 2 1898." A mess sergeant, the story goes, created the stew for a company of soldiers stationed on the island. He followed no particular recipe, using whatever meats and vegetables he had on hand. The stew turned out so tasty that local residents started copying his formula.

It might be true that the first Brunswick stew ever made on St. Simons Island was cooked in 1898 in that now-memorialized pot, but it certainly wasn't the first

Brunswick stew to be made in America. It wasn't even the first in the state of Georgia. Newspaper stories recorded Brunswick stew's being served at various outdoor barbecues around the state in the 1880s. A decade earlier, in 1871, the stew was featured in advertisements for Med Henderson's saloon in Savannah. That summer, Henderson started serving for his daily free lunch such hearty delicacies as clam chowder, okra soup, and "Old Virginia Brunswick Stew."[8]

Henderson's ads point to the real birthplace of Brunswick stew, and the evidence that originated in Virginia is conclusive, including written accounts dating from well before the Civil War. In 1846, a newspaper account of a barbecue at Huguenot Springs, a resort west of Richmond, noted that "a capital squirrel stew—called by some a Brunswick stew—was the favorite of the table." Three years later, the *Alexandria Gazette* described the stew as "a genuine South-side dish, composed of squirrels, chicken, a little bacon, and corn and tomatoes, *ad libitum*."[9]

Whether the dish was devised by a single cook or evolved out of more general hunting stews is less certain. The earliest account of Brunswick stew's origins, which appeared in the *Petersburg Intelligencer* in 1855, doesn't mention the names of any specific cooks. It instead notes that "in the good old county of Brunswick" it had long been the custom during the hot summers "to repair almost every Saturday to some spring, to spend half the day." For entertainment, the men would shoot squirrels, and these (along with some chicken if the hunter came up short) "were placed in a pot with a sufficient quantity of water and set to stewing over a slow fire. In due time were added tomatoes, corn, butter-beans, potatoes, with the requisite condiments of salt and Cayenne pepper."[10]

Over the decades, other accounts added more specific details to the story and linked it to a specific originator. Several accounts published between 1877 and 1907 attribute the creation of Brunswick stew to a man named James Matthews from the Red Oak neighborhood in Brunswick County. A veteran of the War of 1812, Matthews, as one account describes him, was a man of "a roving disposition, and a man of refinement" who bounced around as a guest from one area household to another, making himself welcome through his skills as a squirrel hunter and a cook. Matthews started making his stew sometime around 1820, and his recipe was quite simple. He cooked the squirrels in water along with bacon and onions, stewing them until the flesh separated from the bones, which were skimmed out. He finished the pot with butter and breadcrumbs and seasoned it with salt and pepper. Matthews earned a reputation across the county for his stew, which he was delighted to make at picnics and public gatherings. After Matthews's death, various cooks succeeded him as the local stew master, including Dr. Aaron B. Haskins, Jack Stith, and Colonel W. T. Mason. Each man brought his own innovation to the recipe. Haskins was said to have added a touch of brandy or Madeira wine for flavor. Stith introduced vegetables sometime during the 1830s, adding tomatoes, onions, corn, and potatoes.[11]

By the 1840s, Brunswick stew had spread beyond the borders of its namesake county and had become a staple of barbecues across the state of Virginia. In her account of the 1844 Democratic barbecue outside Richmond (see pages 47–48), Marion Harland recalled a Brunswick stew made from two dozen chickens and cooked in an immense kettle over a log fire. The 1878 cookbook *Housekeeping in Old Virginia*, a compilation of recipes from 250 Virginia housewives, contains four different recipes for Brunswick stew. Three call for either squirrel or chicken, while one calls for a shank of beef. All four include corn and tomatoes.[12]

After the Civil War, Brunswick stew spread beyond the borders of Virginia. It appears in accounts of barbecues in North Carolina in the 1870s. It really didn't show up in Georgia until the last decades of the nineteenth century, and it did so not as a direct descendant of the Virginia-born stew but rather as an amalgamation of several regional barbecue stews. We'll save that part of the story for later.[13]

Brunswick stew pots at a Georgia barbecue. (*Strand Magazine*, 1898)

Two Recipes for Brunswick Stew

IN 1855, THE *Petersburg Intelligencer* offered the following account of the origins of Brunswick stew:

> In the proper season of the year, when Summer's vegetable gifts abound, and when Summer's heats invite cool springs and shady bowers, it was the custom of the different neighborhoods of Brunswick to repair almost every Saturday to some spring, to spend half the day. For the entertainments *inwardly* of the company a sufficient number of squirrels were shot, and in the absence of a supply of them, chickens were to do the duty and often they were used in combination. These articles were placed into a pot with a sufficient quantity of water and set to stewing over a slow fire. In due time were added tomatoes, corn, butter-beans, potatoes, and the requisite condiments of salt and Cayenne pepper, all of which, when properly cooked, furnished to the participators a feast which Apicius might have envied.

Fifteen years later, a Mississippi newspaper offered a more elaborate recipe that included veal and port wine: "Below we publish a recipe for making this famous old-fashioned Virginia stew: First put in one chicken (or squirrel,) a quarter of a pound of bacon, half a pound of veal (or mutton,) and boil them together for half an hour; afterward, put in six ears of corn, one pint of butter beans, one quart of small Irish potatoes, one quart of tomatoes (small size,) and, if you like, about half a pint of port wine, and boil together as long as suitable to taste."

Sources: "A Brunswick Stew," *Alexandria (VA) Gazette*, June 26, 1855, 4; "Recipe for 'Brunswick Stew,'" *Tri-Weekly Clarion* (Meridian, MS), January 6, 1870, 2.

Barbecue in the Life of Enslaved Americans

As with most aspects of American history, barbecue is thoroughly intertwined with the issues of race and slavery, often in contradictory ways. On the one hand, slaveholders used barbecues as an instrument of control, staging Fourth of July and Christmas barbecues for their enslaved workers, purportedly as gifts or rewards for their labor. These displays of supposed generosity helped reinforce the notion that slaveholders were benevolent masters—a notion crucial to the South's conception of its "peculiar institution." Enslaved people's experience with barbecue, though, was much broader than just these officially sanctioned events.

As in earlier decades, enslaved workers had frequently staged their own barbecues on days of rest, but slaveholders curtailed this practice after several incidents—most notably Gabriel's Rebellion in Henrico County, Virginia—where such gatherings were used as cover to plan uprisings. Illicit barbecues with stolen livestock, however, remained a common way for slaves to have entertainment at their masters' expense.

Thirty-one years after Gabriel's Rebellion, on a Sunday afternoon in August, six slaves met at noon in the woods on the plantation of Joseph Travis in the Cross Keys neighborhood in Southampton County, Virginia, bringing with them some brandy and a pig for a barbecue. At three o'clock they were joined by a seventh slave named Nat Turner, a charismatic carpenter and preacher, and—putting in place a plan that had been in the works for six months—they left the barbecue, gathered fifty more slaves, and proceeded on a two-day assault against the white families in Virginia. In the end, fifty-five white men, women, and children were killed before the local militia violently suppressed the revolt, and more than one hundred slaves were killed in retaliation.[14]

The Nat Turner Rebellion was the bloodiest slave revolt in American history, and it marked a turning point in the institution of slavery. News of the revolt caused panic throughout the South, and whites formed vigilance committees and severely curtailed the remaining freedoms of both slaves and free blacks. State legislatures enacted laws prohibiting slaves, free blacks, and mulattoes from being taught to read, preaching without a white minister present, and practicing medicine. Many whites blamed abolitionists and the ongoing Missouri Compromise debates for causing slave unrest, and the Nat Turner Rebellion helped heighten the tensions that eventually led to the Civil War. It also brought to a halt the freedom of movement that had allowed slaves to organize their own barbecues and gather with fellow slaves from other farms and plantations.

But barbecue still played an important role in the social life of enslaved Americans. In the cotton states of the Deep South—especially Georgia, Alabama, and Mississippi—barbecues were common on plantations straight up until the Civil War. At a typical plantation, barbecues were the centerpiece of two holidays: Christmas and either the Fourth of July or a more general late-summer holiday held once the crops were "laid by," meaning cultivation was complete and the hardest labor was over until the autumn harvest. The plantation owner usually supplied the meat for the occasion, which might be a pig, sheep, or even a cow, and the enslaved workers often supplemented this with produce from their own garden patches. In most places slaves were given the entire day off to do as they pleased, and frequently they were allowed to invite friends from other plantations to join in the festivities. The meat was prepared using the standard method, with a long trench dug in the ground and the carcasses placed on long spits or poles over the glowing coals. The smoked meat was the centerpiece of the feast, but there was a range of side items as well. Some of the more common foods appearing in contemporary accounts include chicken pies, sweet potato pies, "light" bread, and cornbread along with desserts like ginger cake, molasses cake, peach cobbler, and apple dumplings.

In some cases, drinking was not a part of the festivities, for owners were wary of alcohol use among the enslaved. Louis Hughes recalled that at the Fourth of July barbecues on the plantation where he was enslaved near Pontotoc, Mississippi, "the drinks were temperance drinks—buttermilk and water." This was not true across the board. Lina Hunter from Oglethorpe County, Georgia, remembered that at the barbecues following the cotton harvest there was "lots of drinkin' and dancin'." When a WPA interviewer questioned Mose Davis's memory of whiskey being available on his master's plantation, he replied, "The Colonel was one of the biggest devils you ever seen—he's the one that started my daddy to drinking. Sometimes he used to come to our house to git a drink hisself."[15]

With or without whiskey, dancing was almost always an important part of plantation barbecues, with music provided by one or more fiddlers. Virginia Tunstall Clay-Clopton recalled visiting "Redcliffe," the South Carolina plantation home of James Henry Hammond, and witnessing the dancing at the Fourth of July and Christmas barbecues. "There is a tall black man, called Robin," she wrote, "on this plantation, who has originated a dance he calls the turkey-buzzard dance. He hold his hands under his coat-tails, which he flirts out as he jumps, first to one side, and then to the other, and looks exactly like the ugly bird he imitates."[16]

Barbecues were also employed as an incentive for collaborative work. Corn shuckings were the most common of such events. After the corn was harvested, it needed to be shucked, dried, and stored or ground into meal. All the hands on a plantation,

A corn shucking on Fred Wilkins's farm near Stem, North Carolina, 1940. This common form of collaborative farm work had its roots in antebellum plantation life and lasted well into the twentieth century. (Courtesy Library of Congress, Prints and Photographs Division)

whether they worked in the fields or in the house, would be enlisted, and the owner would ask neighboring planters to send their workers, too. Hundreds of bushels of corn would be placed in a giant mound fifty or more feet high or in a long row that stretched hundreds of feet. Mahala Jewel, who lived on a plantation in Oglethorpe County, Georgia, recalled that the first thing the workers did at a corn shucking was to "elect a general." He would lead the singing and try to get everyone to join in his songs, which were all about corn, and as they sang faster, "the shucks flew faster too." William Wells Brown, an African American abolitionist and novelist, captured the lyrics of one such song, which included these lines: "I know dat supper will be big /

Shuck dat corn before you eat / I think I smell a fine roast pig / Shuck dat corn before you eat." Once the work was over, all the hands would retire to a barbecue feast, and music and dancing would continue long into the night. Hog killing and cotton picking were similar collaborative occasions where barbecue was traditionally served.[17]

Interpreting the role of barbecue in the lives of enslaved Americans can be tricky. On the one hand, barbecues appear frequently in oral history narratives and memoirs written by formerly enslaved southerners, and those events were often remembered as some of the brightest moments in otherwise bleak, difficult times. Louis Hughes, for instance, who was raised in slavery on a cotton plantation near Pontotoc, Mississippi, recalled that the annual Fourth of July barbecue "acted as a stimulant through the entire year. . . . It mattered not what trouble or hardship the year had brought, this feast and its attendant pleasure would dissipate all gloom." At the same time, white southerners incorporated plantation barbecues into the rhetoric they used to justify the institution of slavery, both during the sectionalist debate leading up to the Civil War and in the postwar moonlight-and-magnolias brand of historiography, which tried to paint slavery as a benevolent institution. The Fourth of July and Christmas celebrations were held up as examples of the generosity of slaveholders, and nostalgic accounts of life on the plantations routinely used sunny depictions of barbecues as proof that African Americans were content in their lives of servitude. Walter L. Fleming, for example, a professor of history at West Virginia University, described plantation barbecues in his 1905 history *Civil War and Reconstruction in Alabama*, emphasizing the singing and merrymaking and concluding, "The slaves were, on the whole, happy and content."[18]

Frederick Douglass, abolitionist leader and author of *Narrative of the Life of Frederick Douglass* (1845), had a different view. He judged the holidays granted to slaves to be not a custom of benevolence but rather "the most effective means in the hands of the slaveholder in keeping down the spirit of insurrection" and "part and parcel of the gross fraud, wrong, and inhumanity of slavery." Such events were "safety valves" that allowed the pent-up spirit of rebelliousness to be released. Douglass noted that many masters not only allowed slaves to get drunk on holidays but actively encouraged it through drinking contests and other means. In Douglass's view, this was not a form of entertainment but a means of enforcing control. The supposed holiday times of freedom became periods of dissipation ending with illness and hangover, so that "we staggered up from the filth of our wallowing, took a long breath, and marched to the field,—feeling, upon the whole, rather glad to go, from what our master had deceived us into a belief was freedom, back to the arms of slavery."[19]

Despite the stricter controls on movements and gatherings enforced after Nat Turner's Rebellion, not all barbecues were sanctioned by plantation owners. Estella Jones recalled that when she was growing up on a Georgia plantation called Powers Pond Place, the men would occasionally steal hogs, barbecue them, and serve them with hash and rice. "The overseer knowed all 'bout it," she remembered, "but he et as much as anybody else and kept his mouth shut." Whether explicitly at white-approved events or illicitly as a subversive form of entertainment, the tradition of barbecue was an important part of African American culture in the decades before the Civil War, and it would only deepen and expand after emancipation.[20]

A Plantation Barbecue

LOUIS HUGHES WAS born into slavery in Virginia in 1832 and was sold at age twelve to a cotton planter from Pontotoc, Mississippi. He worked as an errand boy and house servant and learned enough medicine to be able to treat fellow slaves. He was sent to Memphis in 1850 to work at the planter's new house in the city, and there he married. Hughes twice attempted to escape and was captured before he finally succeeded during the closing days of the Civil War. Hughes and his wife settled in Milwaukee, where he worked as a professional nurse. In 1897 he published *Thirty Years a Slave: From Bondage to Freedom*, his memoirs of life on a cotton plantation. In this autobiography, Hughes captured the following description of a plantation barbecue:

> Barbecue originally meant to dress and roast a hog whole, but has come to mean the cooking of a food animal in this manner for the feeding of a great company. A feast of this kind was always given to us by Boss, on the 4th of July. The anticipation of it acted as a stimulant through the entire year. Each one looked forward to this great day of recreation with pleasure. Even the older slaves would join in the discussion of the coming event. It mattered not what trouble or hardship the year had brought, this feast and its attendant pleasure would dissipate all gloom. Some, probably, would be punished on the morning

continued on next page

continued from previous page

of the 4th, but this did not matter; the men thought of the good things in store for them, and that made them forget that they had been punished. All the week previous to the great day, the slaves were in high spirits, the young girls and boys, each evening, congregating, in front of the cabins, to talk of the feast, while others would sing and dance. The older slaves were not less happy, but would only say: "Ah! God has blessed us in permitting us to see another feast day." The day before the 4th was a busy one. The slaves worked with all their might. The children who were large enough were engaged in bringing wood and bark to the spot where the barbecue was to take place. They worked eagerly, all day long; and, by the time the sun was setting, a huge pile of fuel was beside the trench, ready for use in the morning. At an early hour of the great day, the servants were up, and the men whom Boss had appointed to look after the killing of the hogs and sheep were quickly at their work, and, by the time they had the meat dressed and ready, most of the slaves had arrived at the center of attraction. They gathered in groups, talking, laughing, telling tales that they had from their grandfather, or relating practical jokes that they had played or seen played by others. These tales were received with peals of laughter. But however much they seemed to enjoy these stories and social interchanges, they never lost sight of the trench or the spot where the sweetmeats were to be cooked.

The method of cooking the meat was to dig a trench in the ground about six feet long and eighteen inches deep. This trench was filled with wood and bark which was set on fire, and, when it was burned to a great bed of coals, the hog was split through the back bone, and laid on poles which had been placed across the trench. The sheep were treated in the same way, and both were turned from side to side as they cooked. During the process of roasting the cooks basted the carcasses with a preparation furnished from the great house, consisting of butter, pepper, salt and vinegar, and this was continued until the meat was ready to serve. Not far from this trench were the iron ovens, where the sweetmeats were cooked. Three or four women were assigned to this work. Peach cobbler and apple dumpling were the two dishes that made old slaves smile for joy and the young fairly dance. The crust or pastry of the cobbler was prepared in large earthen bowls, then rolled out like any pie crust, only it was almost twice as thick. A layer of this crust was laid in the oven, then a half peck of peaches poured in, followed by a layer of sugar; then a covering of pastry was laid over all and smoothed around with a knife. The oven was then put over a bed of coals, the cover put on and coals thrown on it, and the process of baking began. Four of these ovens were usually in use at these feasts, so that enough of the pastry might be baked to supply all. The ovens were filled and refilled until there was no doubt about the quantity. The apple dumplings were made in the usual way, only larger, and served with sauce made from brown sugar. It lacked flavoring, such as cinnamon or lemon, yet it was a dish highly relished by all the slaves. I know that these feasts made me so excited, I could scarcely do my house duties, and I would never fail to stop and look out of the window from the dining room down into the quarters. I was eager to get through with my work and be with the feasters. About noon everything was ready to serve. The table was set in a grove near the quarters, a place set aside for these occasions. The tableware was not fine, being of tin, but it served the purpose, and did not detract from the slaves' relish for the feast. The drinks were strictly temperance drinks—buttermilk and water. Some of the nicest portions of the meat were sliced off and put on a platter to send to the great house for Boss and his family. It was a pleasure for the slaves to do this, for Boss always enjoyed it. It was said that the slaves could barbecue meats best, and when the whites had barbecues slaves always did the cooking. When dinner was all on the table, the invitation was given for all to come; and when all were in a good way eating, Boss and the madam would go out to witness the progress of the feast, and seemed pleased to see the servants so happy. Everything was in abundance, so all could have plenty—Boss always insisted on this. The slaves had the whole day off, and could do as they liked. After dinner some of the women would wash, sew or iron. It was a day of harmless riot for all the slaves, and I can not express the happiness it brought them. Old and young, for months, would rejoice in the memory of the day and its festivities, and "bless" Boss for this ray of sunlight in their darkened lives.

Hughes's account of the Fourth of July barbecue at Pontotoc should not be read as overly rosy or nostalgic, for his memoir as a whole is sober and unforgiving. The section immediately preceding this passage describes in detail the barbarous punishments used on the plantation, including stocks and rawhide whippings.

Source: Louis Hughes, *Thirty Years a Slave: From Bondage to Freedom* (Milwaukee: South Side Printing, 1897), 46–51.

Railroad and Booster Barbecues

The 1840s and 1850s witnessed the rise of the railroad, an innovation that transformed American economy and society, and barbecue played an important role in its early years. Though stories of railroad building often portray the enterprise as the province of great individualists, railroad building was very much a community affair, and barbecue was involved on both the front end and the back. Railroad promoters used the prospect of free barbecue to draw citizens to giant rallies in support of their ventures. Once the railroads were built, townspeople would stage grand barbecues to celebrate the completion of railroad lines to their communities, for the arrival of the trains would ensure a town's future economic fortune—and doom those of communities bypassed by the lines.

Building a railroad was an expensive proposition. A mile of track could cost anywhere from $20,000 to $50,000 to build, depending on the difficulty of the terrain. Before the Civil War the federal government provided little in the way of railroad funding, and the large eastern and European banks showed scant interest, too. Some state governments provided loans to railroad corporations, but most early funding came from individual investors. Most railroads were organized as corporations with state charters, and they raised the money to build their lines by selling capital stock or issuing bonds. The charters gave railroads broad powers, including monopoly rights on rail service to defined areas, partial or total exemptions from state taxes, and the right to create banks and sponsor lotteries. In cases where state legislatures did provide loans or other funding to railroads, the money was often tied to the company's success in raising capital, with the state providing matching funds when the company had raised a specified amount from private investors.[21]

And that meant railroad promoters needed to get out in the community and drum up an initial round of committed investments. Many of those who "subscribed" for shares in early railroad companies were farmers and tradesmen living along the proposed routes, or merchants and professional men in the lines' terminal cities. They were motivated not just by the potential of earning income from the investment itself but also by the hope that the railroad would improve land values, open new markets, and lead to a general increase in trade for their city or region. The first generation of railroads were driven by investors in eastern port cities, who saw the lines as a way to

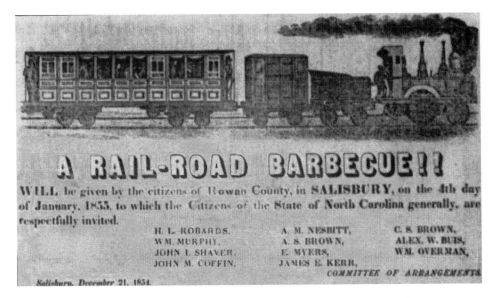

Advertisement for an 1854 railroad barbecue in Salisbury, North Carolina. (*Carolina Watchman*, December 21, 1854)

gain a greater share of the commerce from western markets. They were also supported by farmers along the routes, who sought a cheaper way to get their crops to market than by river or wagon.

To raise capital from these small investors, entrepreneurs needed to gather large crowds and create enthusiasm for their ventures. In midcentury America there was no surer way of gathering a crowd than holding a barbecue. The "railroad barbecue" became a staple of civic life in the South and Midwest during the 1840s and 1850s. In 1847, the citizens of Chester, South Carolina, combined their traditional Independence Day celebration with an event meant to raise money to complete the railroad from Columbia to Charlotte, which would pass through Chester. Following the standard speeches, the assembled citizens "partook of an excellent Barbacue, and again returned to the [speakers'] stand, where the Toasts were read, and the books opened for subscription to the Rail Road." With bellies full of barbecue (and, most likely, a good bit of liquor), the townsmen poured forth their pledges, and the amount subscribed was $150,000—three-quarters of the $200,000 needed to secure the matching pledge from the state delegation. The railroad line was eventually funded in full and reached Charlotte.[22]

By 1850, some $300 million had been invested in building railroads. A decade later that amount exceeded $1.1 billion. Some thirty thousand miles of track had been laid, and railroads served all states east of the Mississippi. Despite these successes, though, barbecues were a relatively inefficient way to recruit subscribers. The lure of free barbecue and whiskey would draw guests from miles around and fill them with "Railroad Enthusiasm" when the sponsors opened the subscription books. But a subscription was not an actual financial transaction, just a promise to buy stock when it was eventually issued. Robert Hubard of Buckingham County, Virginia, who was helping raise funds for a "Straight Shoot" railroad, summed it up nicely in a letter to his brother: "4th of July barbecues afford good opportunities for the sovereigns to eat and drink to excess, but those who drink most liquor are not always most able to pay for the stock which their whiskey generosity and public spirit may tempt them to subscribe for."[23]

After the Civil War, eastern financiers and European banks began to get in on the action, and railroads were increasingly built by corporations dominated by a few wealthy individuals. The federal government also became actively involved, providing massive grants of government land to the railroad companies for each mile of track constructed. The companies could mortgage or sell this land to provide the capital for building additional miles. Public gatherings and subscriptions ceased to be an important means of financing the rails.

Barbecues may have proved an unreliable way to fund railroads, but they were a great way to celebrate their completion. Newspapers from the 1840s and 1850s are filled with accounts of massive gatherings to celebrate the arrival of the first train to a particular city. It was not only a recognition of the labor and effort involved in building the rails but also a celebration of the town and its future prosperity, which the arrival of the railroad helped secure. In June 1842 the city of Columbia, South Carolina, staged a massive assembly to welcome the arrival of the first passenger train from Charleston. The day chosen for this first run, June 29, was also the anniversary of the battle of Fort Moultrie during the Revolution, which at the time was a day of statewide celebration. At 6:00 A.M., two trains left the Line Street depot in Charleston and started for Columbia. Their passengers included prominent Charleston citizens, members of the Artilleurs Français militia company, and two pieces of ordnance. The train arrived in Columbia around 4:00 P.M. and was met by the Washington Light Infantry and some five thousand Midlands residents. Following welcome speeches from local dignitaries, the crowd "adjourned to the adjacent grove" for what was advertised as "a regular old fashioned BARBACUE." The meats for the barbecue were given particular attention, as the prized stock of Congaree planters were contributed for all to enjoy, including Bakewell sheep, Berkshire pigs, and Durham calves, all of which were new breeds recently imported from England.[24]

Barbecue Heads West

Barbecue had long been a feature of life on the American frontier, and as settlers pushed that frontier westward they took the barbecue tradition with them. Indeed, barbecues ended up playing a supporting role in the first major conflict that resulted from American expansionism: the Mexican-American War.

Tensions had been simmering between the United States and Mexico ever since 1836, when the largely American population of the province of Texas declared independence from Mexico and established the Republic of Texas. Things came to a head in 1845 when the United States admitted Texas to the Union as the twenty-eighth state. After several failed negotiation efforts and a border skirmish that killed eleven Americans, the United States declared war in May 1846.

The standing American army was in no shape for the conflict. The regular army numbered fewer than six thousand troops, and many senior officers were too old for active duty. In May, President Polk signed a war act authorizing fifty thousand volunteers to be recruited. Each soldier would be enlisted for twelve months of service and provide his own uniform—and his own horse, too, if he wanted to be in a cavalry unit. And that's where the barbecues came in. The states in the Deep South and the Midwest contributed the most soldiers to the war, and state militia leaders staged grand barbecues to recruit volunteers. Once the volunteer units were assembled, communities organized barbecues to give them a rousing send-off before they headed south to the Mexican border.[25]

Attala County, Mississippi, raised close to one hundred volunteers in the fall of 1846. Because the county had no railroads, the departing soldiers marched on foot to Canton, where they joined detachments from nearby Madison and Holmes. There, the people of Madison had laid out a huge barbecue for the soldiers, and after everyone had eaten their fill, the townspeople organized a convoy of wagons to haul the troops to Jackson, where they could board the only railroad in the state and make their way to New Orleans to board ships to Mexico.[26]

One of the curiosities of the volunteer system was the twelve-month term of service. It was short enough to encourage a lot of volunteers, but, with training and transport time taken into account, it meant a soldier would serve only a few months of active combat duty before it was time for him to return home. So, in the middle of the war, local communities once again staged grand barbecues, this time to welcome the local boys home. In their details, these war barbecues looked much like the standard Fourth of July and political barbecues. What's most interesting about the Mexican War celebrations is their geographical reach, which shows that by the 1840s the institution of barbecue had spread quite far beyond the American South. In a volume titled *Indiana in the Mexican War*, Oran Perry, the adjutant general of Indiana, compiled more than a dozen instances of barbecues held to welcome home volunteers returning from the war. These celebrations occurred in the counties bordering the Ohio River near Louisville, Kentucky, and stretched westward across southern Indiana all the way to Sullivan County on the Illinois border. These southern parts of Indiana had been settled primarily by emigrants from southern states—especially Kentucky, Tennessee, and North Carolina—who brought with them their traditions of public celebration by way of the barbecue.[27]

Texas had been populated largely by settlers from Tennessee and Kentucky, too, and barbecue could be found in the territory even before the outbreak of the Mexican-American War. In 1840, the citizens of Austin invited Colonel John H. Moore to a public barbecue to honor him for commanding companies of volunteers in raids against the Comanche. Moore had been born in Rome, Tennessee, and came to Texas as part of the original "Old Three Hundred" group of settlers led by Stephen F. Austin. The lead member of the barbecue committee, Richard Fox Brenham, was born in Woodford County, Kentucky. Following Texas's admission to the Union in 1845, barbecue's role in the state's civic life would continue to grow, guided by old-timers from the Appalachian states. At Honey Grove in Fannin County, for example, the barbecue pits at the Fourth of July celebrations in the 1850s were overseen by "a Mr. Tate, a Kentuckian, who lived a few miles from town, was an expert in barbecuing meat, and could be had on most occasions."[28]

Texas today has its own distinct regional barbecue style (or, to be more accurate, four distinct styles), but in the early days of statehood its barbecues were almost indistinguishable from the events held back East. Beef dominates modern Texas barbecue, but in the mid-nineteenth century, as was the case throughout the country, the meats used were whatever the community donated to the cause. Early newspaper accounts of Texas barbecues mention beef, sheep, pigs, chicken, goats, and the occasional deer. The same reform movements that were transforming the barbecue tradition in the Old South and Midwest influenced early Texas barbecue as well. In 1848, the first year that Texans could vote in an American presidential election, the Democratic Party held a free barbecue and mass meeting at Paris in Lamar County. An advertisement for the event noted, "The Ladies are particularly invited to attend, and cheer and animate with their smiles." In 1850, citizens of Victoria and surrounding counties were invited to an "an old fashioned Free Barbacue" on the Fourth of July at which the ladies presented a Bible and banner to the Sons of Temperance.[29]

As American settlers pushed westward into the territories gained during the Mexican-American War, they took barbecue along with them. In previous eras, it had taken several decades for barbecue and the social traditions it represented to catch up with the frontiersmen. By the 1850s, settlers were better equipped, and the rituals of barbecue were more ingrained into the national culture. Barbecues could be found on the western frontier from the very beginning—sometimes making appearances even before settlers arrived at their final destinations. On July 3, 1849, a party of immigrants heading westward to the California gold fields arrived at Fort Bridger, Wyoming, a way station on the Oregon Trail. "Being Americans in heart and feeling," the *North American and United States Gazette* reported, "they determined upon the celebration of the Fourth in proper style." A little improvisation was required (the menu for the feast included pork and beans), but they dug a pit in the classic fashion and barbecued plenty of beef for all. As at any July Fourth barbecue, the Declaration of Independence was read, toasts were drunk, and "some fine songs sung." The next day the party departed for the 114-mile trek to the Great Salt Lake and from there on to Sacramento, which they expected to reach in twenty-five days.[30]

Once in California, prospectors and other adventurers continued the traditions they brought with them from more settled places. In 1850, the Fourth of July was celebrated in Sacramento with an "old-fashioned" barbecue, though it had a few frontier twists. Following a grand procession to a shady grove, a traditional Independence Day address was delivered by J. M. Jones—in Spanish. After the assembly retired to the barbecue tables, a guest named Major Dickey received four challenges to duels before he was finished eating his dinner.[31]

Things settled down within a few years. In 1853, the Fourth of July barbecue in Suisun Valley (midway between Sacramento and San Francisco) attracted 800 participants, 150 of them women. The address was delivered by the governor of California, and the barbecue was served on long tables under shade trees on the bank of a creek. For many, the mere fact that such events could be held at all—and, even more remarkable, held without drunken disturbances—was proof that the region was becoming civilized. The reporter for the *Placer Times and Transcript* concluded of the Suisun Valley barbecue, "Nothing can more forcefully demonstrate the rapid advancement of California in those essential elements of natural prosperity and glory than occasions like this in the midst of the country."[32]

As in the East, California barbecues were quickly seized upon by political parties. Five thousand people gathered outside San Jose in 1856 to hear stump speeches by candidates from the Democratic, Republican, and American Parties. Four oxen, ten sheep, and twenty-four hogs were barbecued for the occasion. When the local marshal caught two men carrying away a roasted pig, they tried to argue that "they were Democrats and were bound to go the whole hog," but the marshal made them return it to the tables. The attendees at such events reflected the diverse population of the western frontier, which was made up of immigrants from not only back East in the United States but also from Mexico and Europe, and political barbecues were often their first introduction to traditions of barbecue. The roasted meat at the San Jose event, one commentator noted, was "so sweet and tender that many who had never eaten such meat before, eat as though they never would have a chance to eat any more." A month later, at a Republican barbecue in Oakland, the speeches were delivered in English, French, German, and Spanish.[33]

Barbecues weren't limited to the Golden State. The first recorded barbecue in Nevada was held on New Year's Day 1853 in Dayton, a newly established town on the Carson River, where a few hundred prospectors were working gold and silver claims. One hundred fifty men and nine women attended the celebration. Similar events were held in Utah and the Oregon and Washington Territories. By the time Oregon was admitted to statehood in 1859, barbecue had spread to the most northwestern corner of the country.[34]

It can be fairly said that up until the 1840s barbecue was primarily a southern tradition, but by the eve of the Civil War that was emphatically no longer the case. Whether for political rallies, civic celebrations, or just a good time, barbecues were regular events in communities from the Atlantic coast to the Pacific. Only in the Northeast was the barbecue a relative stranger, and even there a few could be found now and again. Barbecue had become a national institution.

Kansas City's First Barbecue

TODAY, KANSAS CITY, Missouri, is considered to be one of America's great barbecue cities, with its own distinctive cooking style and dozens of legendary barbecue joints. In the early days, though, its residents were still getting the hang of it. The city was chartered in 1853, and five years later it had its first Fourth of July barbecue. There were a few hiccups, as a local historian recorded: "Colonel McGee offered the grove in McGee's addition. 3,000 people attended, 500 of whom . . . were wives and daughters. Banta's Band furnished the music. The celebration commenced at 10 o'clock in the morning, and ended with a ball that night at the Metropolitan hotel. Colonel McGee bought a buffalo for the barbecue, which got away a few days before. Excited neighbors gave chase and captured the buffalo after a chase of a mile or more."

Source: Carrie Westlake Whitney, *Kansas City, Missouri: Its History and Its People* (Chicago: S. J. Clarke, 1908), 657.

4

BARBECUE AND THE CIVIL WAR

ON MAY 19, 1856, Massachusetts senator Charles Sumner, leader of the Radical Republican faction and one of the most outspoken opponents of slavery, took to the floor of the Senate to deliver a stem-winder he had titled "The Crime against Kansas." The chamber was embroiled in the debate over the Kansas-Nebraska Act, which would permit settlers in the two territories to vote on whether to accept or reject slavery. Sumner spoke for five full hours, with the temperature in the Old Senate Chamber reaching ninety degrees in the early summer heat. Sumner declared that Senator Andrew Butler of South Carolina, one of the act's sponsors, was a Don Quixote who "believes himself a chivalrous knight" yet had chosen as a mistress "the harlot, Slavery." Butler had suffered a stroke that left him with speech problems and odd physical mannerisms, which Sumner mocked, claiming that Butler, "with incoherent phrases, discharged the loose expectoration of his speech."[1]

Two days later, as Sumner sat writing at his desk on the floor of the nearly empty Senate chamber, Representative Preston Brooks of South Carolina entered accompanied by two other southern politicians. Brooks, the nephew of Senator Butler, walked with a gold-headed cane because of a wound suffered during a duel. He approached the seated Sumner and declared, "Mr. Sumner, I have read your speech twice over carefully. It is a libel on South Carolina, and Mr. Butler, who is a relative of mine." As Sumner started to rise from his desk, Brooks began pounding him over the head with the cane, continuing until the cane broke and Sumner was left unconscious and bleeding on the floor.

The assault created a firestorm in the press, exposing the depth to which the issue of slavery had divided the country. Northern newspapers denounced the attack as an

Southern Chivalry—Argument versus Club's, an 1856 lithograph by John L. Magee depicting the caning of Charles Sumner by Preston Brooks in the US Senate chamber. Following the incident, Brooks was welcomed home to Edgefield County with a barbecue attended by more than ten thousand South Carolinians.

outrage against democracy and decency, while southern editors lauded Brooks as a noble defender of honor and chivalry. Brooks survived an expulsion vote from the House of Representatives but resigned his seat in July 1856, unrepentant of his actions.

The caning of Sumner on the floor of the Senate remains one of the most infamous incidents in American political history. Less remembered is that upon returning home to South Carolina, Preston Brooks was welcomed with a massive barbecue in his honor at Ninety Six in the Abbeville District. Between eight thousand and ten thousand people attended, and five tons of beef, pork, and mutton were barbecued for the event. Six tables were constructed, each two hundred feet in length, along with a large platform for the speakers and temporary seats for the ladies. Brooks was met at his hotel at 11:00 A.M. by a parade of gentlemen, including the governor of South Carolina, and escorted to the celebration. A band played patriotic tunes, and a series of orators took the platform to praise Brooks for his recent actions. One of these speakers, Dr.

Cain, concluded that the barbecue's turnout "showed plainly that his constituents approved his conduct upon a late occasion, when he prostrated the traducer of his State in the Senate Chamber of the United States. The act was noble; it was daring; and possibly it might be the means of solving the problem whether the South should have an equality in the Union or a separate independence out of it." Brooks was returned to the House of Representatives during the 1856 election, though he died of a sudden infection of croup only a few months later.[2]

Brooks's homecoming was only one of hundreds of barbecues where fierce partisan debates played out during the bitter sectionalist disputes that preceded the Civil War. In the Deep South, they were the venue where hardliners fanned the flames of secession among the general public. In the border states, barbecues played an even more instrumental role, for it was at these events that the debate was played out to determine whether to secede or remain in the Union.

The Election of 1860

The presidential election of 1860 was a four-way race. The Republicans nominated Abraham Lincoln at their convention in Chicago. The Democratic Party was divided along sectional lines over the issue of slavery in the territories, and it split into two conventions, with the northern faction backing Senator Stephen A. Douglas of Illinois and the southern faction nominating John C. Breckinridge of Kentucky, the sitting vice president. A fourth party, the National Constitutional Union, was formed specifically for the election, with a platform based solely on preserving the Union. John Bell of Tennessee was its nominee.

Public barbecues had been a requisite feature of national presidential elections since the Harrison and Van Buren race of 1840. Prior to 1860, though, the nominees themselves did not attend such events, remaining instead at their homes in a show of gentlemanly seclusion. Stephen Douglas broke from this tradition. Known as the "Little Giant" because of his short stature and political prominence, Douglas was a skilled and flamboyant orator, with a booming voice and a penchant for making dramatic gestures to enliven his platform appearances. He traveled widely throughout the country, sometimes delivering as many as twenty speeches a day.

The other three candidates tried to maintain the older tradition of seclusion, but as Douglas stumped his way across the countryside, their supporters increasingly encouraged them to take the field, too. After John J. Crittenden, the senior senator from

Kentucky and a supporter of John Bell, charged Breckinridge in a speech of leading the "disunion party," fifteen of Breckinridge's friends wrote a public letter to the *Lexington Standard*, urging him to address the people of Kentucky at a barbecue "for the purpose of publicly vindicating yourself from the violent personal assaults made upon you since your nomination." Breckinridge accepted, and arrangements were begun for the massive public barbecue that would be his only campaign appearance.[3]

John R. Viley, chair of the Committee of Arrangements, sought to secure the fairgrounds outside Lexington, but its owners refused, saying they did not want the property used for partisan purposes. Viley turned next to Ashland, the former home of Henry Clay and the site of a famous barbecue that had been given for the late Kentucky statesman back in 1837. Ashland was now owned by Henry Clay's son, James, a staunch Breckinridge supporter, who eagerly made his woodlands available. The choice of venue outraged old-time Whigs, who saw it as a sacrilege to allow a Democratic gathering on a spot sacred to the memory of their great leader, but the Breckinridge event moved ahead as planned.[4]

Trenches were dug and enough wood was laid in for barbecuing 5 beeves, 130 sheep, 100 shoats, and 60 hams. Special trains brought attendees from Louisville and Covington, and the crowd was estimated to number between eight thousand and fifteen thousand people. Breckinridge's arrival was hailed by a thirty-three-gun salute, and the candidate took to the stage for a vigorous three-hour defense of his political record, his platform, and his motives in pursuing the presidency. Above all, he defended himself and the southern Democrats against the charge of advocating disunion, arguing that he merely sought to protect the rights of all states and that it was the Republican Party members who were the real sectionalists and disunionists for trying to deny the constitutional rights of the southern states. The barbecue was hailed by the *Washington Constitution* as "the greatest political event of the present campaign."[5]

The Douglas camp was not about to let themselves be outdone by their southern rivals. They took the bold step of bringing the campaign barbecue to New York City for the first time. The Douglas Central Campaign Club announced in early September that a "Monster Democratic Rally, Grand Political Carnival, and Ox Roast" would be held on September 12 at Jones's Wood, a wooded estate on the edge of Manhattan (between present-day Sixty-Sixth and Seventy-Fifth Streets). A great "Kentucky ox" was procured for the occasion, and the animal was paraded through the city streets for two days to generate interest. More than twenty thousand people turned out, many drawn not so much by the chance to hear Douglas speak as by the novelty of tasting barbecued ox. The *New York Herald* declared, "Nothing like it in politics ever occurred here before."[6]

Indeed it had not, and the city's politicos had little experience staging outdoor barbecues. Their attempt devolved into chaos. The featured ox, along with a hog, a heifer, and two sheep, were slaughtered and roasted for the occasion by Bryan Lawrence, a butcher from Centre Market. An Irish immigrant who had arrived in New York City in 1836 at the age of nineteen, Lawrence would later go on to become a bank executive and philanthropist, which was probably for the best, for he showed little talent at the barbecue pit. One newspaperman reported than Lawrence's "well done" carcasses "very much resembled the charred remains which are sometimes seen in this city after the destruction of an old tenement home." The assembled crowd didn't seem to mind, though, for when "feeding time" was announced they quickly degenerated into a mob. Bursting through the pine fences that had been set up around the serving area, they overturned tables, scattered the bread and crackers, and seized whatever bits of meat they could grab. It took three hundred policemen to restore order and allow Douglas to finally take to the platform for his postbarbecue speech (see pages 77–78).[7]

It is not clear whether the Jones's Wood event actually helped Douglas or his cause among New York City's voters. The event and others like it, however, earned him plenty of brickbats from political commentators, who echoed the criticism that had been heaped on backwoods campaigners three decades before. The correspondent for the *Washington Constitution* scoffed at "the public exhibition of candidates for the highest offices in the world before as motley a crowd from the purlieus of New York as any the sun ever shone on." Douglas, he charged, was placing the presidential race "on a level with mountebank performances" by wandering through the country "like a traveling circus, attending clam bakes, barbecues, and tight-rope performances."[8]

In the end, barbecued ox and tireless stump speeches failed to carry the day for Douglas. The Little Giant outpolled Breckinridge and Bell in the popular vote, but the only state he carried was Missouri. Breckinridge carried the Deep South cotton states, while Bell captured the border states of Virginia, Kentucky, and Tennessee. Abraham Lincoln swept the free states, giving him a resounding majority in the electoral college, securing the presidency for the Republicans and pushing the country to the brink of war.

A Description of New York's First Political Barbecue

A CORRESPONDENT FOR the *New York Herald* provided this firsthand account of the Douglas barbecue debacle in Jones's Woods:

> On the left hand side of the pathway a large piece of ground was enclosed with a wooden fence, and about three thousand persons were gathered around (two-thirds of whom were of the "rowdy" class) shouting, waving small flags, and cheering, their greatest anxiety being to get into a position where they could be near the carver, who was preparing to "cut up the bullock." At the centre of the enclosure were eight temporary tables, erected for the purpose of holding the portions of roasted carcass, large piles of crackers, and the heaps of loaves of bread, which were very bountifully provided for the [original illegible], and were very temptingly displayed before the gaze of the hungry multitude. At about one o'clock the onslaught commenced, and the carver set to work with a will. One table, containing the crackers, fronted on the east side of the enclosed space, another, holding the large pieces of oily looking roasted fat pig, faced west; four others, on which the bread, mutton and beef were cut up, fronted on the south, and the remaining two, on one of which were the piles of loaves and on the other rested a whole quarter of the roasted ox, occupied a more central position. The pit at which the ox, the sheep and the hog were roasted occupied a place in the centre of the enclosure, and was about fifteen feet in length by six feet in width and four feet in depth.

DISTRIBUTION OF THE FOOD

> As many of the surrounding individuals were anxious, as soon as the carving commenced, to be within the pine fence, the police were kept actively engaged, running about, driving the intruders out of the "sacred limits," as none but the press were allowed inside the same unless they were legally engaged in distributing the food. The bread, having been cut into huge slices, was handed around on trays, each borne by two boys; and occasionally, in the anxiety of the "famished mortals," to get at the staff of life, the tray would be upset and a scramble ensue. The meat being also cut up in "chunks," were likewise handed round, but as "first come first served" seemed to be the wish of the crowd, a struggle ensued directly any of the provisions were offered, and, as is always

continued on next page

continued from previous page

the case, the "weakest went to the wall," or rather to the background of the mob, for by their conduct this part of the meeting could scarcely be otherwise designated.

DESTRUCTION OF THE FENCE

At last the patience of the mob began to expire, and fearful that they might not be able to get any of the gratuitous supply of roast beef, they resorted to physical force, and tore down the pine fences and burst into the enclosure. The police were in too small a force to keep the crowd now back, and a [most disgraceful scene ensued]. The shouting mob rushed to the not over-steady tables, on which were the provisions, and at once overturned them, with the exception of two, on one of which were large pieces of pork and mutton, and this the police surrounded; and the other, being occupied by the principal carver, the crowd respected as long as he could meet their demands. But at last he was obliged to give way and leave his post, and an onslaught at once commenced. One man attired in a puce colored shirt was very prominent, having secured a hatchet with which he hacked into pieces the quarter of the bullock and the larger joints that had not until then been mutilated. A scramble ensued to get from him portions of the several remains, and as fast as he divided the same so were the pieces wrested from him. At last, having secured a "small morsel" of about twenty pounds weight, more or less, he "left the field" to his unruly neighbors. . . . At one time about a hundred [crackers] were in the air together, coming to the ground in a perfect shower. After the ammunition of wheaten food had been exhausted, the bones and remaining joints of meat were next thrown at one another, followed by portions of the fence, and lastly by the flour or cracker barrels. . . . The police, beginning to see that the fun was likely to prove dangerous, as two or three fights had already ensued, rushed in a body and took the barrels from the crowd and "cast them into the pit," which lay, as it were, yawning to receive them. While they were engaged in this commendable work, the unruly host seized upon the only table that had been preserved and began demolishing the provisions thereon, and really the table itself.

Source: "The Douglas Barbecue," *New York Herald*, September 13, 1860, 3.

Secession and the Onset of War

As soon as Lincoln's election was apparent, white southerners turned their eyes toward secession. In 1860, a daylong debate on abandoning the Union was held in Langdon Hall, the chapel at the Auburn Female Academy in Auburn, Alabama (now Auburn University). In attendance were some of the most noted orators of the South, including Alexander Stephens and William G. Brownlow arguing against secession, and Benjamin Harvey Hill and Robert Toombs arguing in favor. Howard M. Hamill, who was thirteen years old at the time, attended the debates and recalled that people poured in from the towns and countryside within a hundred-mile radius, and for two days and nights in advance there were rival parades with fife and drum bands. Hamill described the great barbecue prepared for the occasion, with "its long lines of parallel trenches in which under the unbroken vigilance of expert negro cooks, whole beeves and sheeps and hogs and innumerable turkeys were roasting." More than anything, Hamill recalled the emotion of the times, writing that "to the small boy there were meat and drink, sights and sounds illimitable, and a tenseness of excitement that thrilled him with a thousand thrills."[9]

On the day of the debate, the two sides alternated speakers. Robert Toombs, the Georgia senator, delivered a stirring prosecession speech in the early afternoon, but then Brownlow, the fiercely pro-Union newspaperman from eastern Tennessee, took the platform, and the Union position seemed to gain the upper hand. William L. Yancey, the Alabama "Fire-Eater," was a fearsome debater and had been one of the most passionate supporters of slavery and Breckinridge during the 1860 presidential campaign, but he lay sick in bed sixty miles away in Montgomery. Seeing the tide of the debate turning toward the Unionists, Yancey's friends sent a special train to carry him from his home to Auburn, where he took to the platform and, despite looking pale and emaciated, made an impromptu, two-hour oration with a "singularly musical voice and an indefinable magnetism" that carried the day for the prosecessionists.[10]

Led by firebrands such as Toombs and Yancey, secession fever swept quickly through the Deep South. On December 20, 1860, the South Carolina legislature summoned a convention, which voted to secede from the Union. Five more states—Mississippi, Florida, Alabama, Georgia, and Louisiana—quickly followed. Texas, though a slaveholding, cotton-producing state, was slower to make the break, for it was home to many powerful Unionists, including Sam Houston, the sitting governor. Houston delayed convening a secession convention as long as he could, and after the eventual convention voted on February 1, 1861, to secede, Houston forced a public referendum to be held to ratify the results.

The vote was scheduled for February 23, and prosecessionists rallied support for their cause through a series of barbecues and public gatherings. On the day of the referendum, the farmers of Port Sullivan, Texas, provided what the editor of the *Austin State Gazette* called "one of the best barbecues I have ever had the pleasure of partaking of." Following two hours of orations, one of the speakers called on all the ladies who were in favor of secession to rise to their feet. "To see who should be first on their feet was the greater struggle," the *Gazette* reported. "For in an instant every lady, even down to the girls of 8 to 10 years, were up; not one kept her seat." Some two hundred miles to the east, near the Louisiana border, the people of San Augustine staged a "sumptuous barbecue" with all the trappings of a Fourth of July celebration, complete with a procession and orations. On the way to the barbecue grounds, the procession stopped off at the courthouse, where the eligible men deposited their votes in favor of secession. This scene was repeated in one Texas town after another, and the results of the referendum were 46,153 votes in favor of secession and 14,747 against. Texas joined the six other seceding states at a meeting in Montgomery, Alabama, to form the Confederate States of America and elect Jefferson Davis as their president.[11]

The mountain and border states moved more slowly than the Deep South cotton states. In a referendum on February 9, 1861, the people of Tennessee rejected a secession convention by a vote of 68,000 to 59,000. Secession was hotly debated in the Kentucky legislature during the months of February and March, too, with ardent support for the institution of slavery but strong opposition to leaving the Union. Then, on April 12, Confederate troops in Charleston began their bombardment of Fort Sumter, and Virginia, Arkansas, and North Carolina quickly voted to join the Confederacy. Unionist sentiment in Tennessee eroded rapidly, and a second referendum on secession was called. The voting was preceded by several weeks of passionate pro-Confederate barbecues and parades, and the state voted on June 8 to leave the Union, 104,913 to 47,238.[12]

The barbecues continued after the referendum as a way to enlist recruits for the war. One notable event took place at Shady Grove Church outside Saltillo in western

Tennessee, where the orator called on the crowd to devote themselves to "the Sunny South." Prior to the barbecue's being served, the men who had already enlisted paraded around the meeting with small stars-and-bars flags attached to the heads of their horses, and then a call went out for more men to volunteer. B. G. Brazelton, in his 1885 history of Hardin County, Tennessee, noted that "few of those volunteers lived to see the war closed."[13]

Wartime Barbecues

As the Confederate states prepared for war, they naturally turned to barbecues to send off the troops. In the summer of 1861, from South Carolina all the way to Texas, companies of new volunteers were honored with barbecues by their communities. It was standard at these events for a young woman to present the company with a banner or flag and to make an impassioned speech in honor of the soldiers' gallantry. The captain of the company would accept the gift and, with equally florid words, express his men's thanks and reiterate their devotion to the cause. Often a minister would offer a prayer for the safe return of the soldiers to their homes once the fighting was over. There were even a few barbecues for Union troops. The Twenty-Third Pennsylvania Volunteer Infantry, for example, was honored with a barbecue near Philadelphia. Flags and swords were presented to the regiment's officers, and a whole ox and fifteen hogs were barbecued, as the reporter for the *Philadelphia Inquirer* noted with a touch of irony, "in this favorite Southern style."[14]

These barbecues, with the mixture of gallantry and optimism displayed in the speeches and ceremonies, reflected the southern mood during the opening months of the conflict. At Bull Run (Manassas) in July, the first major land battle of the war, the Confederate troops repelled the first Union excursion into Virginia, and there was only minor fighting for the rest of the year. The Union blockade was not yet hurting the South severely, and it was not until the fall of 1862 and bloody battles like Antietam (Sharpsburg) that the full weight of the conflict began to be felt.

Barbecues took on a very different purpose and tone during the middle years of the war. Some were held to raise funds for war-related causes. In May 1863, a barbecue given at Courtney, Texas, raised $1,650 for the benefit of soldiers from the local volunteer regiment. The proceeds from a barbecue and fair in Navasota, Texas, in August were used to establish a soldiers' home. Others were held to welcome returning troops, such as the barbecue organized in Richmond, Arkansas, for the Confederate soldiers who had been captured following the four-month siege of Vicksburg and Port Hudson and then paroled by Union officers. All of these barbecues were organized by the women of the community, though it is safe to assume that enslaved male workers still tended the pits. At the Richmond barbecue, the ladies themselves waited on the guests—a remarkable reversal of what was normally a male-dominated tradition.[15]

Barbecues had long been an important part of life on southern plantations, and for the enslaved people on those plantations, Lincoln's Emancipation Proclamation radically changed the nature of those celebratory events. The proclamation actually consisted of two executive orders. The first, issued on September 22, 1862, declared that slaves would be emancipated in any of the Confederate States of America that did not return to Union control by January 1, 1863. The second order, issued on New Year's Day, put emancipation into effect, naming the specific states where slaves were freed.

The arrival of January 1 was a momentous occasion for African Americans in the parts of the South that were already under federal occupation. At Camp Saxton outside Beaufort, South Carolina, a celebration was planned in a live oak grove adjoining the camp, to which several thousand black residents from the surrounding Sea Islands were invited. Ten oxen had been procured to be barbecued for the event. Colonel Thomas Wentworth Higginson, a prominent author and abolitionist, was stationed at Camp Saxton as the leader of the First South Carolina Volunteers, the first Union regiment recruited from former slaves. Barbecue was something new for the Massachusetts native, and he described the preparations with interest in his diaries, noting, "Touching the length of time required to 'do' an ox, no two housekeepers appear to agree. Accounts vary from two hours to twenty four. We shall happily have enough to try all gradations of roasting, and suit all tastes." This was wartime, though, and by the time the skinny oxen were in place over the flames, Higginson noted that "the firelight gleams through their ribs, as if they were great lanterns."[16]

On New Year's Day, the people began to gather around 10:00 A.M., arriving by land and by special steamers sent by the camp commander. The Eighth Maine band played for the ceremonies, and following a prayer, Lincoln's proclamation was read to the assembled multitude. The moment the speaker finished, the assembled freedmen spontaneously began singing "My Country 'Tis of Thee." Following an oration and more patriotic songs, the assembly broke to eat. Apart from the barbecued ox, the provisions

The Emancipation Day celebration at Camp Saxton, South Carolina, on New Year's Day 1863, as captured in *Frank Leslie's Illustrated Newspaper* on January 24, 1863. The color-sergeant of the First South Carolina is addressing his regiment after having been presented with the Stars and Stripes. (Courtesy Library of Congress, Prints and Photographs Division)

were spartan: hard bread and water sweetened with molasses and ginger. Susie King Taylor, a former slave who had become a schoolteacher on St. Simons Island, recalled the feast as "a fitting close and the crowning event of this occasion. . . . Although not served as tastily or correctly as it would have been at home, yet it was enjoyed with keen appetites and relish."[17]

The event at Camp Saxton was just one of many emancipation celebrations. Across the occupied South, Union officers read the Emancipation Proclamation to gathered slaves and announced that they were free. Since the measure could be enforced only in the territory controlled by Union troops, it took several years for emancipation to reach all of the Confederacy. The last state was Texas. On June 18, 1865—some two months after General Robert E. Lee had surrendered the Army of Northern Virginia at Appomattox Court House—General Gordon Granger of the Union army landed with federal troops in Galveston, Texas. The next day he read Lincoln's proclamation to an assembled crowd, formalizing the emancipation of over 250,000 enslaved Texans.

Southern whites greeted the end of the war with barbecues, too, though their events had a somewhat different tone as Confederate soldiers returned home to resume their lives in the newly occupied South. Eliza Frances Andrews, the daughter of a prominent judge and planter in Washington, Georgia, noted in her journal in July 1865, "Barbecues, both public and private, are raging with a fury that seems determined to make amends for the four years intermission caused by the war." Her brother Henry, a former Confederate soldier, got into a bit of a scrape following one such barbecue. Returning home with "more liquor aboard than they could hold," Henry and his friends passed by the hotel downtown where the officers from the occupying federal garrison were lodged. Henry "cussed out" the gathering of officers, which led to an order for his arrest and a twenty-five-dollar fine.[18]

That year, the federal troops in Washington, Georgia, staged a Fourth of July celebration in the traditional southern fashion, organizing a barbecue at the old Cool Spring picnic ground, which was heavily attended by the county's African Americans. White Washingtonians largely boycotted "this anniversary of our forefathers' folly," as Eliza Frances Andrews phrased it, and instead shut themselves in their homes. To show their contempt for the holiday, a group of white men organized a countercelebration on July 6. The commander of the federal garrison threatened to send in a body of African American troops to halt any such "rebel 'cue" but ultimately relented. The barbecue on the sixth came off without incident, though Andrews noted that "it was hot enough to roast a salamander, and nobody enjoyed it very much."[19]

The antipathy with which the white residents of Washington, Georgia, greeted the Fourth of July was shared throughout the South. Though Independence Day—including the traditional barbecue feast—was embraced and widely celebrated by African Americans, white southerners ceased observing the holiday. The traditional Fourth of July barbecue did not return to prominence in the white community for another thirty years, when the onset of the Spanish-American War rekindled patriotic sentiments.

5

BARBECUE, RECONSTRUCTION, AND JIM CROW

"Every year since the signing of that celebrated document," the editors of the *Atlanta Daily World* commented in 1955, referring to the Emancipation Proclamation, "there has been staged among our group some sort of anniversary of grateful expression. Hardly any individual or specific organization can claim credit for the initiation of this practice, for it had its beginning among the early freedmen in every state involved in the slavery question."[1]

Emancipation celebrations played an important role in the civic life of African Americans during Reconstruction, and barbecue was front and center at those events. The date for a community's celebration varied from state to state. January 1—the day on which Lincoln's proclamation went into effect in 1863—was the traditional date in Alabama, Georgia, the Carolinas, and Virginia, but in other states the date varied. August 4 and 8 were the norm in Kentucky, north-central Tennessee, and northeastern Arkansas. In Texas, June 19—the day in 1865 when General Granger read the Emancipation Proclamation in Galveston—became the date for that state's annual celebrations, and it was there that perhaps the most enduring Emancipation Day tradition was established.[2]

The Texas festivities always included a big barbecue along with a reading of the Emancipation Proclamation followed by speeches, prayers, and entertainment like rodeos and baseball games. In the early years, these celebrations were frequently attended by members of the white community, too. Anderson Jones, a formerly enslaved Texan, recalled late in his life that he was just a boy of about nine years old when freedom came, and "we commenced to have the nineteenth celebrations . . . and everybody seems like, white and black, come and get some barbecue." Prominent white citizens were frequently asked to deliver addresses, and they typically lectured—often condescendingly—on topics such as citizenship and self-improvement. Despite the presence of these visitors, the celebrations were clearly organized by and for the African American community. As more and more black Texans became landowners, they began to acquire tracts specifically for holding Emancipation Day and other celebrations. In Houston, for example, Jack Yates, a former slave and the pastor of Antioch Baptist Church, led an effort that raised $1,000 to purchase ten acres of open land that became Emancipation Park.[3]

The Emancipation Day holiday in Texas grew decade by decade. In 1893, the *Dallas Morning News* reported on the festivities not just in Dallas but in a dozen other cities ranging from Tyler to San Antonio. Many celebrations, like the one in Waco, were said to be "on a scale larger than any previous year." Five years later, over five thousand people turned out for a barbecue at Stamps, near the Louisiana line, while fifty miles north in Texarkana a special excursion on the Cotton Belt railroad was chartered to take "almost every negro in town" to the local celebration. The events that year were held on June 18, since the nineteenth fell on a Sunday. It was around this time that the holiday began to be commonly known as "Juneteenth." As former slaves and their descendants began leaving cotton farms and migrating to the growing cities or to other states, they started making annual pilgrimages home for Juneteenth, and the day took on an additional theme of homecoming. One constant was the barbecue pit, which always took the central place at the festivities.[4]

The popularity of Juneteenth ebbed in the early twentieth century, as more and more black Texans were living in cities instead of on farms. July Fourth was already well established as a civic holiday, and nonagricultural employers were less inclined than their rural counterparts to let employees have another day off just a few weeks before. The civil rights movement of the 1960s sparked a revitalization of Juneteenth, as many activists began to look back to the civic traditions of the African American past. In 1980, the Texas legislature made June 19 an official state holiday, and it has since spread well beyond the borders of the Lone Star State as a time to commemorate freedom and civil rights.

Juneteenth has lasted the longest as a formal holiday, but Emancipation Day barbecues were held by African Americans throughout the country in the nineteenth century, even in states that had never permitted slaveholding. In Kansas, for example, the day of the celebration was August 4, following the traditions of Kentucky and Tennessee, since many black residents of those states had moved to Kansas in the wake of Reconstruction to buy farmland and escape worsening racial tensions. Ella Boney grew up in Hill City in the 1870s and 1880s and, in a 1938 WPA interview, recalled that the Emancipation Proclamation Picnic was "one of the biggest events of the year for Negroes in Kansas." It was held for four days in a large grove outside Nicodemus, and African Americans would travel from all over the state to attend. "There are about twelve barbecue pits dug," Boney recalled, "and they are going all day barbecuing chickens, turkeys, ducks, pigs, sides of beef etc."[5]

The Fourth of July holiday also continued to grow in importance for African Americans during the Reconstruction era. These events followed the traditional patterns of antebellum Independence Day celebrations, including grand processions, music, the reading of the Declaration of Independence, and orations, followed, of course, by a barbecue dinner in a shady grove, but these events were organized by and for the African American community. As was the case with Emancipation Day gatherings, prominent white citizens were often invited as guests to African American Independence Day barbecues—dining at a separate, specially reserved set of tables—and were sometimes asked to address the assembly. Whether the speaker was black or white, self-improvement and civic responsibility were the underlying themes of all the addresses, though the speeches delivered by white guests tended to be lecturing and highly condescending. J. A. Turner, for example, spoke at a freedmen's Fourth of July barbecue in Eatonton, Georgia, in 1866 and urged his listeners "to cultivate friendly feelings toward the white people." Turner defended slavery as having been, at the time, in the best interest of African Americans, arguing, "Your forefathers were savages like the wild Indian when they were brought to this country. Now, you, their descendants are civilized, and intelligent, and all enjoy Church privileges. Had it not been for slavery you would now be savages in Africa." The audience's reaction to Turner's sentiments was not recorded.[6]

Appearing at such events was part of a concerted effort by the same white elites who had held power before the Civil War to regain control of southern communities. In 1868, the Democratic Party began staging its own barbecues to try to win over the votes that, with the backing of federal military power, African Americans were just beginning to cast. These events were, on the surface, old-fashioned campaign barbecues, but in the past African Americans had been present only as cooks and workers, not as the targets of the politicians' outreach. In Yalobusha County, Mississippi, where black voters outnumbered whites, Democrats hosted a "grand barbecue" outside the town of Grenada, "designed more particularly for the colored population, whose minds it was sought to enlighten with the gospel of Democracy." The speakers lavished attacks on the current Republican-controlled state legislature and the recently enacted Constitution of 1868, which had instituted universal suffrage. The orations sought to convince the newly empowered voters that the Radical Republicans cared only about exploiting southern blacks for profit and that Democrats were actually the party most concerned with the welfare of black Mississippians—a theme that was omnipresent at Democratic barbecues aimed at African American voters that year.[7]

It took a lot more than barbecued pork and florid rhetoric to sway African American votes. In Tennessee, despite extensive Democratic courting of freedmen, Republican governor William G. Brownlow was reelected in 1867 by an overwhelming majority, including all but forty-three of the state's forty thousand African American votes. Similar results were seen in elections across the South during the late 1860s. Southern whites soon turned to harsher tactics, including violence, intimidation, and the systematic disenfranchisement of black voters through legislative action.[8]

Barbecues remained among the most important social events in the African American community for the rest of the nineteenth century. In the century that followed, as black southerners began migrating to northern cities and to the West Coast, they took their barbecue tradition with them and helped carry it to new parts of the country. Today's barbecue cultures in cities such as St. Louis, Kansas City, and Chicago have their roots in the Emancipation Day and July Fourth celebrations of the Reconstruction days.

At the same time that African Americans were commemorating emancipation and advocating for civil rights at barbecues, white southerners were using the institution to advance their own political agendas. Barbecue was a prominent feature of Confederate veterans' reunions, which flourished in the southern states in the 1880s and 1890s. Most were held by veterans' associations for a particular army unit, and they were a time for old soldiers to renew the bonds of military camaraderie as well as a chance for communities to honor the men who had served in the conflict—and for the younger generations to be instilled with the emerging ideology of the "Lost Cause." Local businesses closed for the reunions, and entire towns were decorated with flags and banners. Organizers canvassed the area for contributions of money and food, and massive amounts of meat were frequently donated for the pits. The 1887 reunion of the Seventh Georgia Infantry served 5 beef cattle, 8 sheep, 5 hogs, and 2,000 chickens, while the 1893 Third Georgia gathering required over one thousand feet of tables to hold the 125 pigs and sheep and 100 gallons of hash served for the occasion. Old soldiers could talk all day about the exploits of their regiments, one veteran observed, but they "can't talk against a barbeque."[9]

As white southerners reasserted political control over the former Confederate states, reunion barbecues began to take on themes of reconciliation with former enemies. In 1888, the Survivors' Association of the Third Georgia Volunteers invited the remaining members of the Ninth Regiment of New York Volunteers, whom they had fought at Antietam, to be their guests at their annual reunion in Fort Valley, Georgia, and "taste the sweets of peace with us in partaking of a Georgia Barbecue." A large delegation of New Yorkers traveled by steamer to Savannah and then by rail to Fort Valley, where the speeches following the barbecue focused on "fraternal greetings, sentiments of good will and patriotic utterances." The events were also used to raise money for veterans' causes. The October 1885 Soldiers' Reunion in Union County, Kentucky, drew five thousand guests to the fairgrounds and raised $640.30 to aid disabled Confederate soldiers and the families of deceased comrades. Stella Guice, president of the Barbour County, Alabama, chapter of the Daughters of the Confederacy, staged numerous barbecues at her family's home on the Chattahoochee River and raised over $3,000 to erect a thirty-five-foot-tall marble Confederate monument at the corner of Broad and Eufaula Streets in Eufaula, Alabama. That monument still stands at the same location today.[10]

The Broadening Footprint of Barbecue

Veterans' reunions were some of the first instances of barbecues being used for fund-raising, a practice that would soon be extended to a wide variety of causes. In just about every part of the United States except New England, the occasions at which barbecue was served expanded during the second half of the nineteenth century. School celebrations, social club gatherings, estate sales, town-boosting land sales, and community betterment efforts were just a few of the events where it was common to find barbecue served.

Cooking meat, barbecue style.

Left: Cooking barbecue in Southern Pines, North Carolina. (*Frank Leslie's Illustrated Weekly*, December 19, 1891)

Below: The barbecue pits at a Masonic picnic, Kissimmee, Florida, 1886. (Courtesy State Library and Archives of Florida)

Stereo view of a Florida barbecue, 1870s. (Courtesy State Library and Archives of Florida)

Pitmasters also began selling barbecue to turn a profit, and barbecue stands were soon common fixtures at fairs, expositions, and other festivals. The Old Settlers Reunion in Perry, Iowa, in 1887 featured a procession, music, and addresses along with roast beef and mutton at the barbecue stand. In addition to vendors of lemonade, popcorn, hot tamales, chili, and chewing gum, the 1900 reunion in Mexia, Texas, featured a barbecue stand. The *Springfield Republican* of Massachusetts noted that county fairs were much more popular in the South than in New England, and that barbecue so dominated events south of the Mason-Dixon Line that "the rates are generally arranged with the barbecue in view: so much for the entrance to the fairground and so

While barbecue remained uncommon in northeastern cities, the New York political machines occasionally experimented with the types of rallies more common in the South and Midwest. This scene, titled "A Democratic Barbecue," shows guests at a Harlem ox roast sponsored by Tammany Hall. (*Frank Leslie's Illustrated Newspaper*, October 18, 1884)

much for the barbecue ticket." Those tickets entitled their holders to all the barbecue they could eat, and since utensils were limited, smart fairgoers often brought their own plates and knives. These early enterprises were precursors of the barbecue restaurants that would appear on the American scene after World War I.[11]

The Rise of Barbecue Men

"A Georgia barbecue," the *Atlanta Constitution* declared in 1895, "is a feast for the gods when it comes from the experienced hand of Jack Callaway. Sheriff Callaway is the king of barbecuists." It was the eve of the opening of the Atlanta Cotton States and International Exposition, and Callaway, the charismatic sheriff from Wilkes County, had set up a massive barbecue operation on the exposition grounds with pits and dining sheds large enough to feed thousands of guests each day. Those guests included lots of visitors from northern states—many of them journalists—who had traveled south to attend the exposition, where they had their first chance to sample genuine Georgia barbecue. The event made Sheriff John W. Callaway a national culinary star.

Callaway was perhaps the most well-known example of a growing phenomenon in southern communities: barbecue men. Following the Civil War and emancipation, hundreds of talented barbecue cooks in rural areas and small towns fed generations of southerners, but many of their names rarely made it into the history books. John W. Callaway was a notable exception. In fact, no man in the nineteenth-century South gained more attention for his barbecue prowess than the sheriff of Wilkes County. Newspapers crowned him the "the prince of barbecuers" and canonized him as "the patron saint of barbecue as it is known in Georgia."

Standing six feet tall and weighing over three hundred pounds, the "Big Sheriff" knew how to play the part. John West Callaway was born in Wilkes County, Georgia, in February 1847. His father, Chenoth Callaway, owned a large plantation with seventy enslaved workers, and he died just a few months before the Civil War began. Still a teenager, John Callaway enlisted in the Thirtieth Georgia Infantry and rose to the rank of third lieutenant. After the war he took up farming on his family's land, but by his early thirties he felt "a desire to lead a life of more zest and adventure," as one later account put it, and accepted the position of deputy to Wilkes County sheriff G. L. Albea. After two terms as a deputy, Callaway decided to run for sheriff himself and narrowly defeated his old boss. A popular and skilled politician, Callaway never lost an election after that. He made friends easily and worked hard to maintain those relationships, and he enlisted the power of food in that endeavor. Whenever he disagreed with someone, Callaway made a point to visit that person's home, and if a short conversation didn't resolve things he stayed over and had dinner. "There is not a better

John W. Callaway at a barbecue in Washington, Georgia. (Courtesy Georgia Archives, Vanishing Georgia Collection, wlk138)

place in the world," he told the *Atlanta Constitution*, "for getting close to a man than when you have got your feet under his dinner table."[12]

The first written account of a Callaway barbecue appeared in the *Atlanta Constitution* in August 1889, though the sheriff's reputation was by then already well established. For that event, a group of prominent citizens in Washington, Georgia, had invited a party from Atlanta, including railroad baron Pat Calhoun, to come sample a "genuine Wilkes County barbecue." They made the excursion via train in Calhoun's private railcar. The barbecue was held in a shady grove where Callaway was "superintending" the work at a long trench filled with live coals over which "shoats, lamb, birds and calves" were roasting. Callaway, the *Constitution* asserted, "knows more about barbecues than any man in the country."[13]

The following year, Callaway took his skills a few counties westward, preparing the barbecue for a large gathering at Stone Mountain. Over three hundred guests arrived via a special train from Atlanta to feast on roasted pigs and lambs and to listen to music and speeches. "The toast of the hour," the *Atlanta Constitution* declared, "is Sheriff Calloway [*sic*] of Wilkes. What he don't know about barbecues isn't worth picking up."[14]

By 1893, Callaway was in demand year round, cooking at no fewer than thirty events a year. His fame began to spread outside Georgia when he presided over the pits at several barbecues that attracted national press attention. For the first of these he returned to Stone Mountain and prepared a "Complimentary Q" for the International League of Press Clubs, whose members were holding their annual convention in Atlanta. "I'll give them something that will make them remember Georgia and the south," Callaway promised as he prepared for the event. "I propose to show them that the reputation we have for our 'cues is thoroughly deserved." It was the first time that many of the northern editors and reporters had ever attended a barbecue, and they were bowled over by "Brunswick stew fit for the gods" followed by a feast of "lamb, goat, shote, pork and chicken" washed down by "kegs after kegs of beer."[15]

Those visiting journalists went home and wrote glowing accounts for their local papers. An unnamed writer for the *Troy Times* was so enthusiastic that he captured his experience in verse:

> When with sleeves rolled up for business, every fellow flashed his knife
> And carved a slice o' honey that just sweetened up his life!

I'll spare you the rest. A more prosaic account was filed by Eliza Archard Conner, a prolific columnist for the New York–based American Press Association syndicate. Published in dozens of newspapers across the country in June 1894, the piece offers a rare outsider's view of a Georgia barbecue. Conner noted that the guests dined under a large white tent, beneath which was "a fine brass band that played 'Yankee Doodle' a little and 'Dixie' a great deal." She described the pit, which was two feet wide, two feet deep, and forty feet long, and a large fire that was kept burning some distance away to provide coals. The lambs, pigs, and sheep were "skinned and split open in front," with "spits put through the joints to make the limbs lie straight," and then placed over the coals on "a rude scaffolding of poles and crosspieces."[16]

When nineteenth-century southerners wrote stories about barbecues, they almost never included any descriptions of how the guests ate the meal. Such details would be as unnecessary to their southern audience as an article today explaining how to eat a cheeseburger. But Conner provided precisely that sort of detail for her northern readers: "The orthodox way to eat barbecue meat is a sort of sandwich. You take a piece of bread—plain bread. The meat is carried around in great bowls. You hold out a piece of bread. The man who carries the bowl gracefully flicks a chunk of meat upon the bread. Another attendant is usually near with what is called 'Brunswick stew.' . . . It appears to be composed of green corn, tomatoes, and red peppers, but I don't know. I do know that it is very good. A spoonful of Brunswick stew is ladled out upon the chunk of meat; then another slice of bread, a good thick slice—none of your fashionable afternoon tea kind—is laid upon the whole. You give them a little squeeze to keep them together and begin to bite." Conner was quite impressed with the results. "The Georgia roast pig was tenderer, juicier than any incubator chicken New York people pay 50 cents a bite for broiled," she wrote. "Chicken indeed! Alongside that incomparable barbecue roast pig a New York broiled chicken is as frizzled india rubber."[17]

Conner's account and other newspaper stories about John Callaway raise the question of exactly what the big sheriff's role was in staging these barbecues. Callaway certainly kept a close eye on the pits. "He knows just when to turn the cooking meats," the *Atlanta Constitution* noted, "and just at the very proper moment he prepares his sauce and paints with it the shining, crispy carcass. He kept his two assistants busy putting on the finishing touches, upon which, oftentimes, depends the taste of the meats after they are served." It's notable here that it was the assistants—not Callaway—who were actually applying those finishing touches.[18]

By the 1890s, African Americans had been cooking barbecue in the South for at least two centuries. In descriptions of the pits in virtually any account before the Civil War, African Americans are the ones holding the shovels and the basting brushes. Though they tended the meat at barbecues staged by the white community, African Americans cooked plenty of barbecue without white supervision, too. It's hard to imagine that the men working Callaway's pits in 1892 needed the great white sheriff to tell them when to turn the meat or how to apply the basting sauce.

But Callaway knew how to play the part. Eliza Archard Conner's account of the Stone Mountain barbecue notes that the three-hundred-pound sheriff, clad in shirt-sleeves and a straw hat, was "standing under a tree, giving directions like a general issuing orders to his army." She watched with fascination the preparation of the meat once it was removed from the pits. A row of African American men stood at a table with hatchets, and when a roast lamb was laid on the table, "one or two sharp strokes

"KEEP THEM HATCHETS AGOIN!"

Newspaper illustration of Sheriff John W. Callaway overseeing a barbecue, 1894. (*Davenport [IA] Morning Democrat*, July 1, 1893)

cut it into halves and two more into quarters. Then a colored brother took the quarter and proceeded to chop it into chunks small enough for individual management while it was being eaten." Sheriff Callaway did make at least one contribution to the effort, though. "As we stared with admiration at the strange scene," Conner recalled, "the sheriff roared in his stentorian voice: 'I don't hear them hammers! You niggers ain't a working them none! Keep them hatchets agoin!'"[19]

Callaway prospered in his dual role as sheriff and barbecue man, in more ways than one. "When he first entered office as sheriff he weighed 180 pounds," one newspaper noted. "Now he positively refuses to be weighed, but at the last account he tipped the beam at an even 300 pounds." Callaway was doing better financially than a typical county sheriff, too. Just two months after wowing the national press at Stone Mountain, "the famous Wilkes county barbecue artist" cooked at a public barbecue where admission was fifty cents, and as part of the draw, it was promised that Callaway would display "his $2,000 diamond shirt stud and $100 cane."[20]

Callaway's star turn on the national stage came the following year at the Atlanta Cotton States and International Exposition. Held on the grounds of the Piedmont Driving Club (now the location of Piedmont Park), the three-month exposition was organized by the Atlanta business community to showcase the New South's products and technological innovations and to foster trade between the southern states and South American countries. Romanesque structures on the 189-acre exposition grounds included the Gallery of Fine Arts, the Manufactures Building, and the Agricultural Building along with a Women's Building. Off in one corner stood the Negro Building, whose presence was required for the organizers to receive federal funding for the exposition. It was the only location that served food to people of color. The Liberty Bell was on display, and performers included Buffalo Bill and composer John Philip Sousa, who wrote the "King Cotton" march for the occasion. On opening day, September 18, 1895, Booker T. Washington delivered what became known as his "Atlanta Compromise" speech, the definitive statement of his so-called accommodationist strategy, which encouraged African Americans to focus on self-improvement through education and commerce instead of agitating for social equality and desegregation.[21]

More than a year before the exposition opened, the *Atlanta Constitution* reported that Sheriff Callaway, "the prince of barbecuers," had "made an application for space for barbecue pits and a barbecue restaurant."[22] In June 1895, three months before the opening, some sixty newspaper reporters visited Atlanta as guests of the city's business community. One afternoon they toured the exposition grounds to check on the construction of the pavilions and other buildings. After the tour they sat down at long tables under the trees and enjoyed a John Callaway spread. In its preview of the exposition, the *New York Times* singled out "Sheriff Callaway, the noted barbecue chef of Wilkes County, who has made a reputation throughout the South for his skill in roasting lamb and shoat." Callaway's barbecue, the *Times* predicted, "is not likely to be despised by a man who had an early breakfast and has acquired an exposition appetite."[23]

In November, Maude Andrews, who had visited the exposition, wrote a glowing profile of "The Georgia Barbecue" in *Harper's Weekly*. "The barbecue is one of the institutions of the South," she declared. "To have known it means happiness; not to have known it means that a link in the chain of life has been lost." She singled out Callaway as "the patron saint of barbecue as it is known in Georgia." Andrews was just one of many northern writers of the period who portrayed barbecue as a symbolic relic of the antebellum South and layered upon the events plenty of romanticized notions of what plantation life had been like a half century before. "The picture is one well worthy to keep within the memory," Andrews wrote, "for the Georgia barbecue is one of the few remaining feasts of antebellum days left to our present generation—a feast typical, indeed, of that lavishness, not elegant perhaps, often barbaric, indeed, but proffered with the generosity and magnificence of monarchs."

The Atlanta exposition and Callaway's barbecue concession struck a chord with the northern press, for it coincided with a renewed interest among northern readers in the culture of the South. Though the tradition of barbecue had long before pushed its way westward and was a vibrant part of social life in the Midwest, the Southwest, and on the Pacific coast, the Northeast and Mid-Atlantic press were seemingly discovering it for the first time.

One of Maude Andrews's colleagues at *Harper's Weekly*, writing the year after the exposition, was similarly superlative in his descriptions, claiming that "a barbecue appeals equally to the stomach and the understanding. Once you have tasted it in perfection, you have a realizing sense of how it smoothes and softens campaign asperities, and makes joint debate not only possible but pleasant." Georgia barbecues even gained recognition in the British press, with John R. Watkins of London's *Strand Magazine* proclaiming, "No one who has had the good fortune to attend a barbecue will ever forget it. . . . England has its roast beef and plum-pudding dinners, Rhode Island its clambakes, Boston its pork and beans, but Georgia has its barbecue, which beats them all."[24]

These sorts of journalistic depictions appeared at about the same time that romanticized fictional accounts of antebellum plantation life were reaching wide national audiences through Thomas Nelson Page's *In Old Virginia* (1892), Charles Chesnutt's *The Conjure Woman* (1899), and Joel Chandler Harris's Uncle Remus tales. While this literary genre helped reconcile the South with the rest of the Union, it also helped establish the sentimental, whitewashed "moonlight-and-magnolias" view of life in the antebellum South.

The Atlanta exposition was the high point of John Callaway's catering career, but he continued his reign as Georgia's "barbecue king" for another two decades. In 1906 he resigned his sheriff's position after twenty-five years in office and became the commissioner of roads and revenues, the most powerful political position in the county. He continued to preside over barbecues, including one for the three thousand attendees of a farmers' club meeting in Washington, Georgia, in 1907. His fame generated many invitations to cook barbecue in far-off places—so many, one newspaper noted, that "if he consented to cook as many from the middle of June until the first of September as he has invitations, he would have time for nothing else." Callaway apparently traveled outside Georgia to cook barbecue on just one occasion, though little record remains of it beyond a few brief newspaper accounts, one of which notes in passing that around 1898 the sheriff "accepted an invitation of the National Press Association, and prepared a barbecue for that body in New York."[25]

John W. Callaway died in 1915 at the age of seventy-one. His obituary celebrated the "Big Sheriff" for being "Far-Famed as 'Cue Artist." Indeed, Callaway had helped establish the Georgia barbecue as an institution in the popular press, cementing the idea that a "barbecue king" was less a cook and more a manager overseeing the outdoor operations.

But what about the men who were doing the actual skilled work at the pit—dressing the carcasses, rhythmically maintaining a pit of even coals, basting the meat and keeping it roasting low and slow until tender and ready to eat? In all of the many accounts of Callaway barbecues, the cooks are inevitably treated as interchangeable "local color" figures characterized primarily by rude dress and the exaggerated dialect in which the period's white writers insisted on portraying African American speech. In all the many accounts, the cooks remain nameless black faces—except in one. That exception is the *Atlanta Constitution*'s story on the first barbecue that John Callaway hosted at Stone Mountain in 1890, four years before the big Press Club event that made him nationally famous. "Sheriff Calloway was the presiding genius at the pits and pots," the *Constitution* noted. "The right-hand man was Henry Pettus, a Wilkes county darky." That's not a lot of information to go on, but sometimes just a name is enough.[26]

Henry Pettus was born around 1855 in Wilkes County, Georgia, most likely into slavery on the plantation of Stephen G. Pettus Jr., who owned fifty-three slaves in 1860. In 1870, the teenage Henry was living with his mother, Elizabeth, a forty-year-old woman employed as a domestic servant, along with six brothers and sisters ranging in age from seven months to thirteen years old. According to census records, Pettus—then just fifteen—was already working as a farm laborer, though two of his siblings, thirteen-year-old Cooper and eleven-year-old Dilla, were enrolled in school. The family was living in the same general area as Stephen G. Pettus's and John W. Callaway's farms, and their neighbors included several black families with the surname Callaway—presumably former slaves now working as farm laborers.[27]

Census records offer only a brief glimpse into Henry Pettus's life. Maude Adams may well have been describing him in her account of the Atlanta exposition barbecue when she portrays "a big fat Negro behind us, who, like the Georgia Colonel, looks as if he had been fed for a lifetime on barbecue." The man in question is clearly in charge, as he instructs other workers, "Turn that pig over, an' put er little mo' fire under his back." Pettus may well have traveled to New York with Callaway around the turn of the century, too, for a newspaper profile of the sheriff noted that "he went to New York with his negro aid to prepare one dinner for the newspaper men of New York State."[28]

Northern writers' accounts of John Callaway's barbecues play up the linkage to antebellum cotton plantations, making it sound for all the world as if Callaway's workers were still enslaved. Maude Adams, for instance, writes that one of Callaway's workers told her that the man stoking the pits was "de leader in de singing on de boss's plantation." It might be a stretch to classify the sheriff's Wilkes County farm as a "plantation." It had just one hundred acres of total tilled land, seventy-five of which were planted with cotton. What is certain is that by 1900, Henry Pettus was no longer working on someone else's farm, much less on a "plantation." The census that year shows him owning his home and cotton farm, free of mortgage. He had been married to his wife, Rhoda, for thirty-four years, and they had at least ten children. A decade later, Pettus's place is described as a "general farm." We know little else about the life of Henry Pettus. John W. Callaway's death prompted long obituaries celebrating the "Famed 'Cue Artist" and "Georgia's Barbecue King." When Pettus died in March 1940 at the age of seventy-three, it didn't receive mention in the papers.[29]

The Great Augusta Barbecue Men

Henry Pettus may have worked the pits in obscurity, but other African American barbecue cooks left more of a record. At least two of these men parlayed their skills into substantial public reputations, though their lives in the Jim Crow–era South wound up taking very different paths.

Augustus Ferguson was born in Pickens County, South Carolina, in 1856, five years before the start of the Civil War. As a young man in 1875, he got into trouble when, as the *Augusta Chronicle* reported, "Mr. W. S. Kirksy, of Pickens county, was struck on the head with a rock, and painfully wounded, by Gus Ferguson, negro." Shortly after this incident—and perhaps because of it—Ferguson became one of the many African Americans who left the countryside to seek better opportunities in the growing city of Augusta, Georgia. There he started working for a white man named John A. Bohler, who was the county tax collector. Bohler lived on a twenty-acre plot of land on Walton Way, a few miles outside Augusta. Politics and barbecue went naturally together in nineteenth-century Georgia, and John Bohler and his son Charles became well known for hosting large barbecue dinners at their home place as well as at other gatherings in the community.[30]

In 1888 the *Augusta Chronicle* announced that a barbecue was to be given to a group of commercial men and would be "under the supervision of that prince of caterers, Charlie Bohler, and the bill of fare will embrace everything that you ever heard of at a barbecue." The following year, a similar announcement declared the younger Bohler to be "the prince of managers," and he presided over large community barbecues in the area for the next three decades. It's notable that the newspaper called him the prince of "caterers" and "managers," not of "cooks," for Bohler's role was to organize and secure the provisions for the gatherings and not to actually work the pits. That role was performed by a number of African American men employed by Bohler, one of whom was Augustus Ferguson.[31]

Throughout the South, the art of barbecuing was passed from one generation of cooks to the next through an informal apprenticeship system. An experienced cook who oversaw the operation would train new workers who came on board to assist, teaching them everything from how to tend to the slow-cooking meat over the pits to the recipes for basting sauce and accompaniments. We don't know much about

Ferguson's work for Bohler—how he learned to cook barbecue, when he became the lead man at the pits—but we do know that he mentored at least one noted cook who followed in his footsteps, a man named Pickens Wells.

Wells, like Ferguson, had been born out in the country—in Wells's case, on a plantation near Plumb Branch in Edgefield County, South Carolina, just across the Savannah River from Augusta. He was drawn to Augusta in the late 1880s by the prospect of regular work in the city's booming textile mills, and he signed on at the John P. King Manufacturing Co., which produced cotton sheeting and shirt material. Wells was employed at the King Mill through at least 1895, and during this period he started working on the side as Gus Ferguson's assistant, learning from him the art of barbecuing meats for large crowds.

As the twentieth century neared, Gus Ferguson stopped cooking for Bohler and set out on his own. By 1898, he was living in Augusta proper with his wife, Alice, and the city directory listed his occupation as "gardener." Ferguson's name appears in the local newspapers for the first time the same year, when he staged a "Hen Barbecue" for the fifty-fifth anniversary celebration of the Trinity Methodist Episcopal Church. "Gus Ferguson always cooks a fine cue," the *Chronicle* noted.[32]

Not long after, Ferguson parlayed his barbecue experience into a career as a professional cook. In December 1898, Jansen's Restaurant on Ellis Street in downtown Augusta began advertising itself as "a nice clean place where you can sit quietly and eat a meal prepared by Gus Ferguson, the best cook in America." Another notice in the same day's paper declared, "It's a big thing for a Restaurant to have a cook like Gus Ferguson. Mr. Jansen says he comes high, but he won't have none but the best cook, and the best that the market affords." Ferguson's tenure at Jansen's was brief. A year later, he was working as a cook for Jacob Phinizy, a wealthy cotton broker and president of the Georgia Railroad Bank, who had a large brick home on Greene Street.[33]

Alongside his regular employment, Ferguson still oversaw the pits at big outdoor barbecues. In 1899 he fed more than three hundred guests at the Knights Templar Conclave, and the menu at that event gives us a sense of Ferguson's repertoire as well as the standard fare at a turn-of-the-century barbecue on the Georgia–South Carolina border. As was the case at John Callaway's and Henry Pettus's events, the meats included "barbecue hash, barbecued lamb, barbecued shoat." Brunswick stew—the classic Georgia barbecue side dish—was missing from the menu, but the presence of lamb is notable, for it was a common barbecue meat a century ago but is rarely found in Georgia barbecue restaurants today. Also notable is the hash, a traditional barbecue stew more commonly associated with South Carolina (see pages 109–10). Ferguson's spread of side items was quite broad, including "cheese relish, pickled beets, mixed pickles, Vienna rolls" along with "chicken with mushrooms, asparagus, stewed corn, rice, stewed tomatoes, English peas, lemonade, cake, coffee, cigars."[34]

After Ferguson stopped working for the Bohler family, Pickens Wells stepped in to fill the role of his former mentor as Bohler's lead cook and the area's top barbecue man. In a 1906 account of two barbecues held at the Bohler place, the *Augusta Chronicle* noted that "both were the work of Pickens, one of the best known chefs in this vicinity." Two years later, a preview of the Fourth of July festivities at Lake View Park promised a "barbecue breakfast," with the barbecue "prepared by Mr. Charles Bohler and his famous cook, 'Pickens Wells.'" In addition to his work for the Bohlers, Wells appears to have had a bit of an entrepreneurial streak. For at least three years, between 1901 and 1903, he was a partner with Anderson Jones in a grocery store called Jones Wells & Co., which was located at 20 Tuttle Street and served the African American community.[35]

In the early years of the twentieth century, the careers of Augusta's two great barbecue cooks diverged. John Bohler died in November 1900, and his will specified a gift of fifty dollars to Gus Ferguson and twenty-five dollars to a man named Jacob Key. "The last two named persons of color," Bohler had written, "have long been my faithful and trusted servants, and to each of them I am very much attached." Not long after, Ferguson and his family moved north. It's not clear exactly when he left town, but neither Augustus Ferguson nor his grown son, Augustus Jr., appear in the 1901 city directory—which, perhaps not coincidentally, was the first edition of the directory to be divided into "White Residents" and "Colored Residents" sections. (Prior editions included all of the city's residents in a consolidated listing, with a small "c" denoting persons of color.) By 1910, census records show that Ferguson, his wife, and their children were living in Red Bank, New Jersey, where Ferguson owned his own home and worked as a cook at a local restaurant. Once hailed as "the best cook in America," Ferguson lived the remainder of his life in obscurity. His death, which occurred sometime before 1920, received no mention in any newspaper I could find.[36]

Pickens Wells's career ended very differently. His grocery venture was finished by

President Taft dining at the head of the table at Charles S. Bohler's home outside Augusta, Georgia, 1909. (Courtesy Library of Congress, Prints and Photographs Division)

1904, but he continued to work as a gardener and cook for Charlie Bohler, who had succeeded his father as county tax collector and continued to stage big barbecues for civic celebrations and political events. By far the most significant of these took place in 1909, when Wells cooked barbecue for William Howard Taft, who had just been elected president of the United States. While waiting to take office (back then the president wasn't inaugurated until March), Taft announced he was planning a tour through the South. Towns throughout the Carolinas and Georgia vied to host the president-elect at "an old fashioned barbecue." On January 4, the *Macon Telegraph* reported that Taft had declined the invitations of all southern cities except Atlanta, though it was likely that he would make a day trip one hundred miles east to the town of Washington. "Judge Taft will be given a genuine Georgia barbecue," the *Telegraph* predicted, "prepared by the 'Barbecue King of Georgia,' Hon. John W. Callaway."

Taft did indeed enjoy a "genuine Georgia barbecue," but it wasn't prepared by the 'Barbecue King' of Wilkes County. Instead, Taft headed a little farther east to Augusta for a barbecue on January 12 at Charles S. Bohler's place. Press accounts described the site as "his extensive cotton plantation," although the tax collector owned only twenty tilled acres and grew no cotton. There, Taft and thirty other guests, the *Macon Telegraph* reported, were treated to "barbecued chickens, lambs and pigs; stuffed potatoes, tomatoes, and peppers; salads and hash and puddings" that were "fit for the palates of kings." The *Augusta Chronicle* added that the president-elect "took occasion to go to the 'cue pit after dinner and personally compliment Pick on the cooking."[37]

Just eight months after cooking for President Taft, Pickens Wells died suddenly. Perhaps fittingly, it happened alongside a barbecue pit. Wells was preparing a barbecue dinner on George T. Barnes's property when he suffered a ruptured blood vessel in his brain and collapsed. "'Pick,' as he was so well known to all barbecue attendants," the *Augusta Chronicle* noted in its obituary, "was the best cook in the country. His fame was not alone in Richmond county, but spread over several states." Indeed, notices of Wells's death appeared in newspapers across Georgia and South Carolina. The *State* in Columbia called him "one of the most famous barbecue cooks in the South." Wells's passing even earned a mention in the *New York Times* under the headline "Taft's Barbecue Cook Drops Dead."[38]

The lives of Gus Ferguson and Pickens Wells pose a tough question. Is it better to die in obscurity with independence and autonomy or to leave the earth with a degree of fame earned beneath the weight of prejudice and in the service of other people? It's a choice that many barbecue cooks had to make in the Jim Crow era. The record that survives offers only brief, incomplete glimpses into the lives of these once-celebrated barbecue men, but they are important glimpses, for they allow us finally to know their names and to begin recognizing the contributions these influential cooks made to one of America's longest and most beloved culinary traditions. Indeed, these figures provide a direct link between the older tradition of outdoor, open-pit barbecue and the commercial barbecue industry that developed in the early twentieth century—an industry that is still a vibrant part of American food culture today.

NOTABLE SOUTHERN BARBECUE MEN

JOHN CALLAWAY, HENRY PETTUS, GUS FERGUSON, AND PICKENS WELLS are just a few examples of late nineteenth-century "barbecue men" who became famous in their communities. These culinary artists were in high demand to cook at public festivals and private functions. Having a noted barbecue man lined up for an event was a big draw, and organizers regularly advertised who would be cooking the barbecue at their functions. Some, like Callaway, gained the attention of the national press and made the jump from local celebrity to national fame. Others remained known only in their home communities, but they strongly influenced the barbecue culture in their regions, for they handed down their techniques to the next generation of cooks who followed.

HEZEKIAH "KIAH" DENT (Columbia, South Carolina)

Born in 1832, Dent was a farmer and a Confederate veteran, and he made a name for himself in the 1890s preparing barbecue for political rallies and gatherings of fraternal organizations such as the Knights of Pythias to Labor Day picnics. He was particularly fond of preparing barbecue for his old comrades at the county Confederate veterans' reunions. Upon Dent's death in 1908, the State newspaper noted that he was "jealous of his reputation as a cook and no one ever partook of a feast prepared by him who went away other than thoroughly satisfied."[1]

JOHN HAYS (Beech Island, South Carolina)

John Hays cooked the barbecue for the monthly meeting of the Beech Island Farmers' Club, an agricultural society that met in a wooden clubhouse about seven miles from Augusta. When President William Howard Taft visited Georgia in 1909, he was the guest at two barbecues: one at John S. Bohler's home where the barbecue was prepared by Pickens Wells (see page 107) and the other at the Beech Island Farmers' Club, where Hays did the cooking. By this point Hays, who had been cooking barbecue for more than half a century, was quite elderly. The *Augusta Chronicle* reported, after the meal "Judge Taft met this old man, shook hands with him, and wished him well."[2]

COLONEL CALVIN JAMES (Easton, Missouri)

James, a staunch Democrat, was heralded the "Barbecue King" of northern Missouri. He was famous across the region for the annual late-summer barbecues he staged at his home near Easton, where he had a dedicated barbecue grove rigged with, as one newspaper put it, "a full set of machinery, ovens, etc. necessary to barbecues." Thousands of Democrats would turn out to hear office seekers make speeches and dine on pit-cooked beef, sheep, hogs, and chicken.[3]

continued on next page

continued from previous page

FRANK T. MEACHAM (Wake County, North Carolina)

Meacham was one of North Carolina's last great barbecue men before the rise of the restaurant era. He was born in Missouri in 1869, but his parents were native North Carolinians, and they moved back to Wake County near Raleigh when Meacham was a small child. He was part of the first graduating class from North Carolina A&M (now known as North Carolina State), and in 1903 he accepted a position as superintendent of the Piedmont Experimental Station in Statesville, where he presided over the experimental farm and assisted farmers throughout the state with agricultural improvement. It was at the Experimental Station that Meacham first started serving barbecue to large numbers of guests, including thousands of diners at the annual Iredell County farmers' picnic. As Meacham's cooking reputation grew, he tended the pit for a wide range of public functions in and around Statesville, including barbecues for the Travelers' Protective Association, the Chamber of Commerce, the Patriotic Order of the Sons of America, the Kiwanis Club, the Boy Scouts, and church gatherings. By 1922 he was well known enough in the area for the Statesville *Landmark* to announce that a Farm Bureau barbecue would be "prepared a la Meacham style." During the 1920s he was traveling throughout the state to cook at big functions, such as the Fourth of July celebration in Taylorsville in 1922 and annual alumni reunions at North Carolina State in Raleigh. Meacham died in 1930.[4]

"OLD ROZIER" (Muscogee County, Georgia)

Rozier, the leading barbecue man of Muscogee County, Georgia, was touted by his local newspaper to be able to "barbecue meats to the queen's taste, and his barbecued chickens cannot be equalled on earth."[5]

JOEL STOWE (Floyd County, Georgia)

One of Georgia's most noted barbecuers, Stowe was widely recognized for his barbecue at the encampment of Confederate and Union veterans at Chickamauga in 1887.

1. "Death of Celebrated Cook," *State* (Columbia, SC), June 23, 1908, 4.
2. "Beech Island Farmers Club Entertain Judge Wm. H. Taft," *Augusta (GA) Chronicle*, January 10, 1909, 8.
3. "The Barbecue King Dead," *Kansas City (MO) Times*, February 28, 1895, 1; *Butler (MO) Weekly Times*, May 14, 1895, 4.
4. "Death Comes to Mr. F. T. Meacham," *Statesville (NC) Landmark*, May 19, 1930, 1. See also the following issues of the *Landmark*: April 25, April 28, November 28, 1921; March 16, May 1, July 6, 1922.
5. "The Colonel in the City," *Columbus (GA) Daily Enquirer*, August 23, 1887, 8.

Tracing the Origins of Hash

IT WAS DURING the era of barbecue men that hash, the classic South Carolina barbecue stew, came into prominence. A thick gravy made from pork and various pig organ meats, hash is generally served over white rice and is usually considered a side dish to accompany barbecue, not a meal unto itself.

Hash originated sometime prior to the Civil War in the counties on either side of the Savannah River, which forms the border between Georgia and South Carolina. Estella Jones, who was born enslaved on Powers Pond Place near Augusta, recalled that when she was a child, some of the men would occasionally steal hogs from other plantations and "cook hash and rice and serve barbecue." In 1861, at the opening of the Civil War, a barbecue was held to honor the Edgefield Riflemen, who hailed from the county in South Carolina just across the Savannah River from Augusta, as they prepared to leave for battle. The menu included "barbecued meats, and hash."

Hash developed as a way to use up all of a pig when it was slaughtered, whether in preparation for a barbecue or at a more ordinary hog killing. A pig slaughtered for a barbecue would be butterflied and prepared to go on the pit. At hog killings in late fall, the pig's fat would be rendered to lard and the hams, shoulders, and belly salted and hung in a smokehouse. In either case, the head, organs, and various other parts were left behind, and these ended up going into a large iron pot and rendered into a thick, savory stew. In nineteenth-century accounts, that stew was often referred to as "giblet hash" or "liver and lights hash"—"lights" being an old term for the lungs. In most early versions, the cook would start with a hog's head, liver, and other organ meats and cook them with water in an iron stew pot over an open fire. Like the original Brunswick stew recipes from Virginia, this combination was slowly simmered for many hours—sometimes a full day—until the ingredients had broken down and merged into a thick, consistent, gravy-like substance. Some cooks would add a few other ingredients—including red pepper, mustard, onion, and potato—but hash has always depended primarily on slow-simmered meats and organs for its rich, hearty flavor.

By the 1880s, hash was being served at barbecues as far north as Newberry, South Carolina, and as far south as Macon in central Georgia—much farther south than hash is found today. In fact, there seems to have been a good bit of confusion in central Georgia about the difference between hash and Brunswick stew. Sheriff

continued on next page

continued from previous page

John W. Callaway of Washington, Georgia, always called his barbecue side dish "hash," but reporters frequently labeled it "Brunswick stew." But there clearly was a difference between the two, for according to a 1907 newspaper account, a Christmas barbecue Callaway cooked for Wilkes County convicts included "several gallons of hash and a like quantity of Brunswick Stew."

It is possible that what Georgians call Brunswick stew today actually evolved out of the hash tradition as a variant of the original recipe. Visiting the Cotton States and International Exposition in Atlanta in 1895, Maude Andrews of *Harper's Weekly* sampled Sheriff Wilkes's famous stew and claimed that it "for reasons not altogether clear even to its maker, bears the mysterious name of Brunswick." Andrews got the recipe from one of the black cooks, and its formula (rendered by Andrews in absurd dialect spellings) seems remarkably similar to that of classic South Carolina hash, with a few additions: "[Y]er jest takes the meat, de hog's haid, an' de libbers, an' all sorts er little nice parts, an' yer chops it up wid corn and permattuses, an' injuns an' green peppers, an' yer stews and stews tell hit all gits erlike, an' yer kain't tell what hit's made uv."

Hash remains an integral part of the Midlands South Carolina barbecue tradition today, where it is served over white rice at barbecue joints from Columbia down to Charleston. The hearty gravy is barely known beyond the borders of the Palmetto State, and visiting diners find it as puzzling as the region's signature yellow mustard-based sauce. In Georgia, Brunswick stew remains the standard barbecue side dish. A lot of hot air has been expended in the debate with Virginia over which state originated the stew—a pointless argument, since the Virginians clearly have the solid historical claim (see chapter 3). Georgians would be better off looking over the Savannah River to their neighbors in South Carolina, for hash and the Georgia version of Brunswick stew are likely distant cousins.

Sources: Louise Oliphant, interview with Estella Jones, Federal Writers' Project, Augusta, Georgia, Slave Narratives (online database), accessed March 22, 2009, http://www.ancestry.com; "The Barbecue at Moore's," *Edgefield (SC) Advertiser*, August 7, 1861, 2; "Wilkes Convicts Eat Barbecue Cooked by World's Best Chef," *Atlanta Constitution*, December 29, 1907, 29; Maude Andrews, "The Georgia Barbecue," *Harper's Weekly*, November 9, 1895, 1072. See also "Treat for the Editors," *State* (Columbia, SC), May 25, 1897, 3; and "The Home of the Barbecue," *Macon (GA) Weekly Telegraph*, April 5, 1887, 2.

The Kentucky Burgoo Kings

Gustave (Gus) Jaubert was the undisputed king of Kentucky barbecue and also of burgoo, a thick stew that is the Bluegrass State's signature side dish. Jaubert was born in New York in 1840, the son of French immigrants, and moved to Louisville, Kentucky, when he was four years old. Jaubert's father was a confectioner and hoped his son would follow in his trade, but at age fourteen young Gus was hired by a pitmaster to help turn the spits at a Know-Nothing rally in Hopkinsville. He determined there and then to "follow the call of the suet pot," a reference to the pots of melted lard that were kept next to the pits for basting the meat.

In April 1861, Jaubert enlisted as a private in the Confederate army. By his own account, he lent a hand "whenever there was any barbecuing to be done" in his regiment. After the war, Jaubert returned to Kentucky, where he opened the Magnolia Saloon on Mill Street in Lexington. He soon became involved with a Captain Beard and Jake Hostetter, two veterans who had already established themselves before the war as noted Kentucky barbecue men. Little is known about Hostetter, a Lexington butcher who was born around 1817 and cooked barbecue for the big political rallies of the antebellum era, and even less is known about Captain Beard. Jaubert began cooking with them for stump speeches, and after they died he inherited the mantle of the region's top barbecuer. In 1866, Senator George H. Pendleton of Ohio traveled to Kentucky to make a speech in support of James B. Beck, a Lexington lawyer running for Congress. For the occasion, Gus Jaubert decided to serve not just the traditional barbecue but also a massive pot of burgoo—perhaps the first time the two dishes were served together at a Kentucky political event.[39]

Popular legend has long credited Jaubert as not just the first Kentucky Burgoo King but also the inventor of the stew. Most accounts have him devising the first version of burgoo for John Hunt Morgan, the famous Confederate general who led a series of infamous raids behind Union lines in Indiana and Ohio. The more fanciful versions of the story have Jaubert making the stew from blackbirds, since other meat was scarce, and the name of the dish has been attributed to either Jaubert's French accent or a harelip that caused "blackbird stew" to be pronounced "burgoo."[40]

These are good yarns, but they aren't true. Jaubert served in the First Kentucky Infantry, not in Morgan's Second Kentucky Cavalry. He was born in New York and raised

Gus Jaubert, Kentucky's first Burgoo King, at a barbecue at Woodland Park in Lexington, Kentucky, circa 1900.

in Kentucky, so it's highly unlikely that he had any sort of French accent. And burgoo clearly predates the Civil War by several decades. R. Gerald Alvey has found references to a stew by that name in Lexington newspapers as far back as 1830. In a newspaper interview, Jaubert himself explained that burgoo originated as a Welsh stew that gained popularity in the British maritime service and was brought by sailors to Virginia and other southern states. As Jaubert tells it, burgoo was once made from a shank of beef, chicken, corn, tomatoes, onions, and bacon. In his version, he eliminated the bacon, increased the amount of beef and chicken, and added potatoes as a thickener.[41]

Gus Jaubert may not have invented burgoo, but he was instrumental in making it a Kentucky barbecue staple. Jaubert tended the pits at so many events for the state Democratic Party that he took to bragging that he had "made more Democratic votes in the South than any other living man." His career as a burgoo king was not limited to political events, either. In the decades around the turn of the century, he cooked frequently at gatherings of tobacco farmers and at public auctions and estate sales. Serving burgoo at public auctions had been a common practice in Kentucky for many years. A 1904 article in the *Central Record* of Lancaster, Kentucky, announced that a

The pits at the 1895 Grand Army of the Republic Barbecue in Louisville, Kentucky, which were presided over by Gus Jaubert and served over one hundred thousand diners. (Courtesy Library of Congress, Prints and Photographs Division)

sale would be held "on the old time plan. That is, a sumptuous dinner will be spread, and everybody invited. Gus Jaubert, of Lexington, whose fame for making the celebrated Kentucky burgoo, has been engaged, and many gallons of this toothsome article will be served."[42]

Perhaps Jaubert's proudest moment came in 1895, when he presided over the barbecue pits at the National Encampment of the Grand Army of the Republic, the famed fraternal organization for veterans of the Union army. It was the twenty-ninth time the organization had held such an encampment, but this one was special. It had been two years in the planning and was the first gathering held below the Mason-Dixon Line, with reconciliation as the theme. Civil War leaders from both sides came to be honored and to speak, and an estimated 150,000 veterans attended. To feed the assembled crowds, Jaubert had 350 cooks and 500 waiters under his direction. They roasted 45 beeves, 383 sheep, and 241 shoats. In addition to the barbecue, Jaubert's crew made 12,000 gallons of burgoo, with some 4,000 pounds of beef, 900 whole chickens, 4,500 ears of corn, 50 bushels of onions, and 100 pounds of peppers going into the pots. Enough tin plates and cups were on hand to feed 30,000 veterans at a time. The Grand Army of the Republic event eclipsed even the national party conventions as the biggest gathering of the year, and it may well have been the largest barbecue ever in the United States.[43]

James T. Looney, Kentucky's Second Burgoo King

AFTER GUS JAUBERT'S death in the 1920s, the crown of Kentucky Burgoo King passed to James T. Looney. Born around 1870, Looney owned and operated a grocery store in downtown Lexington. He learned to cook Kentucky's famed stew from Gus Jaubert himself, and in the early years of the twentieth century he became a fixture at Bluegrass political meetings and horse races. Looney prepared his stews in a massive five-hundred-gallon iron kettle that had been used during the Civil War to make gunpowder. In 1930, he served seven thousand people at a charity horse race at the private track owned by Edward R. Bradley, one of the country's preeminent owners and breeders of Thoroughbred racehorses. Bradley was so taken with Looney's work that he pledged to name a colt after him. Two years later, "Burgoo King" won the Kentucky Derby and Preakness Stakes, helping spread Looney's reputation nationwide.

In 1934, Looney cooked for ten thousand farmers at a tobacco festival in Carrollton, Kentucky. The event earned him a mention in *Time* magazine, which reported his recipe to be made from "800 lb. lean beef with no bones; 200 lb. fat hens; 900 lb. canned tomatoes; 240 lb. canned carrots; 180 lb. canned corn; 200 lb. cabbage; 60 lb. salt; 4 lb. pepper; 'my own seasoning.' Cook 18 to 20 hr. in iron kettle out of doors over a wood fire." The seasoning for Looney's burgoo was supposedly a closely guarded secret, but an Associated Press reporter published the formula in 1948, listing red and black pepper, salt, Angostura bitters, Worcestershire sauce, curry powder, tomato ketchup, and sherry.

As with the great "barbecue men" of the period, it is unclear how much of the cooking was actually performed by Looney. A 1946 photograph of the "Burgoo King" in the *Lexington Herald-Leader* shows Looney in spotless white shirtsleeves and a tie holding the handle of a wooden paddle inserted into a covered iron cauldron. Behind him, though, stand two rather tired-looking African American men with splotched white aprons who appear far more likely to have spent hours chopping vegetables and minding the simmering pots. Looney nevertheless maintained his reputation as Kentucky's top barbecue man and burgoo maker well into his eighties, continuing to cater special events until just a few months before his death, in 1954.

Sources: "Burgoo & Boom," *Time*, November 26, 1934; Horace Ward, "Kentucky in Stew over Real Burgoo," *Kingsport (TN) News*, April 20, 1948, 10.

Burgoo King, the Kentucky Derby–winning racehorse named after James T. Looney, the "Kentucky Burgoo King," May 1937. (Courtesy University of Kentucky Libraries, Special Collections and Digital Programs)

A Kentucky Barbecue

IN 1905, THE Reverend John H. Aughey captured his memories of a Kentucky barbecue and burgoo in Tupelo in his memoirs of life in the South just before and after the Civil War:

THE SOUTHERN BARBECUE

In ordinary times Uncle Jake Hostetter may be an humble citizen in Lexington. Now, as master of the barbecuing, he rules supreme in the cooking lot, for the trenches are enclosed by a tight board fence, and it requires some persuasion to get past the guards. There are only a few favored persons within. The thousands who sniff the odors, and look longingly toward the incense arising from the fires, are wandering through the park wondering when dinner will be ready. The master of the barbecue moves among the trenches and his word is law. He served his apprenticeship away back when presidents came to these Kentucky festivities. Barbecues have not been so frequent of late years. But Uncle Jake feels safe in his experience, and he shows no uneasiness over the fact that 5,000 people are holding him responsible for their dinners, and some of them have gone breakfastless to stimulate appetite. Now and then two of the cooking corps bring up from the trenches to the table under the big tree a carcass to inspect. He cuts into it, slices off bits of the flesh, tastes, and looks knowing.

continued on next page

continued from previous page

Even the president of the day, Hon. W. C. P. Breckenridge, recognizes the authority. The speaking has commenced from a stand in the park, and somebody wants to know when the orators are going to stop for dinner. "Just when Uncle Jake Hostetter says the mutton is done to a turn," replies Mr. Breckenridge, and another statesman is let loose to say a great many pretty compliments about Kentucky, and a very few words about national politics.

The Blue Grass country has contributed to this occasion three great caldrons. Whatever useful purpose they may have subserved about hog killing time, they are now doing duty in the manufacture of 900 gallons of burgoo. Burgoo has a basis, as the chemist says. The basis on this occasion consists of 150 chickens and 225 pounds of beef in joints, and other forms best suited for soup. To this has been added a bushel or two of tomatoes. The heap of shaven roasting ears tells of another accessory before the fact. Cabbage and potatoes and probably other things in small quantities, but too numerous to mention, have gone into the pots. The fires were lighted under the vats before the roasting commenced on the trenches, and the burgoo has been steadily boiling ever since. This boiling necessitates steady stirring, and next to Uncle Jake's ministerial powers the old expert who presides over each kettle comes in for due respect and glorification. "You might not think it," says the old grey-headed Kentuckian whose eye is on the largest of the pots where 500 gallons of burgoo are bubbling, "but a piece of mutton suet as large as my hand thrown into the pot would spoil the whole mess. That shows you that there are some things you can't put in burgoo. Sometimes out in the woods we put in squirrels and turkeys, but we didn't have any this time. I think they've got a leetle too much pepper in that pot down there, so if you don't find what you get is just right

An Aside on Barbecue Sauce

One of the great differentiators in regional barbecue styles today is the sauce. In eastern North Carolina it's thin, spicy, and vinegar based, while in Texas it's sweet, thick, and tomato based. Some variations—like the bright yellow mustard-based sauce from the Midlands of South Carolina and the mayonnaise-based white sauce from northern Alabama—are specific to only a narrow region and are not widely known in other come to me and I'll fix you up with some of this." As the meat boils from the bones the latter are raised from the bottom of the kettle by the paddle and thrown out. Gradually vegetables lose all distinctive form and appearance and the compound is reduced to a homogeneous liquid, about the consistency of molasses. "Burgoo ought to boil about 14 hours," says the old expert, "we've only had about 8 for this, but I think they'll be able to eat it."

Gradually the heap of barbecued meat accumulates before Uncle Jake. He goes over and looks at the burgoo, and consults with the old expert. Then he glances over the fence at the long tables, and finds that two wagon loads of bread have been hewn into rations and strewn along the pine boards. The tin cups, 3,000 of them, are hurriedly scattered with the bread. From all parts of the grounds there is a sudden but decorous movement toward the tables, and the orator on tap runs off a peroration and stops. Uncle Jake's corps of assistants bring out the carcasses still on the stretchers, and every rod of table length finds a smoking sheep and a shoat. Gus Jaubert and a dozen butchers, with their long, sharp knives, shave and cut and deal out with all the speed that long practice has given them. The burgoo, steaming hot in new wooden buckets, is brought in, and as the attendants pass along the lines the hungry people dip out cupfuls and sip it as it cools. There are no knives nor forks. Nobody asks for or expects them. Neither are there spoons for the burgoo. The great slices of bread serve as plates for the meat. There are 5,000 people eating together, and all busy at once. Not a basket has been brought. All types and classes of Blue Grass people are facing those tables, and handling their bread and meat and burgoo with manifestations of appetite which tell of the relish of the fare.

Source: John Hill Aughey, *Tupelo* (Lincoln, NE: State Journal Company, 1888), 397–400.

states. This regional variety is a relatively recent development. In the nineteenth century, the sauces used for barbecue followed a consistent formula across the country.

As early as 1700, colonists had been using a basting sauce when barbecuing, both to flavor the meat and to keep it moist. Edward Ward, the British wit who chronicled a West Indian–style barbecue in Peckham, England, in the early eighteenth century, noted that the cook basted the pigs with "a most admirable composition of Green

Preparing the barbecue at the Coon Dog Field Trials in Henderson, Tennessee, April 28, 1940. The nineteenth-century-style outdoor barbecue remained a characteristic of rural southern life well into the 1950s.

Virginia Pepper and Madeiria wine, with many other palatable ingredients," which he "plentifully dau'b on with a Fox's Tail ty'd to a long stick." This sauce was used only during the cooking, for the pigs were simply removed from the fire, placed on a log, and chopped into quarters for serving. That seems to be the main way barbecue was prepared for the next two hundred years: basted during cooking and served dry.[44]

The earliest instructions for pit-cooking barbecue can be found in Lettice Bryan's *The Kentucky Housewife* (1839), which calls for only the simplest of basting sauces: "nothing but a little salt-water and pepper, merely to season and moisten it a little." Once the meat was done, Bryan instructed, "squeeze over it a little lemon juice, and accompany it with melted butter." Three decades later, Mrs. Annabella Hill, from La-Grange, Georgia, published similar directions in *Mrs. Hill's New Cook Book* (1872), though her recipe incorporates butter and a little mustard into the basting liquid: "Melt half a pound of butter; stir into it a large tablespoon of mustard, half a teaspoon-ful of red pepper, one of black, salt to taste; add vinegar until the sauce has a strong acid taste." At the end of cooking, "pour over the meat any sauce that remains."[45]

This basic combination of butter or some other fat, vinegar, and pepper remained the standard throughout the nineteenth century. An 1860 account of a Virginia event described iron vessels positioned along the side of the pit, "some filled with salt, and water; others with melted butter, lard, etc. into which the attendants dipped linen cloths affixed to the ends of long, flexible wands, and delicately applied them with a certain air of dainty precision to different portions on the roasting meat." An 1896 *Harper's Weekly* account of a Georgia barbecue noted that the meat was cooked for twelve hours and "basted with salt water . . . then, just before it is eaten, plentifully bedabbled with 'dipney'—a compound of sweet country lard and the strongest vinegar, made thick and hot with red and black pepper." Barbecue sauces are very different today on the East Coast than they are in Texas, but an 1883 travelogue titled *On a Mexican Mustang through Texas* described a barbecue outside San Antonio with a sauce almost identical to that used in Virginia and Georgia: "Butter, with a mixture of pepper, salt, and vinegar, is poured on the meat as it is being cooked." The famed regional variations in barbecue sauces do not appear to have developed until the twentieth century.[46]

6

THE RISE OF BARBECUE RESTAURANTS

T HE FAMED BARBECUE MEN of the late nineteenth century straddled the line between the old world of free public barbecues and a new world of barbecue as a commercial product. As more and more schools, commercial organizations, and civic groups began hosting barbecues, cooks began charging for their services at the events. The commercialization continued as barbecue men like John W. Callaway began selling barbecue dinners at state fairs, expositions, and similar venues. By far the biggest factor in the commercialization of barbecue, though, was the rise of barbecue restaurants.

Commercial barbecue businesses first appeared in the closing decades of the nineteenth century. Some evolved out of casual backyard operations, while others sprang up as stands on vacant city lots. A few decades later, still more opened along the sides of the country's new automobile highways. A common pattern can be seen with these early restaurants. They grew slowly from informal trade to permanent business, emerging wherever there were a lot of people who lacked regular sources of food. Be they farmers traveling to the county seat for court and market days, motorists on the highways, or urban workers who didn't have time to go home for lunch, people needed to eat, and barbecue restaurants arose to meet that need. In the process, they permanently altered the nature of the food and the way Americans ate it.

Barbecue Stands

As it had for two centuries, the character of barbecue evolved as it adapted to the shifting social landscape of the United States. In the late nineteenth and early twentieth centuries, America's population was steadily moving from the countryside into towns and cities. They were joined by waves of new immigrants, many of whom settled in increasingly concentrated urban centers. In 1860 some 80 percent of the country's citizens lived in rural areas; by 1900 that number had fallen to 60 percent. Twenty years later, the urban population of the country outnumbered the rural for the first time.[1]

In a rural environment, it took a special occasion like a stump speech or a civic celebration to draw a large enough crowd to justify roasting an ox or a whole pig. Country barbecues were onetime events, with pits dug in the ground for the occasion and supplies provided by the community at large. By the 1880s, it was common to find a "barbecue stand" on the grounds at fairs, expositions, and other gatherings, but these were temporary operations set up for only a few days or weeks. As America's towns and cities grew, their populations provided a reliable enough customer base to support daily operations, and it was in downtown areas that the first barbecue restaurants appeared. The term "restaurant" is used loosely here, for these early operations were little more than impromptu stands put up to sell food to the public. Often they were a sideline to another trade, like selling illegal whiskey. It took several decades for these informal ventures to evolve into full-service, sit-down restaurants.

Some of the first commercial establishments to sell barbecue on a regular basis were meat markets in central Texas. Daniel Vaughn, the barbecue editor for *Texas Monthly*, tracked down a notice in an 1878 issue of the *Brenham Weekly Banner* that observed, "A Bastrop butcher keeps on hand at his stall a ready stock of barbecued meats and cooked sausages." The name of that butcher wasn't recorded, but in August 1886 the *Bastrop Advertiser* announced that Alexander & Gill were selling "barbecued meats, beef, mutton, and pork, morning and evening" at their new meat market. Just two months later another notice in the same paper suggested, "If you want a tender piece of meat fresh or well-barbecued, don't fail to go to John Kohler's market, where Bill will fix it up for you in the good old fashioned barbecue style."[2]

The practice quickly spread to other central Texas towns. In 1888 the editors of the *San Marcos Free Press* commended the "happy thought of one of our butchers, since adopted by the rest, to furnish our people barbecued meats." This was a boon not just to the butchers, who were able to sell more meat, but also to the consumer, since "people should no longer be required to wait for barbecues in order to enjoy barbecued meats." That same year in Waco, J. J. Riddle of the Cheap Cash Market on the public square announced that in addition to his regular selection of steaks, sausages, and roasts, he was offering "a new departure—fresh barbecued meats. Every day direct from the kiln, and delivered to your residence."[3]

Such meat markets were among the earliest purveyors of commercial barbecue, but it would be a stretch to call them restaurants. Selling smoked meats was a sideline to the primary business, and it doesn't appear that customers ate on the premises. So which city holds the honor of having the country's first permanent barbecue restaurant? That answer is a bit hard to pin down, but the best clues can be found in city directories, newspaper advertisements, and the occasional crime report.

The city of Los Angeles is not known as a barbecue hot spot today, but it can boast of having one of the country's first barbecue restaurants. As early as 1894, Peyton W. Lewis was operating what he variously called The Barbecue Stand and Barbecue Delicacy and Lunch Parlor at 124 North Broadway. By 1897 he had moved three blocks south to 348 South Broadway, the same block as the Bradbury Building, though he seems to have gone out of business shortly after that. Texas can beat California's claim, though. In 1890, an African American butcher in Austin named Anderson Maxwell announced in the papers, "I have opened a barbecue stand, opposite the post office," which at the time was at the corner of Sixth and Colorado Streets. Maxwell promised that "the best of barbecue meats will be served at all times of the day," but his stand lasted no more than a few years.[4]

The historical record captures commercial barbecue stands operating even earlier in North Carolina, and the first known of these was the scene of a heinous murder. On July 13, 1888, Howard "Bud" Anderson entered William H. Porter's barbecue stand in Goldsboro and asked to buy something to eat on credit. Porter refused and the two men exchanged angry words. Anderson left the stand, but he returned an hour later and struck Porter with "a ponderous rock," crushing his skull and knocking him senseless. Porter died early the following morning. The newspapers described Porter as "a poor but a quiet and inoffensive citizen," and he left behind a wife and four small girls. The following January, after a sensational trial, Bud Anderson was hanged for his crime. Some three thousand people turned out to the courthouse square to witness the execution.[5]

The existence of another early Goldsboro stand was documented under happier circumstances. On March 12, 1890, the *Goldsboro Headlight* announced that a local couple had been married by a justice of the peace and, immediately afterward, "proceeded to Jim Rhodes' barbecue stand where the wedding feast awaited them. The groom settled the bill of fifty cents and both went home rejoicing." Not much is known about Jim Rhodes, but barbecue was not his full-time trade. Goldsboro merchant Joseph Edwards, "The Champion of Low Prices," regularly listed the names of his salespeople in his ads between 1889 and 1891, and among them was "Jim Rhodes (The Barbecue Man)."[6]

Several towns and cities in North Carolina had early entrants, too. An 1893 ordinance in Kinston, North Carolina, levied a five-dollar tax per stand on barbecue dealers and prohibited the sale of barbecue on Queen Street. An 1899 notice in the *Charlotte Observer* announced that Mrs. Katie Nunn had rented a store on South Church Street, where she planned to run a grocery store and a barbecue stand, with her husband doing the cooking over a pit he had constructed behind the store. Two weeks later, a classified ad in the paper announced, "CALL at the barbecue stand for good barbecued meats, beef, pork, and mutton. Well prepared by the only barbecuer in Charlotte." It's notable that Mr. Nunn specialized not only in pork but in beef and mutton as well—meats not typically associated today with either of North Carolina's two distinctive barbecue styles.[7]

These early barbecue stands were not sophisticated operations. Some of the earliest records of such businesses can be found in the fire reports in the local papers, for they had a stubborn habit of going up in flames. In Dallas, for instance, grease fires were reported in 1897 and 1898 at three separate barbecue stands along Commerce Street in the city's main commercial district. Another fertile source is court proceedings, usually in cases involving illegal whiskey and violence. In 1913, for instance, Walter Faucett was convicted of manslaughter for stabbing John Cox to death with a butcher knife after a fight at Faucett's barbecue stand in Tulsa, Oklahoma. In the court testimony, witnesses repeatedly refer to the restaurant as "the house," suggesting it was a residence that had been converted into a business. One witness testified that he went to the stand "for the purpose of taking a drink," which indicates that whiskey sales were as much a part of Faucett's trade as selling barbecued meat. In the Southwest in particular, liquor and barbecue seem to have gone hand in hand. In 1914, two deputy sheriffs found a large number of empty whiskey bottles in J. W. Kintz's barbecue stand near Convention Hall in Muskogee, Oklahoma, along with three gallons of whiskey "in a trash pile three or four steps from the back door," with "a well defined path from the back door to the trash pile." In April 1915, Phil Gibson got himself into similar trouble when he resold unlicensed liquor from a barbecue stand at the corner of

Thirteenth and Monroe Streets in Fort Worth, Texas. Apart from passing references in court records, no information survives about any of these early ventures. By World War I, though, barbecue stands were common if informal businesses within the larger cities of the South and Southwest.[8]

WANTED—The public to know that I have opened a barbecue stand, opposite the postoffice, where the best of barbecued meats will be served at all time of the day. Anderson Maxwell.

Newspaper advertisement for Anderson Maxwell's barbecue stand in Austin, Texas. (*Austin [TX] American-Statesman*, August 26, 1890)

A Small Fire.

The grease which was on the furnace of the barbecue stand at No. 382 Commerce street caught fire at 12:05 this morning, and the fire department was called out. There was no damage.

Newspaper report of a fire at a Dallas barbecue stand. (*Dallas Morning News*, May 24, 1897)

Barbecue Stand.

Mrs. Katie Nunn has rented No. 1 of the new row of stores on the rear of The Observer lot, and will run, in connection with a grocery store, a barbecue stand. Mr. Nunn will do the barbecuing. He has built a large pit in rear of the store, for this purpose. He will be ready for business Saturday morning.

Notice of the opening of Nunn's barbecue stand in downtown Charlotte, North Carolina. (*Charlotte [NC] Observer*, March 30, 1899)

Kansas City's Streetcar Barbecue Palaces

IN KANSAS CITY, early entrepreneurs converted retired cable cars into barbecue stands, which dotted the city's streets in the early part of the century. Such improvised structures didn't last long. In 1919, the *Kansas City Star* noted the following:

> The old cable car on Vine Street near Eighteenth Street is a cheerful reminder that there have been street cars in Kansas City with a shorter wheel base, a more erratic jerk, and a more limited speed range than the present "kiddie cars."
>
> With many other street cars of its generation, [this one] became the "palace" of a barbecue "king." The dynasty of barbecue kings now has more pretentious quarters; either from a newly acquired dignity, or because the Kansas City Railways company never retires cars. Most of the once familiar street car "palaces" have now disappeared. This one is vacant now.

Source: "A Street Car 'Palace' Is Vacant," *Kansas City (MO) Star*, December 5, 1919, 12.

Restaurants and the Creation of Regional Styles

The first permanent barbecue restaurants evolved out of these sorts of improvised stands as their owners expanded operations. They added brick and cinder-block pits, enclosed dining areas, and started offering all the amenities of full-service restaurants. In doing so, they took a food item that was once found only at large public gatherings and began selling it on a regular basis and in smaller quantities served to order. To make this transition to commercial product, barbecue needed to change, and it changed differently in each part of the country. Early barbecue restaurants were the single greatest influence on the regionalization of barbecue, and it was the rise of commercial barbecue that created the multitude of regional styles we know today.

At old-style outdoor barbecues, diners had a wide choice of meats because local farmers would donate to the cause whatever livestock they had on hand. It is common to see lists like the following in descriptions of such events: "beef, mutton, pork, and fowls were provided in superabundance and barbecued in an excellent manner." As barbecue became a business, things needed to become more standardized. In the days before mechanical refrigeration, a restaurateur could not keep much meat on hand for very long. Many restaurants began as weekend operations, with the proprietor barbecuing a whole hog or a side of beef on Thursday or Friday and selling it through the weekend until the supply was exhausted. It made sense for early businessmen to settle on one or two standard products to serve, and most chose the meat most readily available in the area—hence the prevalence of pork in North Carolina and beef in Texas.[9]

Side dishes needed to be standardized, too. When barbecues were large, community-organized affairs, the dishes that accompanied the meat were easy to carry in bulk and wouldn't spoil in the outdoor heat. Martha McCulloch-Williams, remembering her experiences attending antebellum barbecues as a child, adamantly stated, "The proper accompaniments to barbecue are sliced cucumbers in strong vinegar, sliced tomatoes, a great plenty of salt-rising light bread—and a greater plenty of cool ripe watermelons." This list is typical of the descriptions found in newspaper accounts of old barbecues.[10]

As barbecue cooks began establishing regular businesses, they generally chose a different (but reasonably small) set of side dishes to carry. Many reflected local specialties or preferences; others were simply recipes that the proprietor knew well and felt he could turn a profit on. "Back in the old days," recalls Wayne Monk of Lexington Barbecue in Lexington, North Carolina, "you was trying to have something you could handle in the hot weather but didn't cost an arm and a leg—what is locally available and what's cheap." Initially, sides tended toward things like bread, pickles, and onions. Coleslaw was an early favorite in North Carolina because locally grown cabbage was abundant and cheap, and if you didn't use mayonnaise, it wasn't particularly perishable. As mechanical refrigeration, air conditioning, and electric deep fryers became more common, new items such as potato salad and French fries began to appear on barbecue menus, too.[11]

Another factor in the regionalization of barbecue was the informal apprenticeship system that shaped the trade. Young people would go to work for an established local pitmaster, learn the craft, and then set out to open their own places. In city after city, key mentors can be identified who taught an entire generation of restaurateurs, who in turn passed on their knowledge to the generation after them. Sometimes this apprenticeship occurred within a single family, with parents teaching their children and then their grandchildren. In other cases it was simply a friendship or purely business relationship.

Beyond simply teaching the skills of tending a pit and managing a business, this mentorship system helped codify the style of barbecue served in a particular region. The identifying characteristics of a region's style include the design of the pits, the selection of meats, and the technique used to cook them as well as the way the meat is chopped, sliced, or otherwise prepared for serving. Also key is the type of sauce to be served and the side items that accompany the meat. Over the course of a half century, the menus and styles within particular areas began to coalesce into the unique regional variations that are so treasured by barbecue fans today. This trend can best be seen by looking at the evolution of restaurants in specific parts of the country between 1920 and World War II.

North Carolina Barbecue

It is no accident that so many barbecue restaurants that went on to become eastern North Carolina legends were found in just three towns—Goldsboro, Rocky Mount, and Wilson—for these were some of the region's most important centers of commerce. Goldsboro, originally known as Goldsborough Junction, grew up at the intersection of the Atlantic and North Carolina Railroad and the Wilmington and Weldon Railroad. Rocky Mount was a stop on the Wilmington and Weldon, too, and the establishment of a tobacco market there in the late 1880s and the rising popularity of cigarettes (and therefore, demand for the region's bright-leaf tobacco) made it a commercial hub. Tobacco also made the fortunes of Wilson. The town's first tobacco market was established in 1890, and by 1920 it was recognized as the largest market in the world.

As people began coming into these towns to trade, a group of men started cooking barbecue to feed them. One of the first was Adam Scott of Goldsboro, who got into the barbecue business just after World War I. A janitor and elevator operator, Scott cooked barbecue on the side and catered parties and receptions. As business grew, he began selling smoked meats from his backyard every weekend. In 1933, he enclosed the back porch of his house to create a dining room, and he enlarged the restaurant three times over the years. Scott was a preacher in the Holiness Church, and he claimed the ingredients for his sauce came to him in a dream. The sauce is a classic eastern North Carolina blend, with vinegar, salt, and red and black pepper along with an undisclosed list of other spices. Though Scott's Barbecue is no longer in operation as a restaurant, the Scott family still sells the patriarch's famous sauce in grocery stores throughout the Carolinas.

Some fifty miles to the north in Rocky Mount, Bob Melton's barbecue business grew in a similar fashion. Melton, a merchant and horse trader, started cooking barbecue as a hobby in 1919. In the early 1920s he bought fifty acres of bottomland along the Tar River and started a truck farm, selling vegetables and pecans to neighbors in Rocky Mount. His barbecue business was casual at first—just a pit in the ground where he occasionally cooked pigs for friends. Soon, he was barbecuing by request and selling the meat by the pound, and it wasn't long before townspeople would come down to the river on Saturday to buy lunch. This spurred Melton to build a shed with rough tables, and he screened it in to keep out flies. Two years later he replaced the structure with a permanent restaurant with room for forty people, and he expanded the dining room several more times over the succeeding decades.

Though Adam Scott was probably selling barbecue earlier, Melton created his enclosed dining room first, making his establishment likely to be North Carolina's first sit-down barbecue restaurant. A menu board from 1929 hung in the restaurant until it closed in 2005, and it showed that in the early days a plate of barbecue and boiled potatoes went for forty-five cents, barbecue sandwiches for fifteen, and a soda for a nickel. Melton's trade was boosted by traffic from nearby US Highway 301, which, before Interstate 95 was built, was a main thoroughfare for travelers from northern states to Florida, and the restaurant became well known outside the state. When Bob Melton died in 1958, he was declared by *Life* magazine to be the "king of Southern barbecue." The business changed hands several times over the years, but it remained in the same spot on the Tar River until 1999, when the flooding following Hurricane Floyd forced it to move to a new location in a strip mall. The restaurant closed its doors for good in 2005.[12]

Though neither Scott's nor Melton's restaurants are in operation today, one eastern North Carolina barbecue dynasty—the Jones and Dennis families of Ayden—have kept the restaurant tradition going, and that tradition goes all the way back to the early days of informal barbecue stands. In the late 1800s, a farmer named Skilton Dennis started loading up his wagon on Saturday afternoons and taking home-cooked barbecue into nearby Otter Town to sell to the farm families who had come into town for supplies. (Otter Town changed its name to the more respectable sounding Ayden in 1890). Dennis's son John and grandson Bill followed in his footsteps, carrying the informal business into the twentieth century. Eventually, Bill Dennis rented a street corner booth, where he sold his barbecue along with cornbread made by his wife, Susan. In the 1920s he moved into a permanent building on Second Street. One of Bill Dennis's sons, Emmitt, continued operating the restaurant after Bill passed away. In 1941, a second son, John Bill, set up shop in a seventeen-foot trailer with a barbecue pit from which he sold just pork, cornbread, and drinks. Seven years later he built a dining room around the trailer and transformed it into a permanent restaurant, naming it the J. B. Dennis Café.[13]

Today, Ayden (population 4,932) boasts not one but two barbecue restaurants that trace their roots to these early Dennis operations. Josie Dennis, Emmitt and John Bill's sister, married a man name John W. Jones, and their son Walter B. "Pete" Jones started working at his Uncle Emmitt's place as a boy. When he turned eighteen, Pete Jones set out on his own and opened a curb-service drive-in on the edge of town, calling it the Skylight Inn. As was standard for drive-ins in that era, he sold hot dogs, hamburgers, and sandwiches alongside the barbecue his uncle had taught him to cook, though he later trimmed the menu down to just barbecue, cornbread, and slaw. Latham "Bum" Dennis, Pete Jones's cousin, worked for both Pete and their uncle John Bill. In 1966 Bum bought out John Bill's operation and renamed it Bum's Restaurant. Both Bum's and Skylight Inn today use the same cornbread recipe developed by Susan Dennis back in the 1920s. You can find identical cornbread and wood-cooked whole hog just ten minutes up the road in Winterville, where Pete Jones's grandson opened Sam Jones Barbecue, a large-format restaurant, in 2015.

The style of barbecue served by the Joneses and the Dennises—and previously by the Meltons and Scotts—is now known as the eastern North Carolina style. It starts with whole hogs laid out on metal rods and cooked over an open pit of oak and hickory coals. Once cooked, the meat is finely chopped (almost minced) and served with a spicy, salty sauce that contains only vinegar, salt, black pepper, lots of red pepper, and not a trace of tomato or sugar—a formula that is essentially the same as that used nationwide during the nineteenth century. Though many eastern North Carolina restaurants today have moved from oak and hickory pits to gas cookers, finely chopped whole hog and vinegar-based sauce remain the characteristic style of the region.

Brunswick stew is a common menu item in eastern North Carolina, too. A descendant of the Virginia squirrel hunting stew, North Carolina's version tends to be thick, sweet, and orange and is made with chicken, tomatoes, potatoes, onions, corn, and lima beans. In addition to the cornbread and coleslaw found at Bum's and Skylight Inn, the region's other classic side dishes include simple boiled white potatoes, which Bob Melton was serving as early as 1929, and corn sticks—cornbread batter baked in long, finger-shaped molds and then deep-fried.

Preparing a tray at Scott's Barbecue, 1944. (Courtesy North Carolina Office of Archives and History, Raleigh)

Bob Melton's barbecue restaurant in Rocky Mount, North Carolina, during a flood of the Tar River.

A barbecue tray at Skylight Inn in Ayden, North Carolina, featuring the cornbread recipe created by Susan Dennis in the 1920s. (Photograph by author)

Eastern North Carolina–Style Barbecue

Meats: Whole hog, finely chopped

Wood: Hickory, oak

Sauce: Vinegar based (vinegar, water, salt, black pepper, red pepper, crushed red
pepper; no tomato, no sugar)

Side Dishes:
- Coleslaw: Shredded cabbage with mayonnaise or mayo/mustard mixture. Often includes sweet pickles, celery seed
- Barbecued potatoes: Boiled white potatoes, cut into chunks
- Hushpuppies: Deep-fried cornmeal batter
- Corn sticks: Cornbread fingers baked in a mold and then deep-fried
- Brunswick stew: A thick, reddish-orange stew. Standard ingredients include chicken, tomatoes, corn, onions, potatoes, and lima beans, usually sweetened with sugar. Sometimes shredded pork or beef is added.

Classic Examples:
- Skylight Inn (Ayden)
- Bum's Restaurant (Ayden)
- Grady's (Dudley)
- Wilber's (Goldsboro)
- B's (Greenville)
- Parker's (Wilson)

The emergence of barbecue restaurants in the Piedmont region of North Carolina followed a pattern similar to that of their eastern cousins, but it resulted in a somewhat different style of barbecue. The Piedmont encompasses an area that runs roughly from the fall line near Raleigh westward to the edge of the Blue Ridge Mountains, and its undisputed barbecue capital is the town of Lexington, the seat of Davidson County. In the early part of the century farmers would pour into town for "court week," many staying for several days to transact business. In 1919, Sid Weaver and George Ridenhour began selling barbecue from a tent on a corner across from the courthouse. Soon after, Jess Swicegood erected a tent nearby and began competing for the farmers' business. At first the men cooked barbecue only during court week, but by the mid-1920s farmers were coming into town every Saturday, and the two businesses became regular weekend operations. The tents were soon replaced by more permanent structures with wooden sides and tin roofs.

Weaver and Swicegood perfected the "Lexington style" of barbecue. Rather than using whole hogs, as they did in eastern North Carolina, the Lexington pitmasters used just pork shoulders. Those cuts have a higher fat content than the hams and loins, so Piedmont North Carolina barbecue tends to be juicier and more tender than the eastern variety. In addition to being finely chopped (as it invariably is in the east), pork in the Piedmont can also be ordered sliced or "coarse chopped," which means cut into large chunks. The region's sauce starts off pretty much like the eastern style does, with vinegar, salt, and black and red pepper, but in the Piedmont they add a little tomato ketchup, which gives the sauce a slightly red tinge and a touch of sweetness.

Sid Weaver and Jess Swicegood established that style of barbecue in Lexington, and the men who trained under them spread it throughout the surrounding counties. Swicegood trained Carlton Everhardt, and Weaver trained Alton Beck and J. B. Tarleton, all of whom opened their own restaurants. And then there was Warner Stamey. In 1927, while still in high school, Stamey began working for Jess Swicegood in Lexington. Three years later he moved down to Shelby, North Carolina, and (like his mentor) began selling barbecue from a tent with a sawdust floor. Stamey passed his knowledge on to two Shelby residents, Alston Bridges and Red Bridges (no relation), who later opened Alston Bridges Barbecue and Bridges Barbecue Lodge, respectively. In 1938, Stamey returned to Lexington and bought out Swicegood's operation for $300. There he taught the style to Wayne Monk, who would go on to open Lexington Barbecue, and many, many others. In their book *Holy Smoke: The Big Book of North Carolina Barbecue*, John Shelton Reed and Dale Volberg Reed mapped out a sort of family tree of Piedmont North Carolina barbecue joints, and some two dozen restaurants can trace their lineage back to Warner Stamey, and even more to Sid Weaver and Jess Swicegood.[14]

Stamey ended his journeys in Greensboro, where he opened Stamey's on High Point Road in 1953. In addition to spreading the Lexington method of smoking pork shoulders across the Piedmont, Stamey is credited with introducing hushpuppies to the North Carolina scene, and they are now one of the standard side dishes at barbecue restaurants throughout the state.

Sid Weaver (*left*) at his barbecue stand in downtown Lexington, North Carolina. (Courtesy Davidson County Historical Museum, Lexington, North Carolina)

Warner Stamey (*right*) tending the pits.

Jess Swicegood at his Lexington, North Carolina, barbecue stand. (Courtesy Davidson County Historical Museum, Lexington, North Carolina)

Piedmont North Carolina–Style Barbecue

Meats: Pork shoulders (chopped, sliced, or coarse chopped)
Wood: Hickory, oak
Sauce: Vinegar based, with tomato
Side Dishes:
- Hushpuppies: Deep-fried cornmeal batter
- Coleslaw (a.k.a. "red slaw" or "barbecue slaw"): Cabbage chopped to tiny bits and seasoned with barbecue sauce (not mayo or mustard)

Classic Examples:
- Stamey's (Greensboro)
- Lexington Barbecue (Lexington)
- Barbecue Center (Lexington)
- Bridges Barbecue Lodge (Shelby)
- Smiley's (Lexington)

South Carolina Barbecue

The northeastern part of South Carolina is frequently called the Pee Dee Region, because it encompasses the Pee Dee River basin. The barbecue cooked there is an extension of the style found across the border in eastern North Carolina: whole hogs dressed in a spicy vinegar-pepper sauce. A different style evolved in the central part of the state known as the Midlands. There, barbecue entered the commercial world by way of cooks who offered up their wares to the general public around key holidays—particularly the Fourth of July and Labor Day. As early as 1897, Columbia's barbecue men started running advertisements in the *State* newspaper offering barbecue meat sold by the pound. Their trade was aimed at holiday picnickers, many of whom apparently carried it home in buckets. On July 4, 1923, no fewer than six vendors posted announcements. S. E. Perry offered "Bucket Barbecue" with meat at sixty cents a pound and hash at thirty. The Lakeview Tea Room was hosting a barbecue from 10:00 A.M. until 4:00 P.M., while J. C. Dreher on Broad River Road promised pork "cooked by one with 25 years experience." At McConnell's Market customers could get sauce free with their order of pork, lamb, or hash, while J. D. Perry's Market advised, "Bring your own bucket." Down at the Waverly Church Grove, E. B. Lever was the chair and pitmaster for the church's annual fundraiser, which offered "Bucket Que" starting at 10:00 A.M., and at 11:45 a "Real Barbecue Dinner" for seventy-five cents in the church basement. Notably, all these advertisements featured both pork and lamb. Barbecue in the Carolinas is dominated today by pork, and lamb or mutton is usually associated with Kentucky. As late as the 1940s, however, it was regularly served in South Carolina.[15]

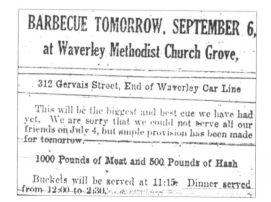

Advertisement for Labor Day barbecue, Columbia, South Carolina. (*State* [Columbia, SC], September 5, 1920)

E. B. Lever would prove a lasting figure on the Midlands barbecue scene. He continued cooking for the church through most of the 1920s, but by the end of the decade he set out on a more commercial path. On July Fourth and Labor Day he set up his own stand on Pendleton Street in downtown Columbia, selling smoked pork, lamb, and hash. "Why do so many demand my barbecue?" Lever advertised in 1930. "Because I select the best meat and cook to suit." By 1935 he had opened a permanent restaurant at the intersection of River Drive and Main Street in the northern part of town, and he eventually moved his operation across the river to Saluda Road in West Columbia. Known as "Barbecue Lever," he was in demand as a caterer for large civic functions, and each year his barbecue stand at the state fair served thousands of guests. Edgar B. Lever died in 1954 at the age of sixty-nine.[16]

South Carolina–Style Barbecue (Midlands)

Meats: Pork
Wood: Hickory, oak
Sauce: Mustard based
Side Dishes:
- Hash and rice: A cross between a meat stew and a gravy served over white rice. Recipes for hash vary greatly from restaurant to restaurant, but it generally consists of pork and/or beef along with vegetables such as onions and sometimes potatoes that are highly spiced and cooked until the ingredients are almost dissolved into a thin, spicy stew. More traditional recipes use various other parts of a hog, including the head, liver, and other organ meats—a throwback to the old days of rural hog killings (see pages 115–16).
- Coleslaw
- French fries

Classic Examples:
- Hite's (West Columbia)
- Sweatman's (Holly Hill)
- Dukes (Orangeburg)
- Maurice's (Columbia)
- Melvin's (Charleston)
- Bessinger's (Charleston)

The Origins of South Carolina Mustard-Based Sauce

THE MIDLANDS REGION of South Carolina is famous for its distinctive yellow mustard-based barbecue sauce, but the origins of that sauce are murky. The members of the Bessinger family, who operate three restaurants in Columbia and Charleston, claim that the now-famed variation was invented by patriarch Joe Bessinger back in the Depression era, when Bessinger was still a farmer and logger in Orangeburg County and had not yet opened his first restaurant in Holly Hill. "In 1933, my dad [Melvin Bessinger] was ten years old," recalled David Bessinger, owner of the two Melvin's Barbecue restaurants in Charleston, in a phone interview. "He came upon his daddy in his shed making this sauce with another man. They were making that mustard-based sauce, and his daddy told him he knew he had something." Eight of Joe Bessinger's eleven children went into the barbecue trade, and they took their father's "yellow gold" recipe down to Charleston as well as up to Columbia and served it in their restaurants.

Other families have staked a claim, too. In 1979, H. O. "Bub" Sweatman, founder of Sweatman's Barbecue outside Holly Hill, told the authors of the South Carolina barbecue guidebook *Hog Heaven* that his family had been cooking whole hogs in their backyard for three generations and that the recipe for his mustard-based sauce was seventy-five years old—which would put its origins back almost to the turn of the twentieth century. Such family stories are the best evidence we have to go on, since no documentary sources from before the 1970s describe a barbecue sauce that is explicitly mustard based. Hardy Childers of Columbia turned up an 1899 newspaper story about a Kiah Dent barbecue that noted, "More delicious than ever was the flavor of mustard and other condiments which make barbecued meat so popular." The phrasing, though, suggests that the meat was being served with prepared mustard, not a tangy yellow sauce. By the 1940s, E. B. Lever, the pioneering Columbia barbecue man, was bottling and selling "Lever's Famous Sauce" at his restaurant and in local grocery stores, but whether it was mustard based is unknown.[1]

We do know that by the 1970s the bright yellow sauce was being used across a wide swath of territory ranging from Newberry County (some fifty miles west of Columbia) all the way down to Charleston on the coast. It even made its way southward into Georgia and down the coast as far as Jacksonville, where it can be found at Jenkins Quality Barbecue, which opened in 1957. And it's omnipresent in central South Carolina, a defining characteristic of Midlands-style barbecue.

1. *State* (Columbia, SC), July 21, 1899.

Puncturing the German Conjecture

MANY WRITERS HAVE attributed the use of mustard in barbecue sauce to the many Germans who migrated to the middle part of colonial South Carolina, settling in the area where the Broad and Saluda Rivers converge, which became known as the Dutch Fork (from "Deutsch"). These Germans, the reasoning goes, brought with them a cultural fondness for mustard that was passed on to later generations. Commentators frequently cite as additional evidence the many families with German surnames who operate barbecue restaurants in South Carolina today. Lake High, for instance, in *A History of South Carolina Barbecue*, notes "names such as Dunn, Fulmer, Hamm, Koon, Kyzer, Lever, Meyer, Mylander, Price, Roof, Seifert, Shealy, Shuler, Sikes, Sweatman, Wise, and Ziegler, as well as six different restaurants run by various Dukes, ten restaurants run by different Bessingers, and three different barbecue houses run by Hites."

But German names are common in the Piedmont of North Carolina, too. The so-called German Conjecture, first advanced by Gary Freeze, a professor of history at Catawba College, postulates that the barbecue families in that region—families with German names like Swicegood, Weaver, and Ridenhour—brought with them a fondness for vinegar-marinated smoked pork and, in particular, the shoulder of the hog. And still others have pointed to the presence of immigrant German butchers in Texas and their fondness for smoked meats to explain the origin of Texas's famous brisket and beef ribs.

It seems curious, though, that German cultural heritage would result in such different barbecue styles in three separate regions. Why no pork dressed in mustard sauce in central Texas, if Germans were so fond of the stuff? This linkage between Germans and mustard sauce collapses under scrutiny. The wave of German settlement that gave Dutch Fork its name occurred during the 1750s, and German immigration to South Carolina effectively ended after the Civil War. Mustard-based barbecue sauce did not exist before the twentieth century, so a fondness for mustard must have lain dormant for generations and emerged only when commercial prepared mustard was readily available on the market. It's also curious that this affinity for mustard was passed down, along with the surnames, via paternal lines only, for census records show that families like the Dukes and Bessingers intermarried with lots of families of British origin over the course of the nineteenth century. It collapses further if you dig into the list of barbecue surnames advanced as being German in origin. Bessinger and Wise (originally, Weiss) are indeed German, according to the *Dictionary of American Family Names*, but Dukes, Sweatman, Lever, Weaver, and Sikes are all English in origin, while Shealy is Irish and Price is a common Welsh surname. But it seems they liked their mustard, too.

Virginia Barbecue

Barbecue doesn't seem to have taken on much of a distinct regional identity in Virginia, which is surprising considering how deep the tradition's roots run in the state. The colony of Virginia was the birthplace of barbecue, the soil where the seed was planted and from which it spread throughout the country. The outdoor tradition remained strong in the state until well in to the twentieth century, and in the 1920s and 1930s, the Old Dominion witnessed as many election and church picnic barbecues as just about anywhere else—and they were often referred to as "old Virginia barbecues."

There was no shortage of commercial barbecue stands in Virginia in the early twentieth century, either. True to form, many made it into the historical record thanks to fires, like the blaze in 1931 that destroyed the Dixie Pig Barbecue Stand on Virginia Beach Boulevard in Norfolk or the one the following year that destroyed Peter Kostopulos's barbecue stand at the corner of High and Rodman. Yet somehow no legendary barbecue restaurants emerged in Virginia that rivaled the reputations of Arthur Bryant's in Kansas City, the Rendezvous in Memphis, or any of the two dozen joints in Lexington, North Carolina. And there isn't a style today that barbecue connoisseurs identify as a distinctively "Virginia style" of barbecue.[17]

You can find good barbecue in Virginia these days, particularly in the Tidewater region, but many of the restaurants there unabashedly advertise "North Carolina–style" barbecue. The website of the Silver Pig Barbecue in Lynchburg, for instance, promises "some of the best Carolina-style Chopped Barbecue, Brunswick Stew and sides known to man, woman or child," while the Three Li'l Pigs in Daleville (just north of Roanoke) declares, "Our NC-style BBQ is made according to time-honored tradition." This stylistic invasion from the south has been going on for quite some time. In 1931 the proprietors of Harry's Place announced the opening of their barbecue stand on Campostella Road in Norfolk, promising "Barbecue Served North Carolina Style."[18]

But if it doesn't quite cohere into a regional style, there are some distinctive elements to the barbecue you find in Virginia. The Southside region—the counties just below the James River—is home to a distinctive reddish-orange, vinegar- and tomato-based sauce flavored with a touch of mustard. At old-school joints like King's in Petersburg, which opened in 1946, that sauce dresses pork and beef that's slow-cooked over oak coals. Farther west, the Shenandoah Valley is home to a long-running

Ad for "North Carolina Style" barbecue stand, Norfolk, Virginia. (*Virginian-Pilot* [Norfolk, VA], June 13, 1931, 12)

barbecue chicken tradition. On just about any Saturday from April to November, you can find a fundraiser staged by a church, volunteer fire department, or Ruritan club featuring chickens split in half and cooked on racks over open charcoal-filled pits. They're basted for hours with a vinegar-based sauce laced with a mixture of herbs and sometimes a little tomato juice—a throwback to the old days of outdoor community barbecues in Virginia.

Is this "Virginia style" barbecue? Perhaps. But not a lot of people outside Virginia know about it.

Georgia, Alabama, and Mississippi Barbecue

The city of Atlanta had barbecue stands in operation by the late 1890s, and these evolved into flourishing restaurants during the early part of the century. One of the best known was operated by Andrew M. Verner. Born in rural Gwinnett County in 1864, he came to Atlanta in his early twenties and worked for a time as an officer on the Fulton County police force and then as a meat and market inspector for the Health

Department. In 1900 he opened a barbecue restaurant on Broad Street, right next to the iron viaduct over "The Gulch," a stretch of railroad tracks that divided the northern and southern parts of downtown. Like many early Georgia barbecue men, Verner cooked more than just pork. For a charity dinner in 1906 he served "Brunswick stew, barbecue veal, lamb, and pig, salads and all the accessories that go with a barbecue dinner." After his building was damaged by smoke and water during the big S. H. Kress building fire in 1922, Verner moved across The Gulch to 37 Marietta Street, where he operated what he came to call "Atlanta's Oldest Restaurant" until his death in 1934.[19]

Savannah had its own barbecue joints, too, including that of Johnny Harris, who opened a white clapboard stand with black shutters and a sawdust floor at the corner of Bee Road and Estill Drive (now named Victory Drive) just outside the city. It was the mid-1920s, and Estill Drive was still a dirt road. The restaurant catered to those traveling from Savannah out to the village of Thunderbolt (home of the Savannah Yacht Club) or to the resorts at Tybee Island. In North and South Carolina, barbecue restaurants tended to be simple places that focused on food only, with no alcohol served and no entertainment. This wasn't necessarily the case in Georgia and the states farther west. Johnny Harris's business was a nightspot, and patrons could dine on barbecue and fried chicken while drinking beer and bootleg liquor and playing slot machines. Harris's cook was an African American man named John Moore, and Moore created the recipe for what became the restaurant's signature barbecue sauce.

After national Prohibition was repealed, Harris and his partner Red Donaldson decided to go big-time. They bought a large tract of land on Victory Drive just to the east of their original location and built a large brick restaurant with three separate dining rooms that could seat a total of two hundred customers. The largest of these was the octagonal Grand Ballroom, ringed by twenty-one handmade cypress booths that seated six guests and had curtains that could be closed for privacy. Customers brought their own bottles of liquor and paid a corkage fee for "set-ups," and each booth had a white call button to summon a waiter when supplies ran low.

In the 1940s, patrons dressed in tuxedos and ball gowns danced in its circular "starlight" dining hall, which had tiny light bulbs embedded in the thirty-foot-high domed ceiling and a revolving bandstand at the center of the floor where big band stars like Harry James and Louis Prima performed. Barbecue and fried chicken remained the house specialties, but an expanded full menu included steaks, seafood, and chops, and eventually everything from omelets to frog legs. Johnny Harris Restaurant remained in

A 1960 postcard for Johnny Harris Restaurant, Savannah, Georgia. Harris's operation began as a barbecue stand selling bootleg liquor during Prohibition and evolved into an elegant nightspot by the 1940s. (Author's collection)

business until 2016, evolving into more of a family-dining restaurant than the night-club of its heyday. Until the end it featured a rarity in Georgia barbecue: lamb, which was served alongside pork on a barbecue plate or as a sandwich on toasted white bread with sliced dill pickle.[20]

Commercial barbecue was not limited to cities. The smaller towns of Georgia, Alabama, and Mississippi began adding barbecue businesses to sell to the growing number of townspeople as well as the residents of outlying rural areas who traveled into town to conduct business. Some of the region's oldest barbecue restaurants date from this period. In 1929, Dr. Joel Watkins opened the Fresh Air Barbecue stand on Highway 42 just outside Jackson, Georgia. It was later leased by G. W. "Toots" Caston, who bought it outright in 1945 after Watkins died. The stand is still in operation today in the same structure, which has changed little since it first opened. The Fresh Air specializes in the two classic items of Georgia barbecue: finely chopped pork lightly dressed in a red tomato-based sauce and Brunswick stew, which, in the Georgia version, is a thick red stew made from pork or beef, potatoes, tomatoes, and corn.

Clement Lamar Castleberry, Barbecue Entrepreneur

SOME BARBECUE MEN took the commercialization of barbecue a step beyond opening restaurants. In Augusta, Georgia, Clement Lamar Castleberry ran a grocery store
on Broad Street in the early part of the century, and on the side he catered large club
gatherings and civic events, specializing in barbecued pork, beef, and hash—the
signature side dish of the region that stretched from the eastern counties of Georgia through the Midlands of South Carolina. In 1926 Castleberry's son, Clement,
started canning his father's hash and Brunswick stew, and the next year the two
men opened a small cannery in a shed on Fifteenth Street, where they produced
six hundred cans a day. Within ten years they had moved to a modern brick factory,
and their thirty-five employees were cranking out ten thousand pounds of food each
day, achieving a nationwide distribution for their products. The business continued
to grow as a private company, expanding into beef stew, chili, tamales, and clams,
and it continues today (under the ownership of Bumble Bee Seafoods) as one of the
country's largest canned meat producers.

Sources: *Federal Writers' Project in Georgia, Augusta* (Augusta, GA: City Council of Augusta, 1938),
158–59; "Food Canner Agrees to Sell," *Augusta (GA) Chronicle*, December 23, 2004.

In Alabama, a unique regional twist emerged in the 1920s: white barbecue sauce. Its
creator was Bob Gibson, a railroad worker for the L&M railway who started cooking and selling barbecue on weekends at his house outside Decatur, Alabama. Gibson
started with a pit dug in the ground and some makeshift tables supported by boards
nailed into the sides of trees. As business grew, Gibson replaced the dirt trench with a
raised brick pit with a flat iron grate. The menu remained simple: pork shoulders and
chickens with coleslaw and potato chips. Between 1930 and 1940 Gibson moved his
restaurant to a succession of increasingly larger buildings before settling in 1952 at a
location that was more permanent and is next door to where Big Bob Gibson's Bar-
B-Q still operates today. Gibson created his signature white sauce to accompany his
barbecue chickens, which he would pull from the pit and dunk in sauce before serving.
"White barbecue sauce" can now be found in restaurants throughout northern Alabama, and it's increasingly making its way southward to Birmingham and beyond.[21]

Georgia-Style Barbecue

Meats: Pork

Wood: Oak, hickory

Sauce: Ketchup based, often fairly thick and sometimes spicy (though pockets of mustard-based sauce can be found in the areas around Augusta and Columbus)

Side Dishes:

- Brunswick stew: While the version of Brunswick stew served in North Carolina and Virginia is almost always made with chicken, the Georgia version is often made with pork, beef, or chicken or any combination of the three, along with corn, pota-toes, lima beans, and tomatoes.
- Cole slaw, generally mayonnaise based
- Baked beans

Classic Examples:

- Fresh Air (Jackson)
- Fincher's (Macon)
- Scott's (Cochran)
- Sprayberry's (Newnan)
- Old Brick Pit (Atlanta)

About the same time that Gibson was setting up shop, James Ollie McClung opened a barbecue stand on Green Springs Highway on the south side of Birming-ham. A year later, in 1927, McClung moved his restaurant to Seventh Avenue, where it would thrive for the next seventy years. Ollie's had both pork and beef on the menu and was known for its homemade pies. (Ollie's would become the subject of a land-mark Supreme Court desegregation case, as detailed in chapter 8.)

Abe's Barbecue in Clarksdale, Mississippi, was founded in 1924 by Abraham Da-vis, a twenty-one-year-old immigrant who had arrived in the United States from Leb-anon eight years before. Originally a snack stand on Fourth Street, the business moved in 1937 to a building at the corner of Highways 61 and 49. Davis cooked Boston butt over pecan wood and then cooled the meat overnight and sliced it. When a customer ordered a sandwich, the pork slices were heated on a griddle, chopped into pieces, and

Big Bob Gibson's Bar-B-Q, Decatur, Alabama. (Author's collection)

served on a bun with the thick, dark red barbecue sauce characteristic of Mississippi barbecue. Abe's featured another Delta specialty on its menu: tamales, which began being sold by street vendors in Mississippi towns sometime around the turn of the century. Davis, following a recipe learned from a local vendor, made his tamales from ground pork shoulder, spreading the meat mixture over a corn shuck that had been lined with cornmeal and then rolling, tying, and boiling it. You can still get a pork sandwich and tamales from Abe's Barbecue today, which is now run by Abe's son, Pat, at the same crossroads location in Clarksdale.[22]

Tennessee Barbecue

Most barbecue styles are defined by state, but two American cities—Memphis and Kansas City—have a barbecue culture that is distinct enough to be considered its own style. Memphis developed its local version in the early twentieth century, when smoked ribs and pork sandwiches became a lunch staple and, because of Memphis's lively nightlife, a late-night delicacy, too. In the decades following the Civil War, the city was an economic magnet that drew thousands of people from the surrounding countryside. A great proportion of these new residents were African Americans looking for better economic opportunities than working on farms. Memphis's black population grew from 3,800 at the time of the Civil War to over 50,000 at the turn of the twentieth century—more than half of the city's total population of 100,000. The city also drew crowds of weekend visitors. Memphis was the hub of the world's largest timber market, and laborers from lumber and turpentine camps in the bottomlands of Mississippi poured into town on their days off, looking for places to spend their hard-earned wages. They were joined by waiters, cooks, porters, and deckhands from docked riverboats along with the more than one thousand men who worked in the city's booming railroad yards.

This in-migration created a significant market for entertainment, and a vibrant nightlife developed in Memphis, with its center on Beale Street. By day, Beale was the heart of black commerce in the city, home to a range of African American businesses including banks, dentist offices, dry goods stores, bakeries, and restaurants. At night, it was a bustling entertainment center, with saloons, theaters, and the music halls that gave birth to the Memphis blues. Beale Street was also home to late-night barbecue joints, the most famous of which belonged to John Mills, an African American who opened a barbecue stand on Fourth Street between Beale Street and Gayoso Avenue in the late 1920s.

John H. Mills was born in Natchez, Mississippi, in 1885. He enlisted in the army around the time of the Spanish-American War and was stationed in various places around the country, including at a base in Minnesota, where he served as a mess cook. He arrived in Memphis around 1919 and worked for several years as a porter and a restaurant cook, residing with his wife, Mary, in furnished rooms on Fourth Street. In 1929 Mills went into business on his own, opening a barbecue stand a few doors down the block from where he lived. By 1932 he had built a brick restaurant in the adjoining lot, and he cooked pork shoulder and ribs over a brick pit in the alley out back. "Mills turns and bastes his meat over a charcoal pit," an Associated Press profile captured in 1938. "It takes a shoulder eight to twelve hours to cook, while ribs can be served in an hour and twenty minutes." While the ribs cooked, Mills mopped them continually with what the reporter described as a peppery "hot sauce," and he served each order with a side dish of sauce, too.

Two decades before Charlie Vergos started selling dry-rubbed ribs at the now-legendary Rendezvous restaurant, John Mills made Memphis famous for ribs. Though located in the heart of the African American district, his restaurant drew both black and white customers, including musicians and celebrities like Bing Crosby, who made it a habit to stop by Mills's place for ribs whenever he was in town. In 1936, the *Pittsburgh Courier* noted that Mills was "often referred to by stage, screen, and musical stars in national radio hook ups 'wishing they had some of Johnny Mills barbecue back in Memphis.'" He regularly shipped barbecue by air express to Kate Smith, Red Mills, and other famous customers, and the Procter and Gamble Company in Cincinnati had a standing weekly order. By 1938, Mills had sixteen employees, including several of his children, and he ran his restaurant on Fourth Street until his death in 1949. Apparently, none of the children wanted to take over the business. A man named John Lewers operated John Mills Bar-B-Q for a few years, but it had closed by the mid-1950s.[23]

Another early Memphis barbecue restaurant is still in operation today. In 1922 Leonard Heuberger opened Leonard's Barbecue at the corner of Trigg and Latham, four blocks south of McLemore Avenue. According to family legend, Heuberger acquired the seven-stool sandwich stand as a barter for a Model T Ford. Ten years later he moved half a mile down McLemore to the corner of South Bellevue and created a drive-in restaurant. Unlike Johnny Mills's restaurant, Heuberger's served only white patrons until segregation ended in the 1960s. The cooks, however, were all black, and they slow-roasted pork shoulders and ribs over hickory charcoal in a brick pit. They cooked overnight, barbecuing up to thirty-two shoulders at a time. One of the cooks was James Willis, who started as a "tray picker" in 1938 at age fifteen and learned the ropes from pitmaster Tom Tillman. Willis recalled keeping the fire going under the meat and turning the shoulders every hour and a half. In between turns, he had to regularly open the pit and make sure nothing inside had caught fire. "You cooking it on an open pit," he told an interviewer in 2009, "that grease gets hot and starts a fire." Leonard's crew would salt the shoulders and cook them a full seven hours, the first four dry and the last three with a mop of basting sauce applied.[24]

Leonard's did a brisk business on weekends, and its busiest time was Sunday evenings, when families out for a drive would stop in for barbecue. Leonard's claims

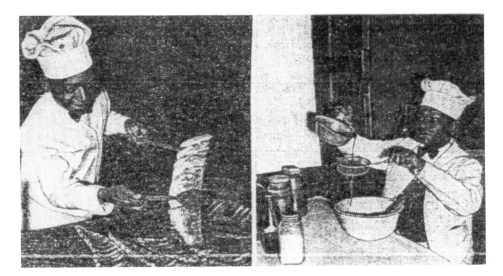

John Mills, Memphis's first Barbecue King, cooking ribs and making sauce, 1938. (*Jersey Journal* [Secaucus, NJ], July 22, 1938)

to have invented the Memphis-style barbecue pork sandwich, which is made from chopped pork shoulder on a bun with finely diced coleslaw and a red, tomato-based sauce. These sold two for a quarter in the 1930s. At its peak in the 1940s and 1950s, Leonard's had twenty carhops working under the canopies, making it one of the largest drive-in restaurants in the country. Although the Bellevue restaurant closed in 1991, Leonard's is still going strong today at its location on Fox Plaza Drive, some ten miles east of downtown.[25]

Many of the early barbecue businesses in Memphis were more beer joints than restaurants. They catered to late-night crowds, with jukeboxes and beer and sometimes areas for dancing. The owners would cook ten or twelve slabs of ribs over small pits in the back, slow-cooking and mopping them all day to prepare for the night's crowd. A popular menu item in the 1940s and 1950s was a rib sandwich, which consisted of three or four ribs served between slices of bread with slaw and a little barbecue sauce. Served with the bones in, the sandwich was meant to be pulled apart with the fingers and eaten.

Though barbecue restaurants flourished in Memphis, the eastern parts of Tennessee did not have much commercial barbecue in the first half of the twentieth century. Charlie Nickens, originally a meat wholesaler, opened a barbecue restaurant at Third and Jefferson in downtown Nashville in the 1930s, where one could get a "Charlie Special"—a pulled pork sandwich served on cornbread—for twenty-five cents and a barbecue plate for forty cents. Chattanooga had a restaurant called the Busy Bee Barbecue in the 1920s, but it was more a downtown café than a barbecue stand, featuring hamburgers, waffles, and the "best coffee in the city" in addition to pork sandwiches. Barbecue restaurants would not become widespread east of Memphis until well after World War II.

Memphis-Style Barbecue

Meats: Pork ribs, pulled pork, some beef, plus barbecued bologna (rolls of bologna smoked on the pit, scored with a knife, and served either as an inch-thick slice on a sandwich or as chunks topped with barbecue sauce)

Wood: Charcoal (oak and hickory)

Sauce: Tomato and molasses based, dark and sweet

Side Dishes:
- Barbecue spaghetti: Spaghetti noodles tossed with bits of pork cooked in a tangy barbecue-like sauce; the best versions, like that at the Bar-B-Q Shop, use sauce that's cooked inside the barbecue pit
- Slaw, often tinged yellow with mustard
- Beans

Classic Examples:
- Leonard's
- A & R Bar-B-Que
- Bar-B-Q Shop
- Payne's
- Cozy Corner
- Jim Neely's Interstate Barbecue
- Charlie Vergos' Rendezvous

Busy Bee Barbecue, Chattanooga, Tennessee, circa 1926. (Author's collection)

Kansas City Barbecue

As an economic center as well as a barbecue capital, Kansas City, Missouri, has many parallels to Memphis. Each is a river city that boomed in the latter half of the nineteenth century, and both developed large African American communities and an active nightlife that included music, dancing, and dining. While Memphis made its fortunes on lumber and turpentine, Kansas City's success was based on beef and grain. In 1867, the town had only twelve thousand people. Two years later, the Hannibal Bridge became the first permanent span over the Missouri River, and Kansas City quickly transformed into a way station for watering and feeding cattle that were being transported on the railroad lines between Kansas and Chicago. Stockyards, grain elevators, and meat packing soon followed. By 1910, with over a quarter of a million people, it had become a major American city.[26]

"Exodusters"—black families fleeing the economically shattered South—started coming to Kansas City in the 1870s, and many found work in the newly built packinghouses. The Great Migration, which began around the time of World War I, increased the size of the African American community to over thirty thousand by 1920. Kansas City was strictly segregated, with most black residents restricted to a few neighborhoods such as Hick's Hollow, Belvidere, and Quality Hill. The latter sat atop high bluffs overlooking the Missouri River and was home to the once-stately mansions of the city's founders. By the 1890s, affluent white residents began moving southward to fashionable homes in newly developed areas, and their old mansions were divided into multitenant rooming houses. It was in these predominantly black neighborhoods that Kansas City's famous barbecue tradition got its start.[27]

The grandfather of Kansas City barbecue is widely acknowledged to be Henry Perry. Perry was a southern transplant, born just outside Memphis in Shelby County, Tennessee, in 1874. He bounced around the Mississippi area for a while, working as a steamboat cook and kitchen hand before settling in Kansas City in 1907. He found work as a porter at a Quality Hill saloon and on the side operated a barbecue stand in an alley off Bank Street in the heart of downtown, where he cooked ribs over a wood-filled pit dug into the ground and sold them wrapped in newspaper for twenty-five cents a slab. As his operation grew, Perry moved several times, first to a location at 1514 East Nineteenth Street and then to an old trolley barn two blocks east at Nineteenth and Highland. Both were in the African American neighborhood known as "The Bowery," but Perry's clientele, the *Kansas City Call* noted in 1932, was about equally divided between black and white, and "swanky limousines, gleaming with nickel and glossy backs, rub shoulders along the curb outside the Perry stand with pre-historic Model T Fords." Perry cooked short ribs, long ribs, ham, and pork over hickory and oak coals, and he was adamant about his technique. "There is only one way to cook barbecue," he insisted, "and that is the way I am doing it, over a wood fire, with properly constructed oven and pit." It was this technique that earned him the title of "The Barbecue King" of Kansas City.[28]

Like Sid Weaver and Jess Swicegood in North Carolina, Henry Perry not only cooked barbecue but also trained an entire generation of Kansas City barbecue men. Charlie Bryant served an apprenticeship at Perry's stand before setting out on his own and opening a restaurant at Fourteenth and Woodland. He borrowed Perry's cooking

HELLO!   HELLO!

Stop in at Perry's during the Holidays for your Barbecued
Turkey, Duck, Pig or Goose.

Don't forget the number.
1514 East 19th Street

HENRY PERRY,   ''The Barbecue King.''

Henry Perry, Kansas City's original Barbecue King. (*Kansas City [MO] Sun*, December 23, 1916)

method but created his own formula for sauce, and he soon gained his own reputation as a notable barbecue man. Bryant moved his restaurant to Eighteenth and Euclid in 1929 and ran it until 1946, when he retired for health reasons. His brother Arthur took over the restaurant, renaming it Arthur Bryant's. He covered the sawdust floors and replaced the wooden tables with Formica-topped ones. He also toned down the spiciness of the barbecue sauce, since he thought that "Old Man Perry and my brother used to make the sauce way too hot." Arthur Bryant was dedicated to his restaurant, arriving at dawn each day and making his own pickles and cutting the potatoes for his French fries by hand. Over time the reputation of Arthur Bryant's grew, helped by a parade of famous diners that included Count Basie, Harry Truman, and many Hollywood stars. In the 1970s, Calvin Trillin declared Bryant's "the best single restaurant in the world." Today, it remains one of the most famous barbecue joints in the country.[29]

The Bryants weren't the only barbecue men who learned their craft from Henry Perry. Arthur Pinkard began working for Perry in the 1930s and later moved to a rundown joint called Ol' Kentuck Bar-B-Q, which had just been bought by George and Arzelia Gates. Pinkard taught his new employers the Perry method of barbecuing, which involved slow-cooking the meats directly over a wood fire so that the juice dripped down onto the coals. The Gateses transformed the Ol' Kentuck into a prosperous restaurant and handed the business down to their son, Ollie, who grew Gates & Son Barbecue into a chain of six restaurants in the Kansas City area.[30]

One last classic Kansas City barbecue joint deserves mention: Rosedale Bar-B-Q. During the depth of the Depression, Anthony Rieke was scraping by selling vegetables from his truck at the city market. In 1932 he rented a small plywood stand and started selling hot dogs and beer. By 1936 he'd moved to a new location and renamed his stand The Bucket Shop, since he sold customers buckets of beer for twenty-five cents, with the customers supplying their own buckets. When Rieke decided to branch out and sell smoked ribs alongside the beer, Rosedale Bar-B-Q was born. The restaurant operates today in the same location, which is just over the Kansas state line on Southwest Boulevard, just a few blocks from Rosedale Park. Rieke ran the restaurant until he died at age ninety-two in 1997, and in the process he became—like Henry Perry before him—one of the city's great barbecue mentors. Rosedale employees went on to

Kansas City–Style Barbecue

"IF IT MOVES, we cook it."
—Carolyn Wells, executive director of the Kansas City Barbeque Society

Meats: Beef brisket, ribs, burnt ends, pulled pork, chicken, ham, turkey (generally sliced)
Woods: Hickory, oak, pecan
Sauce: Tomato and vinegar based, thick and sweet
Side Dishes:
- French fries
- Baked beans
- Coleslaw
- Potato salad
- Pickles
Classic Examples:
- Arthur Bryant's
- Gates's
- LC's
- Rosedale

found a string of restaurants that included Quick's Seventh Street Bar-B-Q, Wyandot Barbeque, Porky's Pit Bar-B-Q, and Johnny's Bar-B-Q.[31]

Entrepreneurs like Henry Perry, Arthur Bryant, and Anthony Rieke helped establish the distinctive Kansas City style of barbecue. The selection of meats is broad, including pulled pork, pork ribs, beef brisket, ham, turkey, and sausage. "Burnt ends" are one of the city's signature offerings. These are the small, crispy bits of meat cut off the ends of a smoked beef brisket. They originated at Arthur Bryant's, where the counter men would slip the trimmed bits of beef across the counter for customers to munch on while waiting for their order to be sliced. Before long, restaurateurs realized they could charge for the tasty morsels, and these day's they're usually served alone with a side of sauce or on a sandwich. Most Kansas City restaurants serve their barbecue with a sweet, tangy sauce made with tomatoes and lots of sugar, a style that was imitated by large food processors like Heinz and Kraft in the 1950s and spread nationwide.

Kentucky Barbecue

Owensboro's first famous barbecue cook was Harry Green. In the late 1880s, he became the regular cook for the Burgoo Club, a group of Owensboro businessmen who got together every two weeks during the summer to eat burgoo and barbecue, drink whiskey, and socialize. The club's first president was Webb David, a minor politico who worked as a whiskey gauger for the US government's Internal Revenue collector. As was typical throughout the South, the white man who organized the barbecues invariably got the public credit for the cooking (an 1888 announcement for one of the club's barbecues promised "cuisine, under the direction of Mr. Webb David, whose burgoo stands unchallenged for deliciousness"). But the residents of Owensboro knew who was doing the actual cooking. The club lasted only a few years, but it established Harry Green's reputation. In 1899, the local paper announced that "Harry Green, of the famous Webb David Barbecue club, will barbecue the meat served at the fair ground." Green was soon cooking for gatherings of the Knights of Pythias and other organizations, and in 1908 he started selling barbecued mutton every Saturday at his home at the corner of Ninth and Hall Streets, advertising himself as "Webb Davis old cook."[32]

Green never made barbecue his full-time profession. He worked during the week as a stemmer in a tobacco factory, and his Saturday business was never more than a simple takeout stand, but it does appear to be Owensboro's first commercial barbecue operation. Through the 1910s and into the 1920s, he regularly posted classified ads in the *Owensboro Messenger* announcing, "Wanted—165 Men to Eat Barbecue." Or 107, or 123—the number changed each time. Green kept his barbecue concession at the county fair for almost thirty years, and each April he traveled to Louisville for the Kentucky Derby and cooked for the big barbecues that were always held on the Sunday after the race. When Harry Green passed away in 1922, the *Owensboro Messenger* hailed him as "the foremost barbecuer in the county" and "conceded to be without a superior in the state."[33]

Green's two sons, John and Pearl, continued selling barbecue on Saturdays for a few years but eventually abandoned the operation. A more enduring barbecue business was established south of town by the Foreman family. Charles Forman was a farmer (early records consistently spell the barbecuer's name "Charles Forman," but the family added an "e" by the 1940s), and he and his son Ollie also operated a blacksmith shop on what was then known as the Livermore Road (and later named Frederica Street). "He did a little barbecuing on the side," recalls his great-great-grandson John Foreman. "Cooked for church picnics and things like that." As the demand for blacksmithing declined in the automobile era, Forman added barbecue to his operation. "The blacksmith shop was on one side and the barbecue on the other side," John Foreman says. "He had a carryout and there was very little room there—he could barely fit in the door."[34]

In 1927, Charles Forman gave up farming altogether and expanded his barbecue operation, naming it Forman's Barbecue Inn. He operated the restaurant until his death in 1941, which brought a pause to the family's barbecue business. His eldest son, Ollie, died just six months later, and his other children didn't keep the restaurant going. But Charles Forman's grandson, Harl T. Foreman, revived the family business after World War II. After serving in the army during the war, he attended the University of Kentucky in Lexington and worked for a time as a draftsman and civil engineer. In 1954, he announced the grand opening of "Harl T. Foreman's Old Hickory" at the corner of Twenty-Fifth and Frederica, the same lot where his grandfather's blacksmith shop and then his restaurant had stood. Touting "3 Generations of Quality Barbecue," Foreman sold mutton, pork, and chicken smoked on a hickory pit, with burgoo on the side.[35]

The Foreman family has been operating Old Hickory Bar-B-Q ever since. A crosstown rival, Moonlite Bar-B-Q Inn, was founded in the late 1940s as a small roadhouse by Sadie Bertram and Betty Stinson, and Catherine and Pappy Bosley bought it in 1963 and grew it into a large-scale, 350-seat restaurant. Old Hickory and Moonlite Inn are both heralded as Kentucky classics today, and barbecue fans argue passionately over which serves the best barbecue mutton in the state.

Advertisement for Harl T. Foreman's Old Hickory restaurant. (*Owensboro [KY] Messenger*, May 8, 1954)

Kentucky-Style Barbecue

Meats: Mutton, pork
Sides:
- Burgoo (see page 111)
- Sliced pickles and onions
- Rye bread
- Potato salad
- Barbecue beans

Classic Examples:
- Old Hickory Bar-B-Q (Owensboro)
- Moonlite Bar-B-Q Inn (Owensboro)

Texas Barbecue

Texas food writer Robb Walsh has observed that "Southern barbecue is a proud Thoroughbred whose bloodlines are easily traced. Texas barbecue is a feisty mutt with a whole lot of crazy relatives." At one point, at least four distinct barbecue styles emerged in the state—East Texas, Central Texas, Cowboy Style (West Texas), and Mexican barbacoa—though the regional distinctions have faded and merged in recent years. The East Texas style was brought by in-migration from other parts of the Deep South, and its pork shoulder, ribs, and thick tomato-based sauce are similar to the style found in Mississippi and Alabama—a descendant of the old Virginia barbecuing tradition. In central Texas, the emphasis is on slow-smoked beef and sausage, while west Texas is known for beef cooked "Cowboy Style" over open mesquite fires. Texas-style barbacoa developed along the Mexican border, where cooks adapted the traditional barbacoa of central Mexico (lamb or goat roasted in maguey leaves) to the ingredients they had on hand, creating a specialty of cow heads wrapped in maguey leaves or burlap sacks and roasted in a pit dug in the ground. All four of these styles were served in restaurants in the twentieth century, but the East Texas and Central Texas styles were the two that became widely commercialized.[36]

During the cotton boom of the 1850s, thousands of planters migrated to east Texas from other southern states seeking new lands to farm. They forcibly brought large numbers of enslaved African American workers and a shared tradition of outdoor barbecues. Following emancipation, many of these rural workers moved into the rapidly expanding cities, especially Houston. The region's barbecue culture received another inflow of eastern influence in the early twentieth century, as streams of former sharecroppers and poor farmers migrated from south-central Louisiana to Beaumont to take jobs in oil fields and refineries in the booming petroleum industry. The city's population quadrupled over the course of two decades, growing from 9,400 in 1900 to 20,600 in 1910, and topping 40,000 by 1920. It was in these urban centers that the first East Texas–style barbecue restaurants emerged.

One of the oldest continuously operating restaurants in Texas is Patillo's Bar-B-Q in Beaumont, which was founded by Jack Patillo in 1912. The Patillo family traces their roots to George Alexander Pattillo, a white man who was an early Texas settler and political leader (Jack Patillo and his descendants dropped the second "t" from their surname). Late in his life, after his first wife died, Pattillo took up with an African American woman who had recently arrived from Louisiana. "They said she was from one of the islands," Robert Patillo told Daniel Vaughn of *Texas Monthly*. "She ran a laundry on Collier's Prairie here in Beaumont. He coaxed her into coming up there and helping him raise those children. She went up there and had three boys with him. My great-great grandfather was their offspring."[37]

Jackson "Jack" Patillo grew up in Beaumont, and just after the turn of the century—in the midst of the city's oil boom—he established himself in real estate, serving as a sales agent and also buying and accumulating lots for himself. Jack ended up losing much of that property—swindled out of it by an unscrupulous developer, according to family lore—and in 1912 he left the real estate trade and with his wife, Roxie, opened a barbecue stand at the corner of Park and Bowie Streets. The building was washed away by a flood in 1915, and Patillo moved first to the corner of Orleans and Forsyth and then two blocks west to a location between Neches and Trinity Streets, a block that at the time was home to many other African American–owned businesses. Advertisements from the early 1930s offered sliced beef, veal, or spareribs for forty cents a pound and sliced lamb or shoulder (meaning beef shoulder clod) for forty-five cents. All were "hickory cooked with plenty of butter sauce." Three "barbecued links" could be had for twenty-five cents. Those sausages, which were made from what Robert Patillo calls "a recipe older than the business," are now known as "Beaumont-style" links (also "juicy links," "garlic bombs," or "grease balls"). A reflection of the Louisiana roots of the Patillo family and other cooks in the city, they're made from beef trimmings ground with garlic, chili powder, salt, pepper, and other spices and stuffed into beef casings and smoked.[38]

Jack Patillo died in 1932, and his son Frank took over the business. In 1935 he moved it to a building he purchased at the corner for Forsythe and Railroad Streets, and in 1950 he opened a second location at 2775 Washington Boulevard. That location is still in business today, operated by Jack Patillo's great-grandson Robert, serving classic Beaumont-style links, ribs, and beef shoulder for over a century.

A hundred miles to the west in Houston, a similar barbecue style developed in the city's Third and Fourth Wards, which include much of the downtown commercial district and the residential areas to the southeast and southwest. These neighborhoods were the center of the city's African American life during the first half of the twentieth century, and in heavily segregated Houston the Third and Fourth Wards functioned almost as separate cities. Dowling Street was the main thoroughfare of the Third Ward, and it was lined with black-owned businesses, theaters, and restaurants. The area's nightclubs included the El Dorado Ballroom, built in the 1930s on Elgin Street, a high-class venue that hosted the likes of Cab Calloway during the 1940s and B. B. King and Ray Charles in the 1950s.

Houston's city directories capture how rapidly barbecue grew as a commercial enterprise in the city. The 1917 directory included for the first time a separate "Barbecue" section in its business guide, and it listed two men, W. E. McCracken at 4607 Washington and Andrew White at 1919 Dowling, the former white and the latter black. By 1929 the number had grown to thirty-seven, and it topped fifty in 1936. By this point the directory's compilers no longer used the mark "(c)" to indicate businesses owned by African Americans, but more than half of the restaurants listed were in the Third and Fourth Wards. A five-block stretch of West Gray Street, between Cushing and Wilson, boasted six barbecue operations.[39]

One of those six restaurants was run by Matt Charles Garner, whose biography reflects the larger migration patterns that shaped the barbecue style of east Texas. Born in Opelousas, Louisiana, in 1879, Garner moved west to Beaumont in the early years of the Texas oil boom. By 1916 he was working as a cook and four years later was operating his own restaurant with his wife, Helen. The Garners moved to Houston's Fourth Ward around 1927, where Garner opened Matt's Barbecue on West Dallas Avenue. He moved the business to 138 West Gray Street in 1934 and soon after initiated a home barbecue delivery via a three-wheeled motorcycle.

Garner taught the craft of barbecue to Joe Burney, who later bought Avalon Barbecue on Dowling Street and then opened Burney's Barbecue on Holman. Burney, in turn, taught Harry Green, who went on to open three of his own restaurants and become a legend of Houston barbecue. Looking back at the original style of Houston barbecue, Green recalled, "Nobody cooked briskets in the old days. I used to go down to the packing house and buy a front quarter of a steer. I'd cut it up myself. And I served mutton, too. But ribs and beef were the biggest sellers." Green also sold "juicy links" made from a recipe he learned from Burney and that Burney, in turn, had learned from Matt Garner, who brought it with him from back east in Beaumont.

Burney's influence wasn't limited to recipes. Many of the early barbecue stand

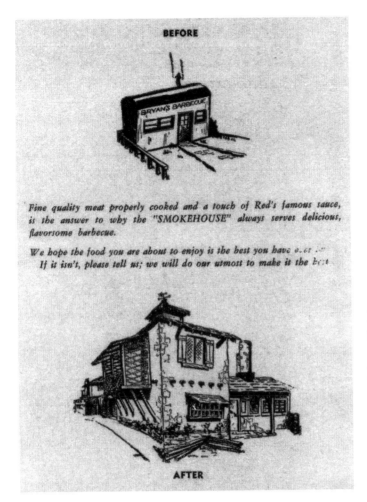

BEFORE

Fine quality meat properly cooked and a touch of Red's famous sauce, is the answer to why the "SMOKEHOUSE" always serves delicious, flavorsome barbecue.

We hope the food you are about to enjoy is the best you have ever ... If it isn't, please tell us; we will do our utmost to make it the best.

AFTER

Illustration from the back of the menu at Red Bryan's Smokehouse, showing the restaurant's evolution from an old converted streetcar in 1930 to a large, stone-sided building in 1947. (Author's collection)

operators in Houston cooked over pits dug in the ground, a method carried over from the outdoor barbecues of the nineteenth century. They began to run afoul of city health inspectors as restaurants began to be more tightly regulated. Burney taught his fellow barbecue men to construct pits out of cinder blocks that would pass city inspection, and their restaurants thrived in Houston's African American neighborhoods until the 1970s, when desegregation started realigning old geographic boundaries.[40]

Over in Dallas, one of the city's first barbecue restaurants was founded by Elias Bryan, who moved from Cincinnati, Ohio, to the town of Oak Cliff, just outside Dallas.

Bryan opened a smokehouse on Centre Street in 1910, where he barbecued untrimmed beef cuts and developed a thick, spicy sauce recipe. Elias's son William Jennings Bryan, known as "Red," opened his own smokehouse on Jefferson Street in 1930 in an old converted streetcar with a sawdust floor, where he sold barbecue sandwiches for a dime and hamburgers for a nickel. In 1947, Red moved from the "tin shack" to a grand building with a stone exterior and calfskin booths where he eventually had eighty-five employees and a flourishing drive-in business, and he later expanded to four other locations. "Sonny" Bryan followed in his father Red's footsteps and founded his own restaurant in 1958, which now has five locations in the Dallas area.

In central Texas, the barbecue business evolved out of meat markets and grocery stores. The tradition there was strongly influenced by the large number of German and Czech immigrants who came to the state in the latter part of the nineteenth century. These immigrants brought with them Old World sausage-making and meat-smoking traditions, and many opened meat markets and groceries in central Texas towns. Prior to World War II, ice provided the only form of refrigeration, and most customers wanted steaks and roasts, since ground beef was not yet widely used. To prevent the less popular cuts from spoiling, butchers would smoke the meatier pieces to make beef barbecue and use the rest in sausage. This barbecue and sausage found a ready market as a takeout lunch. It was sold wrapped in butcher paper, with no sauce, and the customer would often buy a few items from the grocery to go along with it, such as crackers, pickles, and onion.

Some of central Texas's most famous barbecue restaurants got their start in just this way. Kreuz Market in Lockhart was opened by Charles Kreuz in 1900 as a meat market and grocery store. From early on, the market sold takeout meats wrapped in paper as a supplement to the butcher and grocery business. In 1948, Edgar "Smitty" Schmidt, a longtime employee, purchased the market. By the 1960s the barbecue trade had developed into a full restaurant business, and Schmidt closed the grocery side and converted the space into a dining room, but diners still ordered their meat cut to order in the smoke-blackened pit room in the back and carried it to their tables wrapped in brown butcher paper. Schmidt retained some of the more popular takeout items as side dishes, including crackers, bread, pickles, onion, and cheese, which remain on the menu today. After Schmidt passed away in 1990, a rift among his children split the business. Sons Don and Rick Schmidt retained the Kreuz Market name but moved

The brick pits at Smitty's in Lockhart, Texas, fired by blazing post oak logs. (Photograph by author)

the business to a new location about a half mile away. Daughter Nina Sells kept the original building and relaunched it with her sons as a restaurant named Smitty's.[41]

Black's Barbecue, also in Lockhart, grew in a similar way to its crosstown rival. In 1932 the Black family gave up farming to take over running a meat market, to which they added a small grocery section and started selling takeout meat. In 1949 they moved the restaurant into an adjacent building and built a new double-walled pit to handle the volume. Kreuz's, Smitty's, and Black's are all in operation today, giving the small town of Lockhart (population 13,500) three of central Texas's most storied barbecue joints.

As in other states, the barbecue business in Texas was driven by a need to feed hungry people. In the Lone Star State, many of those hungry customers were cotton pickers. The cotton industry had surged in the state during the last decades of the nineteenth century, and thousands of immigrants from the Deep South and Europe moved into the Blackland Prairie section of central Texas to launch cotton farms. The industry peaked in the 1920s, but it remained a key part of economic life in the region for many more decades. Until the widespread introduction of mechanical harvesters in the 1960s, most Texas cotton was picked by hand by migrant workers. An estimated six hundred thousand workers were needed for the 1938 crop, and they moved from farms in the Lower Rio Grande Valley in June to Lubbock in September. These cotton pickers needed to eat, and many went to local grocery stores and meat markets for takeout barbecue and sausages.[42]

In 1918, William Harris Smolik, the son of a Bohemian Czech farmer and sausage maker, opened Smolik's Meat Market in Karnes City, Texas, about fifty miles southeast of San Antonio. Smolik's did a brisk trade during cotton season. "The pickers ate barbecue at our place for breakfast, lunch, and dinner in those days," his son Bill Smolik recalled. "I remember one Saturday we made a thousand dollars in one day, selling barbecue at fifty cents a pound." Edgar Black Jr. of Black's Barbecue in Lockhart remembers that during summers at his father's meat market, the pickers "started coming in the minute we opened at 7 A.M., and they kept coming until we closed. We served nothing but beef and sausage on butcher paper with crackers on the side. That was it. We didn't have time for anything else." At many establishments, cotton workers—most of whom were black or Latino—were not allowed inside the stores and restaurants. Instead, they bought the meat from the back door and ate it sitting on the ground in the store parking lot.[43]

It wasn't just meat markets that got into the trade. Gas stations, grocery stores, and beer halls all made and sold barbecue during the harvest season, and many of these businesses later grew into full-time restaurants. In Taylor, Texas, Louis Mueller added a barbecue shed in the parking lot of his Complete Food Store, and the business became such a hit that in 1959 he moved it across the street into a former indoor gymnasium and installed a brick barbecue pit in the center. The grocery closed in 1974, but Louie Mueller's—now operated by grandson Wayne Mueller—is still selling brisket with a black-pepper rub in butcher paper. Just two blocks away, the Taylor Café got its start as a beer joint, but proprietor Vencil Mares, who learned to make sausage at the

South Side Market in Elgin, soon added brisket and smoked sausage to the offering, transforming his café into a classic central Texas barbecue joint.[44]

The barbecue of east Texas and central Texas was based on the traditional styles brought by immigrants from the southeastern United States and adapted to local circumstances. The barbacoa of the Lower Rio Grande Valley was created through a similar evolution, only the style was brought to the region by immigrants from central Mexico. The original barbacoa was lamb or goat wrapped in maguey leaves and roasted in a covered pit dug into the ground. In Texas, Mexican Americans substituted widely available and inexpensive cow heads and eventually replaced the maguey leaves with burlap sacks. Barbacoa was originally cooked at home for large celebrations, but in the 1930s and 1940s, grocery stores and butcher shops in the Lower Rio Grande Valley started preparing and selling barbacoa to the public. Families would frequently purchase the meat on the way home from church to eat for Sunday dinner.

Making barbacoa was often a family affair, and the grocers' children were enlisted to perform many of the simpler tasks. First, the cow heads were split in half, and the brains and inedible parts of the jaw removed. The brains, which would be cooked separately, had to be rinsed thoroughly to remove any blood clots or bone chips left over from slaughtering, and the heads were thoroughly scrubbed with wire brushes until clean and ready for cooking. In later decades *molinos*—small shops that sold tortillas, beer, soft drinks, and barbacoa—would switch to steaming the heads in stainless steel tubs, but classic barbacoa was cooked in a pit that was dug into the ground and lined with firebrick. The prepared heads were packed along with garlic and salt into metal containers (frequently aluminum lard buckets) and wrapped with wet burlap sacks. The pit was filled with wood, including plenty of aromatic mesquite, and the wood was set ablaze and allowed to burn for hours until reduced to coals, thoroughly heating the brick walls in the process. The metal containers were then placed on the bed of coals, the pits were covered with metal and more wet burlap sacks, and the whole thing was covered with dirt to seal it tightly. Early the next morning, the pit was uncovered and the containers removed. The eyes, tongue, sweetbreads, and cheek meat—now tender and falling from the bone—were separated, cleaned of any inedible portions, and packaged for sale, typically wrapped in white butcher paper—another flavorful variation in the long, rich Texas barbecue tradition.[45]

East Texas–Style Barbecue

Meats: Pork shoulder, pork ribs, chicken, "juicy links" (beef sausage), beef clod, and
 brisket (including chopped brisket sandwiches)
Wood: Hickory and oak
Sauce: Tomato based, sweet and thick
Side Dishes:
- Pinto beans
- Potato salad
- Coleslaw

Classic Examples:
- Patillo's (Beaumont)
- Pizzitola's (Houston)
- Triple J's Smokehouse (Houston)
- Gerard's (Beaumont)

Central Texas–Style Barbecue

Meats: Beef brisket and shoulder clod, beef sausage, pork ribs
Sauce: Thin, tomato and vinegar based
Side Dishes:
- Sliced onions and pickles
- Pinto beans
- Potato salad
- Coleslaw

Classic Examples:
- Louie Mueller (Taylor)
- Kreuz Market (Lockhart)
- Smitty's (Lockhart)
- Black's Barbecue (Lockhart)
- Taylor Café (Taylor)
- City Market (Luling)

Barbecue and Independence

The market demand for a filling, inexpensive meal was one of the forces driving the growth of barbecue restaurants in America's towns and cities. For farmers like Skilton Dennis in Ayden, North Carolina, barbecue was initially a way to earn a little extra income on the side. Smoking meats gave the butchers of central Texas another line of products to sell in their existing retail businesses. African American entrepreneurs who went into the barbecue trade had an additional motivation, for such businesses were a route toward self-sufficiency and independence in a society that offered few other opportunities. In interview after interview, black barbecue restaurateurs cite the desire to not have to answer to anyone as a key reason why they went into the business—and why they stayed in it despite long, physically demanding workweeks.

George and Arzelia Gates, the heads of the legendary Kansas City barbecue family, are prime examples. In the 1920s and 1930s, George Gates worked as a waiter on the Rock Island Line railroad. Over the years he worked his way up in seniority and aspired to be a steward—a position that oversaw all the operations of the dining car, including managing the staff, ordering provisions, and managing the cash receipts. At the time, though, that job was reserved for white men only, and a frustrated Gates eventually quit the railroad. He worked for a while in the post office and as a porter and janitor until 1946, when he and his wife decided to try their hands at the barbecue business. They bought the Ol' Kentuck Bar-B-Q at Nineteenth and Vine, which was little more than a speakeasy, selling more bootleg whiskey than it did food. The Gateses ended the whiskey sales and turned it into a legitimate operation. "It was hard work," Arzelia Gates recalled in an interview with Doug Worgul, "but I didn't mind. I knew that working for yourself is easier than working for someone else. I had worked for somebody else since I was 11 years old. It was a chance to do what I thought was best, not what somebody else told me."[46]

A similar sentiment was expressed in a 1939 interview conducted as part of the Federal Writers' Project. Bill and Geraldine Long, two African American residents of Athens, Georgia, had both worked as domestic servants for most of their early lives, Bill as a houseboy, butler, chauffeur, and fraternity house attendant and Geraldine as a maid and cook. Bill lost his butler's job in the early years of the Depression when the white family who employed him could no longer afford to keep him on. Tired of "house work," he moved to Atlanta and took a job at a barbecue stand. He worked at several different places around the city, learning to cook meat, hash, and Brunswick stew, all the while saving money so he could open his own stand. After two years in Atlanta, Bill Long moved back to Athens, where he married Geraldine. Together they opened their first barbecue stand at their house in downtown Athens. "We dug our first barbecue pit in our own back yard," Bill recalled, "and that good old meat was barbecued in the real Southern style. We done so much business that first summer that we decided to keep our stand going through the winter with home barbecued meat. We already had it screened but when winter come we boarded our pit up."

After two years, increased business forced the Longs to look for a bigger place. They bought a corner lot on Church Street in downtown Athens and moved their stand to the new location. Bill Long printed five hundred circulars, distributed them within a ten-block radius, and over time built a regular clientele that included both black and white customers. The Longs cooked their meat in an outdoor pit behind the stand and sold barbecue sandwiches for a dime. Side dishes included Brunswick stew, cornbread, liver, and bottled beer. Later, they added a small store where they sold fresh meats, groceries, beer, soft drinks, cakes, cigars, and cigarettes. The couple put in long hours and the restaurant was busy for most of the day, but they felt the hard work was worth it, both for the money it provided and, perhaps more important, for the independence. Bill Long drove "a shining new car of a popular make" (as the WPA interviewer described it), and Geraldine Long concluded, "We are making enough to live on, and we don't have to call on nobody for nothing."[47]

Roadside Barbecue Stands

Downtown street corners were not the only places where barbecue started being sold in the twentieth century. In the 1920s, millions of Americans took to the road in newly affordable automobiles, and barbecue took to the roadways as well. The introduction of Ford's Model T and the founding of General Motors (both in 1908) helped make automobiles affordable enough to be purchased by the general public. By 1921, eight million cars were registered in the United States, and by 1931 that number had almost tripled, to twenty-three million. During the 1920s new automobile owners ventured out across the country not just for transportation but also for entertainment and sport.[48]

In the early days of automobile touring, there were almost no restaurants to be

HAMBY'S FAMOUS PIT BARBECUE PLACE — SOUTH BAXLEY, GEORGIA — ON U. S. ROUTES 1 AND 34

Postcard for Hamby's Famous Pit Barbecue Place in South Baxley, Georgia. Many barbecue restaurants got their start as add-ons to gas stations and tourist cottage businesses. (Author's collection)

found outside downtown business districts, and no hotels, either. "Gypsying" motorists would camp out overnight along the roadside, sleeping in tents and cooking their meals over campfires. After a few years, the novelty of roadside camping began to wear off, and tourist campgrounds became popular. Though bare-bones operations at first, these campgrounds started to offer better amenities, including running water, electricity, and bathhouses. It wasn't long before other entrepreneurs saw a chance to make a few bucks feeding the hundreds of thousands of new motorists who were taking to the road each year.

The first roadside food stands were flimsy wooden structures, often homemade, that were thrown up quickly to capitalize on the auto boom. Unlike the more elegant tearooms, which had flourished in the previous decade and catered to the first wave of wealthy automobile tourists, the roadside stands of the 1920s targeted the growing number of middle-class car owners. The menu was similar to that found at county

Roadside barbecue stand made of galvanized tin, Corpus Christi, Texas, 1939. (Courtesy Library of Congress, Prints and Photographs Division)

fairs—hamburgers, hot dogs, ice cream, sandwiches—but one menu item was more popular than any other, especially in the South: barbecue.

Barbecue was an ideal food for roadside stands. It did not require expensive equipment, just a pit dug in the ground and filled with glowing wood coals. Wrapped in brown paper or placed between slices of bread, barbecue was easy to serve and easy to take away. As *Collier's* magazine observed in 1937, the smoke from a barbecue pit was often the only advertising needed. "Down South," the authors wrote, "the mingled savor of pork and hickory wood rising from the pit sets the traveler's nose to twitching half a mile away . . . small wonder that barbecue stands have grown as thick as filling stations, especially as we cross the Mason and Dixon Line." In the early days, most roadside stands were seasonal operations, with the exception of Florida and California, where the warm climate allowed for a year-round auto trade. Cecil Roberts, a

British travel writer who toured Florida in the 1930s, noted, "Everywhere one sees 'Joe's Barbecue' or 'Tom's Barbecue.' It may be an elaborate pseudo-Spanish bar, with gay awnings and aluminum stools, a soda fountain, or a mere wooden shanty on the roadside." By 1934, *Fortune* magazine estimated the total annual revenue from roadside restaurants to be $630 million.[49]

Many barbecue restaurants got their start when the proprietors of another roadside business began serving barbecue on the side, and many found the sideline enterprise more profitable than the original. In 1928, for example, Alex and Gladys McClard, owners of the Westside Tourist Court in Hot Springs, Arkansas, constructed a barbecue pit and started selling slow-cooked beef, ham, and goat to their guests. The barbecue business took off, and soon they were selling to nonlodgers, too. In 1942 they moved the restaurant into the whitewashed stucco building that it still occupies today, which evolved into a drive-in with carhops and a jukebox that broadcast music over an AM band for diners to hear in their cars. Today the carhops are gone, but the restaurant remains in the same building as a sit-down establishment and is a landmark of Arkansas barbecue. Owens' Bar-B-Q in Lake City, South Carolina, followed a similar evolution. In 1946 Mellon Owens opened a grocery store and filling station on Highway 378, about a mile east of the small South Carolina town. Six years later he started cooking barbecue and selling it in the store. Before long the Owenses gave up the grocery business altogether and began running a barbecue restaurant, which remained in operation until the 1990s. Other legendary barbecue restaurants that evolved out of roadside businesses include the Golden Rule in Irondale, Alabama, which started off as a pit stop for travelers on US 78, the main highway from Birmingham to Atlanta. Sprayberry's in Newnan, Georgia, was originally a gas station on Highway 29, just north of Newnan, but owner Houston Sprayberry closed his pumps in 1925 to focus on barbecue.

A few of these early restaurants, like McClard's and Sprayberry's, thrived and became long-standing local institutions, but most were short-lived. Barbecue was a natural adjunct to the gasoline trade, since motorists needed to fuel both their automobiles and their bellies, and filling stations with barbecue pits out back could be found all across the South and Midwest. Burlington, North Carolina, a medium-sized town midway between Greensboro and Durham, had some twenty thousand residents in 1930. Several of its Main Street restaurants—including the Barbecue Lunch and the

Sprayberry's Bar-B-Q, 1143 North Park Street, Carrollton, Georgia. This second Sprayberry's location—the original opened in Newnan, Georgia, in the 1920s—was sold to the Moore brothers in 1959. (Courtesy University of West Georgia Special Collections)

Community Shoppe—featured barbecued pork on their menus, but even more barbecue was found along the highways on the outskirts of town. Eat the Pig Barbecue at W. S. Oakley's gas station between Burlington and nearby Graham sold meals to travelers on NC Highway 10, the original Central Highway that connected the mountainous western part of the state with the coast. In July 1930, Oakley sold the business to Henry M. Johnson, a transplant from New Orleans, who renamed it Henry's Place. On the other side of town, at the intersection of Alamance Road and Highway 10, Bobby's Café offered two kinds of service twenty-four hours a day: gas and oil for cars and "all pork barbecue" curb service for drivers. In 1932, C. W. Harper placed a want ad in the paper offering for sale his "Barbecue Café, Filling Station, and Grocery Store" at the corner of Highways 62 and 54, explaining that he "must devote time to other business."[50]

Burlington was typical of small towns on main highways, and by the 1930s barbecue could be found at tens of thousands of roadside stands throughout the country. Many of these were in business for only a few years before changing hands or fading away altogether, and only a small number lasted past the 1950s. For the moment, though, barbecue was king of the American highway.

Barbecue and Early Restaurant Chains

Today, hamburger chains like McDonald's and Burger King dominate the takeout market, but the country's first drive-in restaurant chain was devoted not to hamburgers or hot dogs but to barbecue sandwiches. The first Pig Stand opened in Dallas in September 1921 at the corner of Chalk Hill Road and the Dallas–Fort Worth Turnpike. Its founders were Jesse G. Kirby, a candy and tobacco wholesaler, and Reuben W. Jackson, a local physician. The Pig Stand was an unassuming operation—a small, white wooden stand on a corner lot—but it had a revolutionary feature. Jesse Kirby was reported to have said, "People with cars are so lazy they don't want to get out of them to eat!" and his restaurant was likely the first in the country to offer curb service for motorists. Customers could pull up to the curb in their automobiles and be served by "carhops," young men in white shirts and black bow ties who would hop up on the running boards of arriving cars and take passengers' orders even before the car had come to a stop. The carhops worked for tips only, and the competition was fierce to get to each car first and return with the sandwiches as quickly as possible.

The Pig Stand's menu was simple—a pork or beef sandwich wrapped in paper and served with a bottled soft drink—but the curb service was a hit. There was a traffic jam at the grand opening, and Kirby and Jackson opened five more Pig Stands in the Dallas–Fort Worth area by 1925. Their first restaurants had curbside service only, and customers had to either stop their cars along the street or walk up to the stand on foot. By the late 1920s, the newer Pig Stand restaurants had evolved into pagoda-like buildings set back from the street so motorists could pull in headfirst and park, making them true "drive-in" restaurants. The chain began franchising and continued to grow, and by 1934 over 120 Pig Stands were in operation, stretching from Florida along the Gulf Coast through Texas and also in Southern California.[51]

Other operators soon latched on to the drive-in concept. A&W Root Beer, whose roadside stands had been around since 1919, added carhop service to its parking lots, taking heavy glass mugs of root beer and food straight to customers' automobiles. Other pioneers included Carpenter's in Los Angeles, whose octagonal restaurant at the corner of Sunset and Vine in Hollywood, California, was a dressed-up version of the Pig Stand. J. D. and Louise Sivils, owners of a sit-down restaurant in Houston, opened a "Drive-Inn" branch on the outskirts of the city in 1938 and became perhaps

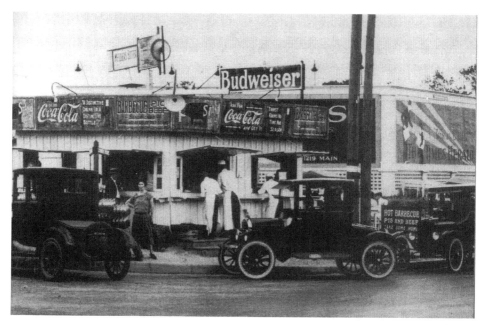

Curbside service at the Pig Stand #2, Dallas, Texas, 1920s. (Author's collection)

the first business to use what would become the universal term for restaurants that serve diners in their cars. Many early drive-ins ran a basic operation along the Pig Stand model, selling sandwiches wrapped in waxed paper and drinks in glass bottles. Others added fancier trappings like window-mounted serving trays and, later, long serving boards that diners would stretch from door to door inside the car, making it possible for meals to be served on china plates with glasses and silverware. Menus remained varied, too, and barbecue was one of the leading items. Once found only at large rural gatherings, barbecue was now being eaten daily in cars from the East Coast to the West.

The Expansion of Barbecue

By World War II, barbecue was standard fare in restaurants from eastern Virginia all the way to the West Coast. Many of these establishments were nothing more than improvised wooden stands erected on street corners that sold smoked meat that had

Roadside barbecue stand near Fort Benning, Georgia, December 1940. (Courtesy Library of Congress, Prints and Photographs Division)

been cooked in a hole in the ground and wrapped in brown paper. Others were sit-down restaurants, where barbecued pork or beef was listed on the menu alongside steaks and chops. Still others were nightspots, where the barbecue was a sideline to beer and liquor sales and provided late-night fuel for dancers and revelers. These many styles of restaurants had one thing in common: they created stable, fixed locations where barbecue was sold on a regular basis.

As the restaurant industry matured, the equipment used to make barbecue was transformed, too. The "pit" evolved from a trench dug in the ground into permanent structures that reduced the intensive labor required to lift and baste meat. By midcentury, a typical barbecue pit was elevated above the ground, with brick or cinder-block sides supporting a metal rack or grill at about waist level. Glowing hardwood coals were shoveled below the grill, and the meat placed on top, some two feet or so above the coals, where it would be loosely covered and cooked for hours until tender. In some pits, a sheet of tin was also placed above the meat so that coals could be shoveled on top to provide heat from both sides. As the century progressed, restaurateurs hired masons to build custom pits out of firebrick, with steel doors enclosing the cooking chambers and chimneys rising high above.[52]

Barbecue restaurants today tend to be specialized operations, with barbecue as the prime attraction and the other menu items being mostly side dishes like beans, French fries, or coleslaw. In the 1930s and 1940s, however, countless large-format restaurants added barbecue pits out back for cooking pork, ribs, and chicken. The South and Midwest were dotted with signs advertising "Steaks—Chops—Barbecue," and many drive-in restaurants included barbecue sandwiches alongside their offerings of hamburgers, hot dogs, and fried chicken. Barbecue had entered the mainstream of American restaurant dining.

7

BARBECUE FINDS THE BACKYARD

These days, the word "barbecue" means different things to different people. When many Americans—especially those in northern states—invite guests to a barbecue, they may well serve hot dogs or hamburgers that have been cooked on a charcoal or gas grill. Other Americans—especially those in the South—insist that such an event is a "cookout" and that the hosts are "grilling," not "barbecuing." For purists, barbecue has the very specific meaning of slow-cooking large cuts of meat over a wood-fired brick or metal pit, not cooking brats or chicken breasts on a grill.

As different as those two ways of cooking seem today, they both descended from the same common ancestor: the outdoor community barbecue. Around the same time that the older form of barbecue was being modified for commercial sale at barbecue stands, it was also becoming a fixture of the American backyard. Over time, new ingredients, equipment, fuel, and commercial sauces pushed the backyard version further and further away from its original ancestor, and in the process it acquired its own set of trappings and conventions. In the decades just before and after World War II, the backyard barbecue became a routine part of the suburban family experience and an iconic image of the good life in America. Not everyone may call it "barbecue" today, but historically it's part of the country's long barbecue tradition.

"An Unusual Way to Entertain"

In the 1920s, general interest magazines started publishing travel narratives from the Southwest that described outdoor barbecues as a curious regional experience. "An unusual way to entertain informally during the late summer or fall is to give a barbecue," a 1924 article in *Woman's Home Companion* opened. The writer provided instructions for staging an event for up to thirty people, including digging a pit in the backyard, and she depicted the barbecue as a very western kind of thing, complete with a recipe for "Cowboy Sauce" that she learned from "a Colorado cowboy, famed years ago on the plains for his expert skill in barbecuing meats." These sorts of western-inspired parties grew in popularity during the 1930s as suburban residents adapted the pit-cooking tradition from the South and West and turned it into a small backyard event for family and friends.[1]

Backyard barbecuing initially took hold on the West Coast, where the warm climate allowed year-round outdoor cooking. In 1936, *American Home* magazine noted that barbecue was "a word dear to the heart of a Californian, and in almost any sheltered garden one may find an outdoor grill, and on most any rancho, a barbecue pit." In 1939, the editors of *Sunset* magazine, a California publication dedicated to "Life in the West," created *Sunset's Barbecue Book*, the first full-length book on the subject of barbecue. The volume opened by asking, "Why is it that practically everybody in the West has a barbecue, is planning to have a barbecue, or wishes he had one?" *Sunset* defined a barbecue as not just a social gathering but also the fireplace or stove used for outdoor cooking, and the majority of the book focuses on instructions for building a backyard pit or fireplace.[2]

To explain the appeal of backyard barbecues to Californians, *Sunset's* editors pointed to the element of escape inherent in outdoor cookery. "The barbecue satisfies our desire to get away from hectic daily routine," they noted, awakening "impulses that hark back to pioneer days and put us 'right with the world.'" The barbecue became an important part of the image of California that West Coast "lifestyle" magazines like *Sunset* promoted to eastern readers during a period of great economic hardship. "Sunset fought the Depression by ignoring it," the California historian Kevin Starr has observed, "by holding before the middle class an image of the good life as it was surviving even in dire times."[3]

This image of the California "rancho" life was linked to a highly romanticized view of the Mexican influence in early California. A 1933 article in *Touring Topics* claimed that history was responsible for the growing popularity of outdoor barbecue fireplaces and grills, which dated "back from the days when a caballero rode from hacienda to hacienda summoning the Señors and Señoritas to gather for the great fiesta." Wealthy Californians (including part-time Californians from back East) purchased

THIS CURVED-TOP brick barbecue is at the W. P. Botkin home, Hillsborough, Calif. Note the raised platform, side work shelves and chains at either side that regulate the grill.

A RAISED CORNER PIT in Napa, Calif., built of light-weight concrete units. It's part of a garden wall. The wing walls form ample counters for pushing things around.

HERE'S A SIMPLE brick unit built against a wall at the Z. E. Page home, Lindsay, Calif. The step back construction is both decorative and useful for cooking equipment or ornaments.

A VARIATION on the outdoor fireplace shown on *Page 30* (Plan 9) is this brick and stone structure in the garden of Landscape Architect Charles Gibbs Adams, Los Angeles.

Sunset's Barbecue Book (1939) provided readers with dozens of examples of brick barbecue pits from California backyards, complete with plans for constructing them.

ranch estates in places like Carmel Valley and the Santa Ynez Valley, where they constructed houses with adobe walls and red-tiled roofs. No rancho would be complete without a brick barbecue fireplace, and the more elaborate versions were equipped with iron spits, utensils, and other decorations intended to evoke Old Mexico. Before long, upper-middle-class Americans in other parts of the country began imitating the trappings of the relaxed, easygoing California lifestyle. Hosting a barbecue for family and friends around an outdoor fireplace was an enjoyable way to escape the pressures of the business world. By 1941, Genevieve Callahan could write in *Better Homes and Gardens*, "Indoors, outdoors, and year-round barbecues have the whole country's mouth watering."[4]

Backyard Barbecues in Wartime and After

During World War II, the interest in outdoor cooking spread beyond the professional classes. "With the entire nation seeking simpler means of entertainment because of wartime requirements," noted a 1942 article in New Mexico's *Deming Headlight*, "backyard barbecues are becoming quite the style from California to Maine." An article on new types of outdoor grills in the *New York Herald Tribune* strongly recommended such devices "in these harsh times" because they "afford an economical means of entertainment al fresco; good food, fresh air and the kind of relaxation that goes deep; i.e., a momentary return to primitive modes." The focus on economy was essential not only because of high wartime prices but also because of rationing. With gas limited to only three gallons a week, picnics in the country became an inaccessible luxury, and Americans turned to their backyards for entertainment. Buying steak required twelve ration points per pound, but ground beef needed only seven, so the foods of choice for barbecuing were often hamburgers and frankfurters.[5]

After the war ended, permanent home barbecue pits continued to grow in popularity among the upper middle class, who proceeded to take it one step further. Magazines such as *House and Garden* and *House Beautiful* ran articles offering plans not only for permanent brick barbecue pits but for entire "barbecue rooms"—extensions to a house's patio or porch that provided a covered dining area built around a large brick fireplace. In 1947, Herbert Coggins in the *Atlantic Monthly* satirized the temptation of a homeowner building a barbecue pit to add more and more features to it. Starting with a simple outdoor fireplace, Coggins's narrator added rustic chairs

Dining in a suburban barbecue room. (*Better Homes and Gardens*, May 1941)

and tables and a motorized rotating spit and then enclosed the fireplace in a glass room. Gradually adding one gadget after another, he ultimately migrated the entire kitchen—sink, refrigerator, and all—"outdoors" and then turned the old kitchen into a sunroom with wide French doors opening outside. Now the family could take the food cooked "outdoors" in the enclosed barbecue room and eat it "indoors" in the open-air dining room.[6]

The menu for backyard barbecues was much broader than at traditional pit-cooked events. The recipe section of *Sunset's Barbecue Book* begins with steaks, veal sati, chops, hamburgers, and shish kebab along with a range of potato, corn, and bean recipes for sides. In California, the backyard barbecue was not just for grilling dinner: "If you've never used your barbecue for outdoor breakfasts," the *Sunset* editors insisted, "you've missed a good part of its charm." Recommended menus included grilled ham and sausage along with eggs and pancakes, which could be cooked in skillets placed directly on the grill.

Grilling burgers on a backyard grill, of course, is quite different from cooking over an old-fashioned barbecue pit, and calling this backyard pastime "barbecuing" drew the ire of traditional barbecue fans very early on. "Many Georgia epicures insist that this is an insult to the honorable name of barbecue," Rufus Jarman wrote in the

Mr. and Mrs. Fred Hammond of Nashville, Tennessee, grilling in their backyard over a permanent brick barbecue, 1952. (Courtesy Tennessee State Library and Archives)

Saturday Evening Post in 1954. "You cannot barbecue hamburgers, roasting ears, potatoes, onions, tomatoes, wieners, or salami, and it is a shame and disgrace to mention barbecuing in connection with such foolishness." For an increasing number of Americans, though, this was the definition of barbecuing, and they couldn't get enough of it.[7]

Backyard Barbecue Equipment

The first commercial barbecue equipment for backyard chefs appeared on the market in the 1930s. By the 1940s, a wide array of barbecue grills could be found for sale in hardware, sporting goods, and heating supply stores. Many of these were dual-purpose devices that could be used as a grate within a living room fireplace and also as a portable barbecue grill for picnics and other outings. Most were simple in design—a metal tray for holding wood or charcoal with a gridiron above it for holding meat—though a few more sophisticated models featured accessories such as adjustable grill levels and spits for turning meat. Early grills tended to be small, so that they could be packed up and easily taken on outdoor picnics.

In 1952, George Stephen, a backyard barbecuer from Mount Prospect, Illinois, grew frustrated with battling wind and uneven, hard to control flames when cooking with his brazier grill. Stephen, an employee of Weber Brothers Metal Works, fashioned a grill from metal parts that were being used to make buoys. He cut a spherical buoy in half to create a bottom and then added a dome-shaped lid and a three-legged stand to support them. The design worked, and Stephen soon launched a "barbecue division" at his company. Selling at close to fifty dollars (at a time when a brazier-style grill could be had for ten), the Weber grill was a premium product. It gained popularity first in the Midwest, then throughout the country, and inspired numerous imitators of its "kettle grill" design. In the late 1950s Stephen bought Weber Brothers Metal Works, renamed it Weber-Stephen Products, and over the next two decades transformed it into one of the leading producers of equipment for the home barbecue market.[8]

Along with new types of grills, new fuel sources were introduced to make cooking easier. At first, most barbecuers fired their grills with wood or lump charcoal. The latter product was made by piling wood in a large mound, covering it with dirt, and setting it afire. It would burn slowly with little oxygen present, losing all its water and gradually breaking down over the course of three or four weeks until virtually nothing but pure carbon was left. Many barbecuers found lump charcoal to be superior to wood, for it burned hotter and more cleanly, but it also tended to crumble in a bag, leaving behind lots of powder and small chips rather than large lumps. Orin F. Stafford, a professor at the University of Oregon, set out to fix that problem.

In the early part of the twentieth century, Stafford patented his "retort" method of making charcoal. This involved passing wood continuously through a series of ovens until it had become lump charcoal, then grinding it into powder, mixing it with starch, and compressing it into a briquette shape. Stafford's method was popularized by Henry Ford, who started producing charcoal briquettes as a way of achieving economy in his automobile manufacturing. Back in the 1920s, cars still used a lot of hardwood in their bodies, and with Stafford's retort method Ford could convert leftover wood scraps into something he could sell.[9]

At first, Ford's charcoal was used for firing ovens and stoves in railroad dining cars and hotel kitchens. In the late 1920s the company started marketing the product to household consumers through coal and ice dealers, who encouraged their customers to use the briquettes for starting furnaces and grate fires. It took another decade before

A 1940 newspaper advertisement for Ford charcoal briquettes and grills. (*Valparaiso* [*IN*] *Vidette Messenger*, August 13, 1940)

Ford found the natural market for the product. In the 1930s, coal dealers started adding blurbs to their newspaper ads suggesting, "On that week-end camping trip use Ford's Charcoal Briquettes for steaks and bratwurst roasts" and "Ford Charcoal Briquets in convenient paper sacks. Ideal for picnic roasts." Within a few years, the briquettes were being sold through Ford's network of automobile dealerships. "Going riding" was a popular form of evening and weekend recreation for entire families, and the automobile retained strong connotations of outdoor adventure and escape. Automobile dealers in the years just before and after World War II stocked a full line of camping and cooking equipment that could be used for weekend rambling. Ford's charcoal fit perfectly into this mix, and it was common in the 1940s for a Ford dealer to sell a portable grill for two dollars and a five pound bag of charcoal for twenty five cents. Through the 1950s, automobile dealerships would be the primary sales outlet for Ford's charcoal.[10]

Ford's charcoal was produced near Iron Mountain, Michigan, at the site of the company's body part works. A company town grew up nearby and was named Kingsford after E. G. Kingsford, a relative of Ford's who helped found the charcoal works and later managed them. In 1951, Ford Motors sold the charcoal operations to a group of local investors, who renamed it the Kingsford Chemical Company. The company later moved to Louisville, Kentucky, and began placing its products for sale in supermarkets. Acquired by Clorox in 1973, Kingsford remains the largest-selling brand of charcoal in the country.[11]

In the early 1960s, the backyard barbecue took another step further away from the wood-fired pit when the first gas-fired grills were introduced. Promising "the ultimate in cooking convenience for the backyard chef," early models were built of aluminum with ceramic briquettes that were heated by gas burners, and they were designed to be installed permanently in backyards or on patios. The grills were sold by local gas companies that were eager to find new ways to sell natural gas, and barbecue grills joined a line that already included gas lamps for permanent outdoor lighting and gas-powered air conditioners. One of the first models of gas grills was manufactured by the Arkla Air Conditioning Company, a subsidiary of the Arkansas Louisiana Gas Company, which sold natural gas to customers in Arkansas, Louisiana, Oklahoma, and Texas. Around the same time, competing models were brought out by Charmglow Products of Antioch, Illinois, Char Glo by Waste King Universal of Los Angeles, and Falcon Manufacturing of Dallas.[12]

Gas grill manufacturers touted their products as being easier and cleaner than charcoal models. With a three-position burner, the advertisements promised, controlling the heat was a snap, and the ceramic briquettes minimized flare-ups from dripping grease. For $0 down and thirty payments of just $2.60 a month, Lone Star Gas Company customers could have either an Arkla or a Falcon gas grill installed in their yards. Within a few years, Char Glo and Charmglow introduced portable models that could be moved around the yard. Charcoal grill pioneer Weber introduced its own gas-powered version, the Gas Barbecue Kettle, in 1971, and fifteen years later brought out

revolutionary new
ARKLA GASGRILL
nothing down,
$2.60 monthly

Here's Space Age barbecuing! Gasgrill gives you tasty outdoor flavor and complete heat control! Permanent ceramic briquets glow clean — fast, flexible gas starts them radiating instantly! No more messy charcoal to handle — grubby ashes to take out. Smoke meats easily by closing the hinged dome cover. Made of heavy-duty cast aluminum, Gasgrill is weatherproof . . . can't rust . . . outlasts a dozen old-fashioned grills. Installs easily in your yard . . . free up to 50-ft. Get your Arkla Gasgrill (by the makers of famous Arkla Gaslites and Gas Air Conditioning) now! Makes a great gift, too!

ONLY
$78.00
plus tax

LONE STAR
GAS
COMPANY

*Hear
PEGLER
speak out!
Nov. 8   Statler-
8 p.m.   Hilton

Left: A 1966 newspaper advertisement for the Arkla Gasgrill. (*Dallas Morning News*, November 6, 1963)

Above: Advertisement for Georgia Barbecue Sauce. (*Atlanta Constitution*, January 31, 1909)

its Genesis line, which promised cooks more precise heat control. The popularity of gas-fired models continued to grow over the years. In 1985, 3.1 million gas grills were sold in the United States, compared to 7.8 million charcoal models. Two decades later, gas grills were outselling charcoal, with 10.1 million gas models sold in 2006 versus 6.8 million charcoal.[13]

Barbecue Sauce

As postwar manufacturers started producing new grills and fuels aimed at the backyard cook, the food industry finally took notice of the huge potential market offered by outdoor cooking. It had taken a long time for barbecue sauce to become a commercially manufactured product. By the 1870s dozens of prepared sauces such as ketchup and Worcestershire sauce were being sold, but barbecue sauce was not among them. Early barbecue cooks helped define regional sauce variations at their restaurants and barbecue stands, but few had shown any interest in bottling and marketing their secret recipes. The handful of early entrepreneurs who did try to enter the bottled sauce business found only limited success.

The first of these, the Atlanta-based Georgia Barbecue Sauce Company, began advertising in the *Atlanta Constitution* in 1909, promising "the finest dressing known to culinary science for Beef, Pork, Mutton, Fish, Oysters, and Game of every kind." The company's ads disappeared after only a few months. Two decades later, Eddy's Strictly Pure Barbecue Sauce began to be carried in grocery stores nationwide, and Bayles and Topsy brands appeared in the Midwest around the same time. None of these brands was long lived.[14]

At first, most backyard barbecue cooks made their own sauce, and the cookbooks and magazines of the 1920s and 1930s offered a steady flow of recipes for them to try. In the days of rural barbecues, sauces had been very basic and prepared in bulk, relying on only a few staples such as vinegar, salt, and pepper for ingredients. Sugar was usually absent from the list. That began to change as mass-circulation magazines popularized the backyard barbecue, and in the 1920s sugar began to creep into recipes along with commercially prepared products such as ketchup and Worcestershire sauce.

Mrs. S. R. Dull, editor of the *Atlanta Journal*'s Home Economics page, included the following recipe for barbecue sauce in her 1928 book *Southern Cooking*:

2 1/2 lbs of butter	1 pint chili sauce (medium size)
2 quarts of apple vinegar	
1 pint of water	2 lemons, juice only
1 tablespoon dry mustard	1/2 lemon put in whole (seed removed)
1/2 cup minced onion	
1 bottle of Worcestershire sauce	3 cloves of garlic chopped fine and tied in bag
1 pint of tomato catsup	2 teaspoons of sugar

Two teaspoons is a relatively small amount of sugar. Two decades later, Dorothy Malone tripled that amount in her barbecue sauce recipe in *Cookbook for Brides* (1947),

During the 1950s, food manufacturers sought to capitalize on the popularity of backyard barbecues. This example from *Best Foods* is from 1954.

which calls for two tablespoons of brown sugar along with onion, butter, vinegar, lemon juice, catsup, Worcestershire sauce, prepared mustard, parsley, salt, and pepper. By World War II, recipes such as these had become standard, and homemade barbecue sauce had evolved from a thin, peppery basting liquid to a sweet, cooked product with a mix of many flavors.[15]

Magazine advertisement for Kraft's new barbecue sauce. (*Woman's Day*, June 1961)

Around this time, the large commercial food producers entered the barbecue sauce market. Heinz was the first major company to put a brand on grocery store shelves, introducing Heinz Barbecue Sauce in 1940. General Foods soon followed with its "Open Pit" brand. Kraft got into the game much later—around 1960—but advertised widely, using full-page color spreads in women's magazines, and its brand quickly became the leading bottled barbecue sauce—a position that it maintained for five decades. (It was eclipsed by Sweet Baby Ray's in the 2010s but remains the second best-selling sauce today.) Ads from the 1960s show sauce being poured on top of steaks, hamburger patties, and hot dogs, often while they are still cooking on the grill. Kraft's advertisements advised cooks to brush on its sauce throughout the grilling process, claiming, "Kraft Barbecue Sauce simmers real cook-out flavor right into the meat!" All of these bottled sauces were similar in style and borrowed heavily from the traditional Kansas City variety. Tomato based with lots of sugar and molasses, the thick, orange-brown concoctions continued the century's trend of increasing sweetness, and their mass marketing helped them gain acceptance nationwide.

By the 1960s, charcoal grills were almost universal on Americans' backyard patios, and bottled barbecue sauces could be found in kitchen pantries across the country. While "barbecuing"—used in the sense of cooking on a charcoal or gas grill—resulted in a very different type of food than its hickory-pit forebears, the backyard version continued barbecue's centuries-old tradition of bringing people together for relaxation and community, though on a much smaller and more personal scale. In only a few short decades, "grilling" or "cooking out" had become an entrenched part of American home life. More than just a favorite meal, the backyard barbecue was synonymous with "the good life," one of the favorite forms of entertaining in the postwar suburbs. It still is today.

8

THE FIRST GOLDEN AGE OF BARBECUE

THE TWO DECADES FOLLOWING the end of the World War II may well be considered the First Golden Age of American barbecue. Barbecue during these years was no obscure regional specialty or a craft practiced by a few skilled cooks. Instead, it was one of the most popular food items in the American culinary repertoire. It could be found in fancy steak and chop houses, at drive-ins and cafés, and at countless backyard events throughout the country. And the number of restaurants specializing in barbecue kept growing. A typical medium-sized American city had a handful of barbecue stands or cafés in the 1920s; by 1950, that number could easily be in the dozens.

The late Nick Vergos, the son of Charlie Vergos and owner of the legendary Memphis rib joint Rendezvous, observed that many of the people who took barbecue mainstream were not old-time barbecue men who decided to open their own restaurants but rather established restaurateurs who decided to branch out into barbecue. These restaurateurs often enlisted the help of an employee or a friend who knew the craft of barbecue from the precommercial days. The Rendezvous itself, which many credit with inventing Memphis-style dry-rubbed ribs, is a perfect example.[1]

Charlie Vergos's family emigrated from Greece to the United States in the early 1900s. His father, John Vergos, tried his hand at many trades before settling on selling hot dogs in Memphis, Tennessee. Charlie followed in his father's footsteps, running a meat-and-three restaurant called Wimpy's with his brother-in-law. In the late 1940s Vergos decided to set out on his own and open a snack bar in the basement of the building that housed Wimpy's. There was an old, unused coal chute in the corner of the basement, and he had the bright idea of converting it into a smoker. His original plan was not to make barbecue but rather to smoke hams and slice them for

"BBQ Pete" Petroff's Circle Room Restaurant in Inglewood, California. Opened in 1947 and specializing in barbecued chicken and spareribs, the Circle Room is an example of barbecue's becoming a staple of mainstream, high-end restaurant menus nationwide. (Author's collection)

sandwiches. Vergos had learned from his father that the restaurant business worked best if you kept it simple, so he would sell ham and cheese sandwiches on rye bread along with beer and little else. The Rendezvous was located in what was then the main downtown shopping district, and Vergos figured that in a city with so many one-car families, he could draw a regular clientele of men who would stop in for a sandwich and beer while their wives did their shopping. He would sell the sandwiches almost at cost and make his profit off the beer.

The sandwich idea was only a modest success, and over time Vergos started experimenting with other items in his smoker. He added salami first, which sold well, and then tried chickens and oysters, both of which flopped. In the late 1950s, the Rendezvous's meat distributor suggested he try pork ribs. Vergos didn't know anything about barbecuing, but one of his employees, a man named "Little John," did, and together they created a Memphis classic. Most barbecue joints slow-cooked their ribs, but the Rendezvous cooked theirs eighteen inches above a hot fire for only an hour and fifteen minutes. Little John suggested basting the meat in water and vinegar to keep it moist, and Vergos came up with a spice rub based on the combination his father had once used for Greek chili: salt, pepper, bay leaf, cumin, chili powder, and oregano. To give the ribs more color, he added paprika. Memphis-style dry-rubbed ribs were born.[2]

The Vergos family weren't the only Greek Americans to get into the barbecue trade. Opening a restaurant was a common way for recent immigrants to start their own businesses. Though they may not have grown up eating barbecue, many of these new restaurateurs were eager to learn how to cook one of America's most popular foods. Birmingham, Alabama, was home to a large number of Greek American restaurateurs, and many of them—such as Angelo Serandos of Eli's Bar-B-Q and Aleck Choraitis of Andrew's Bar-B-Q—learned the southern art of pit-smoked barbecue and turned it into a career. John and Dale Reed have noted a strong Greek American barbecue trend in North Carolina, too, including Simos Barbecue Inn in Winston-Salem (founded by Apostolos "Pete" Simos in 1939), the Red Pig Café in Concord (founded in 1945), and Mr. Barbecue, also in Winston-Salem (founded by Tom Gallos in 1952).[3]

These entrepreneurs entered a barbecue restaurant market that was booming. Indeed, it was in the postwar decades that the majority of the restaurants that are today considered classic American barbecue joints were founded. Of the twenty-four restaurants named on the North Carolina Barbecue Society's "Historic Barbecue Trail"—which were chosen by the NCBS board as "representative of the distinctive methods and barbecue cooking styles" of North Carolina—fourteen opened between 1945 and 1965. (Two others, Richard's in Salisbury and Stamey's in Greensboro, opened during the 1930s.) The story is the same in other states. The list of famous restaurants opening during this period includes, to name just a very few, the Ridgewood in Bluff City, Tennessee (1948); Boyd 'N' Son in Kansas City (1949); Starnes in Paducah, Kentucky (1954); Sconyers in Augusta, Georgia (1956); Dreamland in Tuscaloosa, Alabama (1958); and the Moonlite Bar-B-Q Inn in Owensboro, Kentucky (1963).[4]

The Continuity of Barbecue

By the middle of the twentieth century, barbecue was firmly established in the world of commerce and in the suburban backyard, and it had been transformed in

Gable's Motel and Restaurant, Florence, South Carolina. (Author's collection)

the process. But the older barbecue tradition was still going strong, too. Through the 1950s and into the 1960s, the outdoor barbecue remained as important to social life in rural America—particularly in the rural South—as it had been in the nineteenth century, and the methods and conventions were largely unchanged.

"The traditional time for a Georgia barbecue," Rufus Jarman reported in the *Saturday Evening Post* in 1954, "is when crops are 'laid by,' when cultivation is finished and the farmer has only to wait for the harvest." Throughout the rural South, barbecues remained a popular way for farmers to show appreciation to the hands that worked their fields. Ed Mitchell, one of North Carolina's most famous pitmasters, remembers, "In the hard days of putting in the tobacco or picking the cotton, everybody came together. . . . It didn't make any difference who owned the crop, but the one purpose in mind was to finish it and to do an excellent job. And when you finished, the farmer rewarded you by throwing a barbecue."[5]

Newspaperman Roy G. Taylor grew up in rural eastern North Carolina, and he captured his memories of late-August tobacco farm barbecues in one of his columns for the *Wilson Daily Times*. Though the events took place in the twentieth century, the details could easily have been from a century earlier. The preparations began late on

Menu from Red Bryan's Smokehouse, Dallas, Texas, 1950s. (Author's collection)

a Friday afternoon, when the men killed a pig and prepared it for the pit, which was usually dug under "a backer barn shelter" and filled with coals from green oak. The meat was basted with "vinegar with red pepper cut up in it," and it was served not with coleslaw or cornbread but rather with fresh cucumbers, deviled eggs, and hoecakes along with a big wooden tub of lemonade. "It's just too good to be true," Taylor recalls himself thinking. "All that good food and no more backer to 'put in' either. Everybody's in a good mood with clean clothes and washed hair and looking good except for the hands that still carry the stain gathered over the barning period. And Saturday night and Sunday coming up too. What a great world!"[6]

As textile manufacturing spread across the South in the early twentieth century, the practice of staging barbecues as a reward for laborers was extended to mill workers. In 1907 such barbecues were still unusual enough that the South Carolina Department of Agriculture said of the Middleburg Mills in Batesburg, "This company makes an

Tenant farmers and their families dining at the annual barbecue at Braswell Plantation, North Carolina, 1944. (Courtesy North Carolina Office of Archives and History, Raleigh)

innovation by giving its help an annual barbecue." Within a few years, the mill barbecue had become a regular management practice—and an attempt to earn the goodwill of workers without doing something more costly like raising wages or improving working conditions. In 1933, O. Max Gardner, the owner of the Cleveland Cloth Mill and a former governor of North Carolina, staged a "barbecue, dance, and love feast" for his workers to head off a drive for unionization. But barbecues could be enlisted on the other side of the labor struggle, too, and they became potent tools for union organizers. In 1919, more than one thousand unionized textile workers from mill towns across the Piedmont of North Carolina assembled in Charlotte's Electric Park for a barbecue "jubilee" to celebrate the end of a sixteen-week strike at the Highland Park and Johnson Mills.[7]

Employee picnic, American Thread Company, Tallapoosa, Georgia, 1944. (Courtesy Special Collections Department and Archives, Georgia State University Library)

Barbecues were soon adopted by workers in other industries and became an iconic feature of Labor Day celebrations. That holiday had originated in the labor movement of the late nineteenth century. The first celebrations and gatherings were organized by various unions and other labor organizations starting in the 1880s, and it was made a federal holiday in 1894. In the early years, Labor Day was specifically linked to unionism, and its celebration usually included massive parades with prolabor banners and music, as well as lots of American flags and other patriotic symbols. During the conservative 1920s, the celebrations were stripped of their more radical trappings, and marches were replaced by more general gatherings, festivals, and speeches. In the Midwest and the South in particular, barbecue was frequently served at the events.[8]

Over time, Labor Day evolved into a more general public holiday. During the

Men cooking Brunswick stew for the employee picnic, American Thread Company, Tallapoosa, Georgia, 1944. (Courtesy Special Collections Department and Archives, Georgia State University Library)

1950s, the American Federation of Labor and Congress of Industrial Organizations still hosted massive barbecues on Labor Day. In 1955, for example, the organizations hosted a Labor Day rally at Denison Dam that drew union members from all over Texas and was capped by a keynote address by Sam Rayburn, speaker of the US House of Representatives. By this time, though, the Labor Day barbecue had lost most of its connotations of unionism, and the events gradually shifted from the pit-cooked to the backyard variety and became part of a long weekend of relaxation. In 1956, the *Dallas Morning News* reported that members of the city's country clubs were "preparing for a gala and final summer fling over Labor Day weekend," with events including dances, swim meets, and barbecues. Newspapers and magazines in the 1950s and 1960s were filled with advertisements for charcoal grills and discount meat to supply families' Labor Day barbecues. Cooking out in the backyard remains an inseparable feature of the Labor Day holiday today.[9]

Labor Relations and Barbecue Jurisprudence

IN 1914, HENRY M. Williams, a weaver at the Cotton Mills Company in Columbia, South Carolina, asked to be excused from work for two days because he wanted to prepare and give a barbecue. The request was denied, but Williams left work to barbecue anyway. When he returned to the mill a few days later, he was told that his loom had been given to someone else. Williams was offered another position at a lower wage, which he declined, and he was subsequently evicted from his company-owned house in the mill village.

Williams sued the mill company for wrongful eviction and won. The mill company appealed and the case made it to the South Carolina Supreme Court. One of the key issues was whether Williams should have been allowed to testify about the reason he missed two days of work. The mill's lawyers had objected, apparently recognizing that—in South Carolina, at least—knowing that a man skipped work to barbecue would likely bias any jury in his favor. Williams won the appeal.

Source: "Williams et ux. v. Columbia Mills Co. et al.," *Southeastern Reporter* 85 (1915): 160.

Barbecue had been used by churches and other organizations to raise funds during the late nineteenth century, and that practice only picked up steam in the twentieth. The Poplar Tent Presbyterian Church near Concord, North Carolina, held its first fund-raiser in 1946, starting with five hogs cooked in a ditch in the ground, which netted the congregation eighty dollars. More than seventy years later, the annual event is still going strong. The Episcopal Church of St. Hubert the Hunter in Bondurant, Wyoming, held its first Bondurant Barbecue in 1941. Beef is donated by local ranchers, and the church members cook baked beans, homemade cakes, and potato salad for the event, which raises money to maintain the church building as well as support local charities.[10]

Perhaps the largest and most famous church barbecue is the annual October affair held by the Mallard Creek Presbyterian Church outside Charlotte, North Carolina. The event began in 1929, just after the stock market crash. The congregation had borrowed money to build their first Sunday School classrooms and found themselves in danger of defaulting. J. W. "Will" Oehler, a longtime member, offered to barbecue three whole hogs and a goat, which the congregation sold to the public for fifty cents a plate. The event raised $89.50, and it became an annual fund-raiser. From the start, it was always held on the fourth Thursday in October. In the early days, the pigs for the barbecue were donated by farmers who were members of the congregation, and they were slaughtered and dressed by H. Y. Galloway at his house. The meat was cooked in open pits dug in the ground over coals from hickory wood that was also donated by church members. Things evolved over time. In 1946 the organizers started taking the pigs to an abattoir for slaughter, and a screened-in cookhouse with cement-block pits was built. After Oehler died in 1944, his son J. W. Oehler Jr. took over the pitmaster duties, and he in turn passed them on to his son Donnie, who still oversees the cooking today.[11]

The Mallard Creek barbecue now draws more than twenty thousand people each year. It serves some fourteen thousand pounds of pulled pork (at nine dollars a plate) along with 2,500 gallons of Brunswick stew, which is still cooked in a row of iron kettles stirred by volunteers with big wooden paddles. The money raised goes to support the church's local and international mission projects. Over the years, North Carolina politicians discovered that the Mallard Creek gathering was an ideal place to meet and talk with voters, and—in a merging of the political and religious traditions—the barbecue has become an obligatory campaign stop for anyone aspiring to a local or statewide office. As the political traffic increased, the church began corralling hopeful office seekers to a separate area roped off with colored flags, but walking the line and shaking politicians' hands remains an essential part of the Mallard Creek experience.[12]

"Barbecue men"—pitmasters who had gained fame in their region and even beyond—continued to play a key role in traditional outdoor barbecues, and they remained in demand for fund-raising and celebratory events. A lot of these men, as we have seen, ended up opening restaurants and making barbecue a full-time career, but many remained freelancers who traveled around a region cooking for large gatherings and public events. A. B. "Bud" Foster, the sheriff of Fulton County, was considered the top barbecuer in the Atlanta area, keeping alive the Georgia tradition of barbecue-cooking sheriffs that had been started by Sheriff John W. Callaway of Wilkes County back in the 1880s.

To some extent, the persistence of the barbecue tradition in rural areas reflected the sharp divide that still existed between urban America—which had changed dramatically in only a half century—and rural America, much of which had seen minimal progress since the end of Reconstruction. Newspaper and magazine accounts from the middle of the twentieth century play up this distinction, depicting rural barbecues as quaint relics of an earlier age. Describing a barbecue held by the Euharlee Farmers Club of Euharlee, Georgia, for example, the *Saturday Evening Post* commented, "In such an atmosphere one almost expected to see Uncle Remus, Br'er Rabbit, Br'er Fox and 'de yudder critters' emerge through the early-morning haze out of a blackjack thicket across the cotton patch." But for those who lived out in the countryside, barbecues were more than just local color. They were central institutions of social and political life, and—as they had been a century before—they would become the venues where many of the painful transformations of the twentieth century would be played out.[13]

Barbecue and Twentieth-Century Politics

Campaign barbecues were still essential to politics in rural America, and the automobile helped accelerate things. The 1930s and 1940s saw the rise of the "political caravan," a convoy of cars and buses filled with candidates for statewide office that would crisscross the countryside, stopping at one town after another along the way for speeches, hand shaking, and plenty of barbecue. In the 1950s, Herbert O'Keefe, a former editor of the *Raleigh Times*, warned, "No man has been elected governor of North Carolina without eating more barbecue than was good for him."[14]

Barbecues also became important means of celebrating political victories, frequently on a massive scale. John C. "Jack" Walton, mayor of Oklahoma City and a lively and colorful platform speaker, ran for governor of Oklahoma in 1922. Though a Democrat, he ran on a populist platform with enough progressive planks to draw support from the Farmer-Labor Reconstruction League, the Socialists, and even a few Republicans. As he campaigned across the state, Walton promised that if he were elected there would be no "pink tea party" for his inauguration but rather an old-fashioned barbecue to which the entire state would be invited. Walton won the election, and he kept his word.

The two-day celebration was set for January 10 and 11, 1923. Dan V. Lackey, a prizefight promoter, served as chair of the committee of arrangements, and the Central Barbecue Committee included "Pawnee Bill" Lillie and Colonel George Miller

Jr., both producers of famous Wild West shows. The center of a half-mile racetrack was floored in to be used for dancing, but Walton announced that no waltzes or other "citified" dances would be permitted. Instead, there would be old-fashioned square dancing, Virginia reels, and cowboy hoedowns. The Democratic headquarters in each county were asked to recruit "old fashioned fiddlers who know how to play 'Turkey in the Straw.'" A thousand Native Americans from various Oklahoma tribes were enlisted to perform war dances.[15]

Just before Christmas, Walton sent out a call for Oklahoma farmers to contribute enough meat to serve two hundred thousand people. In addition to thousands of beeves, hogs, sheep, and chickens, the donations included 103 turkeys, 1,363 rabbits, 26 squirrels, 134 opossums, 113 geese, 15 deer, 2 buffalo, and 2 reindeer, which had been "shipped in from the North." A man from Sayre, Oklahoma, captured a live bear and donated him to the cause. The bear won the sympathy of Oklahoma City school-children, who pooled their pocket change, bought him for $119.66, and donated him to the Wheeler Park Zoo, where he was a crowd favorite for more than a decade.[16]

For the less fortunate creatures, six parallel trenches were dug at the Oklahoma state fairgrounds, stretching almost a mile in total. An estimated five hundred butchers, slicers, and pitmen were recruited to cook and serve. Six gigantic coffee percolators were constructed for the event, each the size of a boxcar with a capacity of ten thousand gallons. The rest of the provisions secured for the crowds, according to the *San Antonio Express*, read like "an emergency ration order to furnish food for the American expeditionary force": 339,000 buns, 55,000 pounds of sugar, 450 barrels of salt, 450 barrels of pepper, and 3,000 pounds of onions.[17]

By the night before the barbecue, it was estimated that some fifty thousand people had already arrived in Oklahoma City, traveling in cars and trains from even the most remote parts of the state. The *Dallas Morning News* considered one hundred thousand to be "a conservative estimate" of the crowd that showed up at the fairgrounds on the morning of January 9. The official inauguration ceremonies, which had been performed the day before in the capitol, were repeated for the crowds, and following a few short speeches, fiddlers began to play over a novel electrical amplification system. The feeding continued through the afternoon. From the leftover meat, twenty-two thousand gallons of soup were made and distributed along with the remaining bread to the poor of Oklahoma City. The Walton barbecue was the largest political barbecue

Pappy O'Daniel's inauguration barbecue, Austin, Texas, January 1941. (Courtesy Texas State Library and Archives Commission)

of the twentieth century, and it competes with the 1895 Encampment of the Grand Army of the Republic as the largest public barbecue in American history.[18]

In the decades that followed, inaugural barbecues were commonplace in the capitals of southern and southwestern states. The Louisiana gubernatorial race of 1940 marked the end of the twelve-year hold on the office by Huey P. Long's political machine. Long's brother Earl was defeated in the 1940 Democratic primary by Sam Houston Jones, a reform-minded attorney who promised to roll back the excesses of the King-fish era. Jones's inauguration on May 12, 1940, was celebrated with what was billed as "the greatest barbecue ever seen in storied Louisiana." Held in the football stadium at Louisiana State University, the barbecue featured a thousand beef cattle cooked over the pits. The following year, Governor Wilbert "Pappy" O'Daniel of Texas stumped across the state, closing his reelection campaign speeches by imploring Texans to "come down to dinner at the Governor's mansion some time." Twenty-five thousand did just that in January 1941 for the inaugural celebration. A fifty-foot pit was dug in the yard of the governor's mansion, and 17,000 pounds of barbecued beef were served along with half a ton of potato chips, 6,000 pickles, and lemonade squeezed from 24,000 lemons.[19]

The political barbecue was an inherently populist institution. Politicians who mastered the art of the campaign barbecue could use it to propel themselves to great heights. One such master was Eugene Talmadge, who served four terms as Georgia's governor in the 1930s and 1940s. Talmadge had a minimal political organization (one biographer called it "primitive by almost anyone's standards"), but unlike most Georgia politicians he managed to sidestep the "courthouse gangs" that dominated the state's political machinery. He did so by appealing directly to the people, and there was no better way to do that than with free barbecue.[20]

In 1932 Talmadge kicked off his first gubernatorial campaign with a massive Fourth of July barbecue in his hometown of McRae. Norman Graham, the "Barbecue King" of Telfair County, was recruited to oversee the pits, and letters were sent out to area farmers asking them to contribute pigs, goats, cows, and chickens. Three days before the meeting, farmers began arriving with donations, which were taken to City Park in downtown McRae for slaughter and cleaning. Graham started cooking early in the morning on the day before the event, with over ten thousand pounds of meat smoking over the shallow pits and one thousand gallons of Brunswick stew bubbling in iron kettles. He kept the fires going overnight, illuminated by a string of bare light bulbs. According to the local paper, those bulbs drew so many insects into the stew pots that Graham didn't need to add any pepper, since "bugs was good spice."[21]

An estimated ten thousand people turned out for the barbecue. They cheered wildly throughout Talmadge's speech and carried him from the platform on their shoulders at its conclusion. Talmadge repeated the performance on a two-month campaign tour through rural Georgia. Nine other candidates were competing in the Democratic primary that year, and in the Solid South that primary winner was guaranteed victory in the general election. Talmadge swept the crowded field, winning a majority of the votes cast and securing the nomination without a runoff.

Barbecues were the centerpiece of Talmadge's campaigns for the rest of his political career. Along the way, he attracted a band of regular followers, including the

Eugene Talmadge addressing a political rally, Gainesville, Georgia, July 4, 1946. (Courtesy Special Collections Department and Archives, Georgia State University Library)

"Tree-Climbing Haggards of Danielsville." For rallies, the elder Haggard and his eight sons dressed like Talmadge in black suits with wide-brimmed hats and red suspenders and climbed to the top of tall pine trees around the grove where the barbecue was being held. From these high perches they shouted down scripted cues for their candidate—like "Tell us about the schoolteachers, Gene!" or "Tell us about the old folks!"—prompting Talmadge to launch into his canned remarks on each topic. One afternoon, the story goes, one of the Haggard boys, having eaten too much barbecue at the previous campaign stop up the road, fell asleep in his tree and tumbled to the ground amid the onlookers, bringing Talmadge's speech to a crashing halt and illustrating the dangers of too much political barbecue.[22]

CHAPTER 8

The Great Migration

In the early twentieth century, a wave of African American southerners had moved from rural areas into growing cities like Memphis, Houston, and Kansas City, where they were instrumental in shaping their adopted cities' barbecue styles. The Second Great Migration, which began during World War II and continued through the 1970s, was even larger than the first. More than 1.5 million black Americans left the South during the 1940s—almost double the estimated 800,000 who had migrated in the 1920s. By 1950 some 2.5 million southern-born African Americans had moved to other parts of the United States, and that figure reached a peak of just over 4 million in 1980.[23]

Out-migration was driven largely by dire economic and social conditions in the South. The general collapse of southern agriculture during the Great Depression and the subsequent transition to mechanized farming eliminated the need for millions of workers. At the same time, Jim Crow and racial violence was only worsening. The economic mobilization of World War II, which created millions of wartime manufacturing jobs in America's industrial cities, drew many families north and west. Those families usually chose places where they had existing connections—namely, people from their home communities who had already made the move. African Americans from South Carolina and Tennessee tended to go to New York and Philadelphia, while Texans headed west to California and those from Mississippi and Louisiana went to Chicago. As in the prior wave of migrations, these southern residents brought their traditions of cooking and eating barbecue along with them.

Chicagoans were not totally unfamiliar with barbecue, which had long been a staple of midwestern roadside dining. The city area had its share of barbecue stands before World War II, but most were found outside the city proper along the suburban highways in Cicero or Chicago Heights. A great many were connected to gas stations, and during Prohibition they were frequently fronts for selling illegal beer and liquor. A British-born man named Ruel J. Siegel, who came to the United States from Liverpool at the age of six, was described by the *Chicago Tribune* as "a Chicago pioneer in the barbecue stand wave which swept the country" in the first two decades of the twentieth century. Siegel got rich running what were variously described as barbecue stands or lunchrooms, but it's unclear how much his and similar establishments sold pit-cooked meat versus other lunchroom fare like hamburgers and hotdogs. A 1928 newspaper profile of "The Spic and Span Barbecue Stand" on Garfield Boulevard describes one Mrs. O'Connell "frying hamburger over a gas plate."[24]

During World War II, the inbound wave of African American migrants—many of whom came from the Mississippi Delta—brought a new style of barbecue to Chicago. Among them were the Lemons family, who hailed from Indianola, Mississippi. In 1942, Myles Lemons and his teenage brother James headed north to seek work. Though many of their fellow Mississippians had taken jobs in Chicago's booming wartime factories, the Lemonses found employment at Greek restaurants—Myles at the Highway Restaurant on Madison Street and James at the Lakeside Restaurant on Bryn Mawr. Their brother Bruce joined them in Chicago a few years later. In 1951, Miles and Bruce decided to open a restaurant of their own, a barbecue place on Fifty-Ninth Street. They christened it with Myles's nickname, calling it Lem's Bar-B-Q. Their brother James came to work with them a few years later.

Postwar Chicago restaurants like Lem's were usually small operations. Continuing the long-running tradition of urban barbecue stands, many were takeout operations with no seating areas for customers. The Lemons brothers had grown up on a farm back in Indianola, and their parents had a smokehouse as well as a barbecue pit (which they called a "grill") where they would cook whole hogs at Thanksgiving. The kind of barbecue the brothers cooked in the city, though, was quite different. They served ribs, rib tips, and hot links—now the signature specialties of the South Side Chicago barbecue style—with French fries and sliced white bread as the side dishes, the ribs often piled on top. The Lemonses made their own barbecue sauce, too, a sweet, tomato-based mixture based off a recipe for "spicy gravy" that their mother made back in Mississippi. As James Lemons put it in a 2008 interview, "It was created from Mississippi, but it's Chicago barbecue."[25]

Indeed, the town of Indianola—which had only 3,600 residents in 1940—could very well be said to be the birthplace of Chicago barbecue, for another pioneering South Side barbecue family hailed from there, too. The Collins brothers—Harvey, Caesar, Argia B., Stoop, and Earl—all came to Chicago and ended up opening barbecue restaurants. Their menus focused on pork, since that is what they had cooked back home in Mississippi, but like the Lemonses they cooked not whole hogs or shoulders but spareribs, which could be bought cheaply from the city's many stockyards, and rib tips, which were knobby scrap cuts filled with cartilage that the stockyards often gave away for free.

In the 1960s, the Collinses were among the many South Side restaurateurs who adopted a unique style of barbecue cooker that came to be known as the "aquarium pit." The first versions were made by Leo Davis of Fulton Metal Products, who designed metal-bottomed pits with a chamber of tempered glass on top in which the meat cooked. Most Chicago cooks fired those pits with a combination of wood and charcoal—oak and hickory to impart smoky flavor and charcoal for consistent heat. Unlike in Texas or the Carolinas, where meats were typically slow-cooked at low temperatures, Chicago barbecue was cooked fast and hot, with burning logs just a few feet below the meat. Ribs could be finished in forty-five minutes, and rib tips, which needed longer to break down the tough cartilage, in an hour and twenty minutes.

Argia B. Collins often provided free meals to the Reverend Jesse Jackson and his fellow organizers of Operation Breadbasket, which sought to improve the economic status of African Americans by boycotting businesses that refused to employ African Americans or to sell products from African American–owned businesses. Collins himself was one of those business owners, for in 1957 he had designed a label and bought the equipment needed to bottle and sell the barbecue sauce he made for his restaurant. But he hit a brick wall when he tried to get wholesale distributors to put Mumbo Sauce in their warehouses. Six years later, after Operation Breadbasket started putting pressure on the warehouses, he was finally able to get his sauce onto grocery shelves and into restaurants. By 1970 Mumbo Sauce was the third best-selling barbecue sauce in the Chicago market. "My father was among a group of black men who saw starting a business as a way of improving their community," Allison Collins told the *Chicago Tribune* in 2007. "The sauce is more than about barbecue. . . . It was also a way to help build the black community."[26]

Perhaps the most intriguing figure on Chicago's South Side barbecue scene was Leon Finney. Like so many of the city's barbecue men, he was born and raised in Mississippi, but unlike the Lemonses or the Collinses, he did come from a family with a tradition of cooking barbecue. He was the son of T. J. Huddleston of Louise, Mississippi, a prominent and well-connected entrepreneur who founded the first African American–owned hospital in Mississippi and later established a chain of three dozen funeral homes that made him the state's wealthiest African American. Huddleston had seven children by his first wife and several more, including Leon Finney, out of wedlock with other women. "He was a bit of a rogue," recalled Huddleston's grandson Mike Espy, who became the first black congressman from Mississippi since Reconstruction, as well as secretary of agriculture during the Clinton administration.[27]

It's a testament to the conditions in midcentury Mississippi that the children of the richest African American man in the state decided they were better off seeking their fortunes up north. "Back in the forties when African Americans were leaving," Espy told an interviewer, "he gave each one of his seven children who left Mississippi a building in Chicago." Huddleston didn't buy buildings for his out-of-wedlock children, but in 1940, at the age of thirty-four, Leon Finney headed north to Chicago, too. He lived with an aunt, Bertha Brody, who worked as a cook at a Garfield Avenue restaurant that was actually a front for a bookie joint. When the police raided the basement gambling parlors and shut them down, the owner offered to sell the restaurant to Finney's aunt for $700. Finney called his father back in Louise, Mississippi, who wired the money that set his son up in the barbecue business. "We had a lot of hogs in Mississippi," Finney later recalled, "but I'd never heard of barbecue until I got here."

Finney learned the ropes quickly, selling ribs for thirty cents an order, but business hit the rocks in 1947 when President Truman reinstituted price controls on meat. Finney's father urged him to come back to Mississippi to make caskets in the family business, but after having tasted life in Chicago Finney had no desire to go back south. He spent the 1950s working a series of service jobs, including busboy, checkroom attendant, and restroom attendant at the Stevens Hotel (later the Conrad Hilton). In the early 1960s he went to work for a man who owned a barbecue restaurant on Eighty-Third Street, and Finney helped grow it to $7,000 a week in sales and expand to a second location. Through years of hard work and thrift, Finney managed to save $30,000, and he used his savings to buy out his boss and rename the restaurant Leon's Bar-B-Q. He eventually added three more locations. Finney made a point of driving downstate to the packing plants in southern Illinois to procure his meat, so he could buy it right after the hogs were killed. His signature sauce, a blend of Worcestershire sauce, ketchup, mustard, vinegar, sugar, and seasoning, was described by one reporter as "slightly sweet, slightly sour, with some tang to it."[28]

Finney helped other Chicagoans get into the barbecue trade, too. "He came along at a time when it was hard for African-Americans to get loans," his son Leon Jr. recalled in his father's 2008 obituary. "He was always very willing to make loans to help people start businesses." When he was a youth, Mike Espy, Finney's half-nephew, would travel to Chicago every summer and work at Leon's Bar-B-Q, making the sauce. Espy recalled that Finney had a Rolls-Royce automobile with a picture of a pig painted on the side. "I remember saying 'Uncle, why do you have this pig?'" Espy told an interviewer. "He said, 'The pig bought this goddamned Rolls Royce.'"[29]

The pioneering generation of Chicago pitmasters has since passed away, but it taught the craft to the generations that followed. Rib tips and sausage cooked on aquarium smokers live on today at South Side stands like Lem's, Honey 1 BBQ, and Uncle J's BBQ—a distinctive regional variation in the long American barbecue tradition.

The Evolution of Political Barbecue

The political barbecue reached its height of national and international attention with the presidency of Lyndon Baines Johnson. Johnson bought his LBJ Ranch in 1951, two years after being sworn in to the US Senate, and he held his first barbecue there in 1953. After a few years, he decided that a grove of trees along the bank of the Pedernales River was his favorite barbecue location. For Johnson, these barbecues were not just social events but political tools, allowing him to project an image of himself as an ordinary man. The LBJ Ranch offered national and, later, international visitors a mythologized version of rural America, one that put suspicious urban politicians at ease and allowed Johnson to work his charm on them. Johnson consciously styled his barbecues with western instead of southern imagery. Richard "Cactus" Pryor, the Texas broadcaster and humorist who was a frequent emcee at LBJ Ranch barbecues, recalled that they "had the look and feel of a chuck wagon dinner." Guests dined at round tables with checkered tablecloths and coal-oil lanterns. Servers wore western gear, and Stetson hats were frequently given away to out-of-state guests. Such images helped Johnson brand himself as a "western" politician and distance himself from the poverty and racial strife then associated with the South.

Johnson's caterer of choice was Walter Jetton, a man whom Texas barbecue historian Robb Walsh called "the last of the open pit barbecuers and probably the single most influential pit boss in Texas barbecue history." Jetton started in the barbecue business in 1930 as a sideline to his meat market, cooking for church picnics and other

Barbecue guests along the bank of the Pedernales River at the LBJ Ranch, April 1, 1967. (Courtesy Lyndon Baines Johnson Library and Museum)

civic functions. By the early 1950s, even before his association with Lyndon Johnson, Jetton had established himself as the Fort Worth "barbecue king." In 1951 and again in 1952, he took his catering rig—a motorized chuck wagon—all the way to Washington, DC, to serve pit-cooked beef, ranch-style beans, potato salad, and coleslaw to eight hundred members of the Texas State Society.[30]

Jetton's highly publicized barbecues at the LBJ Ranch earned him a national reputation, but he remained an unrepentant devotee of the open pit and hardwood coals, even for casual backyard cooking. "To barbecue, you need a pit," he wrote in his 1965 *LBJ Barbecue Cookbook*, "and it definitely shouldn't be one of those backyard creations with a chimney. You want your smoke, you don't want to draw it off." Jetton advocated a portable pit made of four pieces of sheet metal, with the fire built right on the ground inside the pit and a big metal grill laid over the top. He initially cooked whole steers for large gatherings, although—like most Texas pitmasters—he eventually switched to briskets.[31]

Walter Jetton's Barbecue Menu

IN *WALTER JETTON'S LBJ Barbecue Cook Book* (1865), the acclaimed Texas caterer recorded President Johnson's favorite barbecue menu:

Texas Beef Barbecue with Natural Gravy
Smoked Ranch Beans
Cooked Country Corn
Country Potato Salad
Texas Cole Slaw
Sliced Dill Pickle Spears
Spanish Sweet Onions
Modern Day Sourdough Biscuits
Fried Apple Pies
Six-Shooter Coffee
Soft Drinks

Source: Walter Jetton, with Arthur Whitman, *Walter Jetton's LBJ Barbecue Cook Book* (New York: Pocket, 1965).

As Jetton's fame grew, he expanded his catering business and opened two cafeterias in Fort Worth. He continued to travel widely to cater barbecues, including serving pork ribs, beef brisket, chickens, and fried pies at Gracie Mansion, the official residence of the mayor of New York City, for a Young Citizens for Johnson campaign event. By the time of his death in 1968, Jetton had a fleet of eighteen catering trucks that could supply barbecue for up to ten thousand people, and he estimated he was serving 1.5 million dinners each year. But the barbecues at the LBJ Ranch remain his primary legacy. Over the course of his presidency, Lyndon Johnson hosted nearly one hundred barbecues at the ranch. Heads of state treated to Texas hospitality included Chancellor Ludwig Erhard of West Germany, President Gustavo Díaz Ordaz of Mexico, and Prime Minister Levi Eshkol of Israel. Barbecue had achieved international stature, being served at state dinners by the president of the United States.[32]

Through cowboy imagery and western themes, Johnson tried to distance his political barbecues from the racial strife engulfing the South, but it is impossible to disentangle the institution of barbecue from the subject of race and civil rights. In some ways, barbecue was a food that brought whites and blacks together. It was a tradition shared by all southerners, and many public events were attended by a broad mix of residents from across a community, regardless of skin color. Some barbecue joints, like Red Bryan's Smokehouse in Dallas and Abe's in Clarksdale, Mississippi, were among the few restaurants in the South that served an integrated clientele prior to the civil rights movement, and white patrons would often seek out African American–owned restaurants like that of Johnny Mills in Memphis to enjoy great barbecue.

More often, though, the same social divisions entrenched in southern society at large were reflected in the world of barbecue. African American pitmasters may have earned fame in their regions and were invited to preside over massive events for the white community, but they and their families were usually excluded from dining at the main tables. At countless restaurants across the South, like Leonard's in Memphis and Ollie's in Birmingham, black men tended the fires in the pit houses but were not allowed to eat in the dining rooms. Some African American–owned joints, like Scott's in Goldsboro, North Carolina, had segregated dining rooms.

The civil rights activists of the 1950s and 1960s were determined to change that, and barbecue restaurants took center stage for some of the key legal battles for desegregation. Title II of the Civil Rights Act of 1964, which President Johnson signed into law on July 2, prohibited discrimination in hotels, restaurants, and other places of public accommodation that engaged in interstate commerce. In the case of a restaurant, that meant "it serves or offers to serve interstate travelers or a substantial portion of the food which it serves, or gasoline or other products which it sells, has moved in commerce."[33]

Barbecue restaurants were at the center of several landmark rulings about the act's public accommodation provisions, and that didn't happen by chance. Barbecue was a commercial food that had a long history in both the black and white communities, and its very nature challenged assumptions about regional culture and interstate commerce. In Alabama, the Birmingham Restaurant Association had started planning its challenge to the Civil Rights Act months before Johnson signed it. Association members considered the act's interstate commerce provisions to be its most vulnerable aspect, but most members could not volunteer for test cases because they clearly served interstate travelers. So, the association turned to forty-eight-year-old Ollie McClung, the white man who owned Ollie's Barbecue on the predominantly black south side of Birmingham. His restaurant did not advertise, and it was located well away from any interstate highway, railroad, or bus station. Two-thirds of Ollie's thirty-six employees were African American, but they served only white patrons in the dining room. African American customers had to use a takeout window. The federal government had not yet taken any action to desegregate Ollie's, but Ollie McClung—at the urging of the Birmingham Restaurant Association—sued in federal court, seeking an injunction to prevent Title II from being enforced against his restaurant in the future.[34]

McClung won the initial case in the district court, but it was appealed to the US Supreme Court, which delivered its landmark *Katzenbach v. McClung* ruling on December 14, 1964. Ollie's, the justices determined, had purchased 46 percent of its food—most of it meat—from a local wholesaler, who in turn had purchased it from Hormel meatpacking plants outside the state. That fact, the court decided, meant that "a substantial portion of the food served in the restaurant had moved in interstate commerce." Discrimination at the restaurant, the ruling argued, indeed affected interstate commerce, since the fewer customers Ollie's served the less food it purchased from suppliers outside the state. In addition, it concluded that discrimination made it difficult for African Americans to purchase prepared food while on trips, which discouraged travel and obstructed interstate commerce in a significant manner. Ollie McClung peacefully desegregated his business two days after the Supreme Court handed down its decision, telling reporters that "as law-abiding Americans, we feel we must bow to this edict." Black and white customers ate side by side in the dining room until Ollie's Barbecue closed in 2001.[35]

A second test case of the Civil Rights Act involved barbecue restaurants in Columbia, South Carolina. A few days after the act was signed, J. W. Mungin, an African American minister, filed a complaint with the FBI after being refused service at a restaurant owned by L. Maurice Bessinger. Bessinger at the time operated Little Joe's Sandwich Shop on Main Street in downtown Columbia as well as five Piggy Park drive-ins around the city. He was also the chair of the South Carolina campaign committee for the segregationist presidential candidate George Wallace. It took almost two years for the case to come before US District Court judge Charles Simons, who began hearing testimony in April 1966.

Bessinger's arguments invoked the regionalism of barbecue as well as religion. He claimed that his restaurants were not engaged in interstate commerce in any form. He testified before Judge Simons that his barbecue was "made exclusively for the taste of central South Carolinians," and that his business was never meant for interstate travelers because "people from New York or North Carolina or Georgia have entirely different tastes for barbecue." Merle Brigman, Bessinger's bookkeeper and food buyer, testified that Piggy Park Enterprises purchased all its meat from South Carolina processing plants, that items such as paper plates that originated from outside the state were not sold but given away with the food, and that the drive-ins refused to serve cars bearing out-of-state license plates. Perhaps most sensational was Bessinger's claim that the Civil Rights Act "contravenes the will of God" and violated his constitutional right to free exercise of religion.[36]

The district court dismissed Bessinger's religious arguments outright, and it disagreed with him on most of the interstate commerce points, too. It ruled that Little Joe's Sandwich Shop, which was a traditional sit-down restaurant, had indeed violated the Civil Rights Act by refusing to serve African Americans. The five drive-ins, however, were ruled to not be covered by the act because they were not "principally engaged in selling food for consumption on the premises." The Piggy Parks had no tables, chairs, counters, or stools, and, as Bessinger had testified, about half the customers ate their barbecue in cars while parked on the premises, while the other half took it away.

A year later, the decision on the drive-ins was overturned by the Fourth Circuit Court of Appeals, which ruled that Congress had not intended for civil rights to depend on a head count of customers eating on-site. The qualification of "selling food for consumption on the premises" was meant to differentiate restaurants from other businesses such as grocery stores or bars. A technical ruling about whether the prevailing party could be awarded attorney's fees made it all the way to the Supreme Court, which decided in 1968 that such awards were not only valid but also an important means to ensure that people who had been discriminated against could seek redress in the court system.

Maurice Bessinger lost his case, but he remained a divisive figure in the world of barbecue until his death in 2014. The tables in the entryways to his restaurants were stocked with religious tracts with proslavery themes. Through the 1970s, he was president of the right-wing South Carolina Independent Party and in 1974 made an unsuccessful bid for governor, campaigning in a white suit and riding a white horse. After his defeat, Bessinger focused on running his chain of barbecue restaurants and faded somewhat from public attention, but he thrust himself back into racial politics in the year 2000, when the South Carolina legislature voted to remove the Confederate flag that flew above the statehouse dome in Columbia. Bessinger responded by hoisting the Stars and Bars over each of his nine area restaurants. This action led to a boycott by the NAACP, and several large grocery and retail chains removed Bessinger's bottled barbecue sauces from their shelves.[37]

While white-owned barbecue restaurants were enlisted as testing grounds by one side of the civil rights struggle, barbecue restaurants—especially those owned by African Americans—played an important role on the other side of the struggle, too. Brenda's Bar-B-Que Pit in Montgomery, for instance, became a hub for the local civil rights movement in the 1960s. "My mother and my sister and my auntie would help the NAACP," the founders' son recalled in a recent interview. "We had a printing machine, and we could put out fliers about when different meetings were going to be." At the time of the marches from Selma to Montgomery in 1965, Lannie's Bar-B-Q Spot—a small barbecue stand in an African American neighborhood—was just around the corner from a home known as the Freedom House, where many of the activists stayed. Founder Lannie Travis regularly prepared barbecue sandwiches and took them to Freedom House to feed the guests.[38]

Even more central to the civil rights movement was Aleck's Barbecue Heaven in Atlanta. Located on Hunter Street, it was the third of six barbecue restaurants that Ernest Alexander opened in the city, and he built his pit using cobblestones taken up from nearby Raymond Street when it was paved with asphalt. The restaurant was next door to the West Hunter Street Baptist Church, home of the Reverend Ralph Abernathy, cofounder of the Southern Christian Leadership Conference and a close friend and adviser of Dr. Martin Luther King. Aleck's was famous for its ribs, which were served atop slices of white bread with a spicy "comeback sauce" made from mustard, ketchup, and lots of cayenne. On the second floor was a lounge with live music and a space where activists like Stokely Carmichael regularly held meetings.

By the mid-1960s Aleck's had become a hub of civil rights activity in the city. "All of the morning business was carried out at Paschal's [Motel and Restaurant]," recalled Andrew Young, a civil rights activist who went on to become mayor of Atlanta. "But in the evening and late at night, you'd always stop at Aleck's." Martin Luther King lived just six blocks away and was a regular customer, frequently talking strategy in a back booth. Whenever he was working on a big speech, he would fuel himself with a takeout order of ribs. After King's assassination in 1968, his regular booth was turned into a memorial decorated with a large black-and-white portrait and various mementos. Even though it was one of only four booths in the tiny restaurant, no customer ever sat there again. Hunter Street was renamed Martin Luther King Jr. Drive shortly after the civil rights leader's death.[39]

9

≡

THE DECLINE OF AMERICAN BARBECUE

The Fate of Barbecue in a Fast-Food Era

In the 1950s and 1960s, barbecue was riding high, the most popular menu item in American restaurants and an essential element of the country's culinary life. It wasn't obvious at the time, but changes were brewing that would soon challenge the preeminent status of pit-cooked meats. The American restaurant industry was expanding, and it became increasingly standardized and corporatized as it did. Early burger franchises like McDonald's and Burger King were still infants in the 1950s, but they were growing fast. McDonald's expanded from a single restaurant in 1955 to over a hundred in 1959. Burger King, which had only five outlets at the end of the decade, all in the metropolitan Miami area, was poised for explosive growth, too. At this stage, though, hamburgers were by no means the clear leader on quick-service restaurant menus. Franchised chains were increasing their share of the restaurant market, but the types of foods that lent themselves to the evolving fast-food culture were still being sorted out.

Early in his restaurant career, Dave Thomas, who would later found the Wendy's Hamburgers chain, thought barbecue was a promising option. In the mid-1950s, he was managing a restaurant called the Hobby Ranch House in Fort Wayne, Indiana, and he and the restaurant's owner, Phil Clauss, went to visit Mac McKenny's barbecue operation in nearby Evansville. They were impressed. Mac's Barbecue seated two hundred people and had a very limited menu: ribs and chicken served on paper plates and accompanied only by potato salad, rye bread, pickles, and onions. They cooked 100 chickens and 150 pounds of ribs at a time over hickory coals in enclosed pits. Thomas

Dave Thomas (back) preparing barbecued chicken at his Hobby Ranch House restaurant in Fort Wayne, Indiana.

noted that even with the limited menu, McKenny was doing more than $2,000 a night in carryout orders alone.[1]

So, Thomas and Clauss signed on as franchisees of Mac's. In an informal arrangement typical of early restaurant franchising, they paid no royalties and didn't even use the Mac's name. All they did was buy their sauce from McKenny—or, more accurately, the flavoring for the sauce, since they received dry powder from Mac's and added ketchup, vinegar, and water to it. Thomas spent a few months in Evansville learning the ropes and then returned to Fort Wayne to open the franchise, which they christened with the rather unmelodious name of Hobby Ranch House with Barbecue. Like Mac's, the Hobby Ranch House started out with a simple menu of chicken and ribs on paper plates, though it did add baked beans alongside the potato salad.

Advertisement for the opening of the Little Pigs of America franchise in Asheville, North Carolina, 1963. (*Asheville [NC] Citizen Times*, April 20, 1963)

Little Pigs of America, Pioneer of Barbecue Franchising

MORE THAN A few aspiring entrepreneurs, witnessing the early success of hamburger chains, tried to follow suit with barbecue. In the early 1960s, the Memphis-based Little Pigs of America began selling franchises for barbecue restaurants nationwide. Asking for an up-front investment of $6,000, Little Pigs promised franchisees a net return of $18,000 per year, with no prior barbecue experience required. The company provided training for franchisees at its Memphis headquarters and also helped with location selection and the design for the restaurants' brick pits. A typical Little Pigs of America outlet sold a pork basket for 59 cents, a pork plate for 69 cents, and a rib platter for $1.59.

The company announced a bold goal of opening one thousand total restaurants, and by 1965 some two hundred franchised units had been sold in the United States and Canada. (By comparison, in 1963 the eight-year-old McDonald's hamburger chain had opened unit number 500.) Despite the company's rapid initial growth, 1963 was the only year it turned a profit, and it filed for bankruptcy before the end of the decade, ending the brief run of what was at the time America's largest barbecue chain. Most Little Pigs franchisees closed their doors within a few years of the parent company's folding, but a few operators stayed on in the business. You can still find restaurants named Little Pigs in operation today that trace their roots to the Memphis chain, including businesses in Columbia, South Carolina, and Asheville, North Carolina.

Sources: "New Barbecue Establishment Opens," *Burlington (NC) Daily Times News*, April 24, 1965; "Profits for Mom & Pop," *Time*, May 24, 1963; *Securities and Exchange Commission News Digest*, no. 66–64, April 4, 1966, 1.

Making such adjustments was the seed of its downfall, and barbecue did not turn out to be the moneymaker that Thomas had hoped. In retrospect, he blamed their deviation from Mac's bare-bones operating formula. "When customers complained about the paper plates we switched to china," Thomas recalled. "But china and silver ran our costs up. When customers said they would prefer rolls to rye bread, we gave them rolls and butter. . . . The variety killed our focus and made the business much harder to manage." The lessons Thomas learned from his barbecue experience—and from subsequently working with Colonel Harland Sanders during the early days of the Kentucky Fried Chicken chain—were put into practice in 1969, when he founded the first of his Wendy's Hamburgers restaurants, which today generate over a billion dollars in annual revenue from more than six thousand restaurants. None of them serves barbecue.[2]

Dave Thomas wasn't the first restaurateur to recognize the inherent problems with barbecue in what was increasingly becoming a low-margin, high-volume industry. Perhaps no story is more emblematic of the fate of barbecue as a roadside food than that of Richard and Maurice McDonald, whose drive-in in San Bernardino, California, launched the fast-food revolution in America. The brothers' original restaurant was typical of the era: an octagonal wooden building with carhops serving a broad, twenty-five-item menu that included ham, chili, and tamales in addition to hamburgers and French fries. Like many drive-ins at that time, its menu also featured barbecue—specifically, beef, ham, and pork sandwiches, made with meat that was slow-cooked behind the restaurant over a hickory-chip pit.

The McDonalds were barely breaking even, and in the late 1940s the brothers took a hard look at their operations. The carhops were a problem: their service was too slow, and they were easily distracted by other customers. Groups of teenage boys had adopted the drive-in as a hangout, repelling families and older customers who were just looking for a bite to eat. Operating costs were high, too, especially because of broken china and flatware that disappeared on a regular basis.

In the fall of 1948 the McDonalds closed down their restaurant for three full months. When it reopened, the carhops were gone, and the windows where they used to pick up their orders had been converted to self-service portals. Also gone were the china and silver, replaced by paper wrappers and cardboard cups. The most significant changes were to the menu. Wood-cooked barbecue was too slow and labor intensive, so the hickory pit was extinguished. The only sandwiches remaining were hamburgers, with the toppings limited to cheese, ketchup, mustard, onion, and two pickle slices. Side items were equally limited: French fries, coffee, milkshakes, and sodas. The patties had been reduced from eight to the pound down to ten to the pound, but the prices had been reduced even more: from thirty-five cents for a hamburger down to just fifteen.

The principles of the McDonalds' "Speedy Service System" were simple: focus on a

A 1943 menu for McDonald's Famous Bar-B-Q, prior to the restaurant's conversion to a fast-food hamburger stand. (Courtesy Ray Quiel)

basic, low-cost menu, sell convenience and low price, and make money through volume. It was a flop at first. Their old customers missed the drive-in features to which they were accustomed, and they were underwhelmed by the streamlined menu. Within a few months, though, the McDonalds noticed that they were attracting a new customer base made up of commuters, workers, and families—diners who wanted a cheap, fast meal without having to deal with the overhead of a full-service restaurant and the annoyances of loitering teens.

The business model also caught the eye of Ray Kroc, the distributor of a new five-spindled milkshake machine called the Multimixer. In 1954, Kroc noticed that the McDonalds had purchased eight of his mixers for their hamburger stand, and he paid them a visit to see what could possibly be driving such volume. Fascinated by the

Richard and Maurice McDonald in the midst of converting their drive-in from barbecue stand to hamburger bar, 1948. (Courtesy Ray Quiel)

speed of service and unending parade of customers, he convinced the brothers to start franchising, and he signed himself up to be their agent. The first McDonald's franchise opened in Des Plaines, Illinois, in 1956.[3]

What was a big success for the McDonalds and for the hamburger was the beginning of the end of barbecue as a fast food. As fast-food chains grew in the 1950s and 1960s, they focused on speed, standardization, and low labor costs, which is to say being able to use low-skilled labor. Barbecue scored poorly in all these areas. Hamburgers were pretty much the same from one state to the next, but barbecue differed greatly from location to location, with each region having its own style of cooking and its own favorite type of sauce. Barbecue took hours to cook, and it required a skilled pitmaster who knew how to tend the fire, turn and baste the meat, and control flare-ups. Barbecuing was a skill learned through an apprenticeship system over the course of years. You couldn't hire a couple of sixteen-year-olds off the street, give them an afternoon tutorial, and turn them loose on the pit.

The same challenges that prompted the McDonald brothers to discard the car-hops and limit their menu were being felt throughout the restaurant industry. By the late 1950s drive-in operators knew they needed new ways to attract more customers, serve them more efficiently, and sell bigger orders, but they weren't sure what would work. They tried all sorts of innovations, like adding metal canopies to provide shade for diners and electronic ordering systems that reduced the number of carhop trips per customer and allowed operators to shrink their workforce. In the end, such improvements could not offset the inherent inefficiencies of the drive-in model. Rising land prices in cities made large parking lots an expensive proposition, and trade fell off dramatically during winter months, even in the southern states. Those big lots were prime hangouts for teenagers, and operators had to contend with large crowds of nonpaying youths and the drinking, fighting, and vandalism that often accompanied them. Cruising teens would make a loop from one drive-in to another, creating traffic jams that blocked not only the operators' lots but the adjoining streets as well. City residents began lodging complaints, and many municipalities enacted ordinances that held drive-in owners liable for the activity on and around their premises and required landscaping, fences, and other facility changes.[4]

The drive-in didn't stand a chance against the efficiency of self-service outlets, where customers left their cars and stood in line for food. Limited hamburger-based menus were more cost-effective, customer turnover was twice as fast, and the number of employees needed was much lower. In most cities, the number of drive-ins declined precipitously during the 1960s. Of those that remained, few served pit-cooked barbecue anymore. Once the king of the American roadside, barbecue had taken a back seat to the hamburger.

The Decline of American Barbecue

It wasn't just drive-ins and roadside barbecue stands that were feeling the pinch in the 1960s and 1970s. Operators running more traditional barbecue restaurants faced their own set of challenges in continuing to do business as they had. By the 1970s, hardwood was becoming increasingly scarce, which drove up costs for log-burning pitmasters. Keith Stamey of Stamey's Barbecue in Greensboro, North Carolina, used to get his hickory from a local man who delivered it in an old pickup truck. As business increased, he had to turn to sawmills and furniture factories for leftover scraps before he finally secured a supplier who could regularly provide the volume he needed. "I won't tell you who they are," Stamey's son Chip told an interviewer. "Used to be that we wouldn't give out our recipes, but we're now more secretive about our wood." Some classic barbecue joints, like Melton's in Rocky Mount, North Carolina, turned away from wood altogether, installing gas cookers instead. Willie Bob Melton, nephew of founder Bob Melton, explained that his restaurant made the switch in the early 1970s because "wood was getting hard to get. You couldn't get anybody to cut your wood for you."[5]

When Allie Patricia Wall and Ron L. Layne surveyed South Carolina barbecue joints in 1979, they found that more than half used either electric or gas cookers. The cost of wood wasn't the only factor driving the change. "More and more restaurateurs are turning to gas or electric heat as a way out of the labor predicament," Kathleen Zobel reported in 1977. "Besides being less trouble, it is a faster and cheaper method." Others pointed the finger at government meddling, citing increased pressure from local health departments on restaurants that used open pits. Alton Beck of Beck's Barbecue—a classic Lexington, North Carolina, joint—predicted in 1977 that good barbecue was on its way to extinction. "The state'll stop it," he told the *Charlotte Observer*. "You can't build a new pit now and use it in Lexington. The ones here now are operating under the grandfather clause."[6]

But it seems unlikely that the health department was the real villain. If actual state regulations were ever drafted forbidding cooking on wood-fired pits—much less rules "grandfathering in" existing pits—no one has ever been able to find them. In its regulations for retail food establishments, the South Carolina Department of Health and Environmental Control defines detailed requirements for "Barbecue Pit and Pit-Cooking Room Construction." Nothing in the rules mentions allowable fuel sources, and the requirements themselves seem geared specifically for traditional wood cooking. These include rules for the construction of pit rooms—they must be completely enclosed, can have screening above four feet of solid walls, and must have a floor constructed of "smooth, durable materials"—as well as the pit or cooker, which must have a floor constructed of concrete, firebrick, or "compacted clay with a top layer of clean sand to absorb grease drippings." In 1969, Dr. E. Kenneth Aycock, South Carolina's state health officer, announced that his department was cracking down on barbecue restaurant operators who didn't have a permit from the local health department. But the standards he highlighted had nothing to do with the pits, focusing instead on hot and cold running water, facilities for washing hands, and meat inspected by the USDA or Clemson University's meat inspection service.[7]

The only government official I have ever been able to identify who actively discouraged the use of wood-fired barbecue pits was Robert Fulp, though he had nothing to do with the health department. Fulp was the director the Environmental Affairs Department in Forsyth County, North Carolina, which includes the city of Winston-Salem, and in the 1970s he led a drive to encourage barbecue restaurant owners to switch from wood to electric cookers to help the county comply with the federal Clean Air Act. This effort earned him the nickname "Barbecue Bob" in a derisive cartoon in the *Winston-Salem Journal*, but his admonitions hardly carried the force of law. (Indeed, in 2017, someone writing under the name Clayton Moore started emailing officials at the North Carolina Department of Environmental Quality to complain about "unregulated point source smoke stacks" sending clouds of matter into the air. Local officials, the *Winston-Salem Journal* reported, responded that "federal and state laws prevent them from doing much of anything about smoke coming from restaurants.")[8]

Blaming the government seems more of a convenient excuse adopted by operators who had plenty of other reasons to switch to something less expensive and less labor intensive than wood-fired pits. Entrepreneurs had started promoting electric barbecue cookers to restaurateurs as early as the 1930s. Most of the early models were essentially rotisserie ovens with electric heating elements, and they made little headway in the market. By the 1970s, however, the designs had evolved and began to gain wider adoption. These cookers were usually made of stainless steel with a lid that could be closed during cooking. On electric models, heating elements similar to those in an electric oven were positioned on the lid and near the bottom of the cooker, while on gas models liquid propane jets provided the cooking heat. Most versions had a sloping bottom that drained grease to a pan underneath while the meat cooked. To give the meat smoke flavor, there was either a smoke box or a metal plate that would burn chips of hardwoods like hickory or oak to infuse the cooking chamber with smoke. With such equipment, an attendant could simply put the meat on a metal rack in the cooker, close the lid, and set the desired temperature on the thermostat. No close watching or shoveling of coals was required.[9]

Changes in America's food distribution system also had a shaping effect on the nature of commercial barbecue. In the 1950s and 1960s, meatpacking—once a local business—became increasingly industrialized and national in scope. Earlier in the century, Texas meat markets had ordered whole forequarters of beef and butchered them in-house. The sirloin and rib sections went into the meat case to be sold as steaks, while the low-demand cuts like the chuck and shoulder were smoked on the barbecue pit. By the 1960s, though, barbecue cooks could order the cuts of their choice from companies like Iowa Beef Products (IBP), the nation's largest meatpacker. In most cases that choice was untrimmed brisket. Pork was changing, too. Although the vertical integration and health concerns over pork were still some years away (those changes occurred mostly in the 1990s), pork was beginning to fall out of favor with American consumers. Per capita pork consumption in the United States fell from a peak of 81.1 pounds in 1944 to just 42.9 pounds in 1975, while both chicken and beef increased greatly, the latter reaching a peak of 88.2 pounds per person in 1975.[10]

Running a profitable barbecue operation in the era of fast-food chains was difficult, but traditional barbecue did not disappear completely from the American restaurant landscape. Instead, it became more of a specialized product. A few diners and drive-ins today still include barbecue alongside their menu of hamburgers. The Beacon Drive-In in Spartanburg, South Carolina, and Doumar's in Norfolk, Virginia, are notable examples. Starting in the 1970s, however, most restaurants either dropped pit-cooked barbecue from their menus or decided to focus on barbecue exclusively. Those that took the latter route tended to be modest establishments that didn't advertise widely and didn't get much attention from anyone except the local customers who had been eating there for years.

By the 1970s, the word "barbecue" had taken on a new meaning for much of America. For many, it had less to do with the way the meat was cooked than it did with the sauce with which it was served. Over the course of the twentieth century barbecue sauces had grown progressively sweeter, particularly when large producers began selling bottled sauces in grocery stores. Such sugary condiments were thicker than their vinegar-based forebears and could be glugged onto meat like ketchup. On the grill, however, that sugar would caramelize and burn to a charred crust, so backyard chefs didn't baste their meat with sauce while it cooked but rather waited until serving time to pour it on. The thick, sweet flavor of commercial sauces overwhelmed the natural smoked flavor of the meat, so cooks could devote less attention to the cooking part of the process, since it wasn't as important to the final result. In both restaurants and backyards, as the fuel used for barbecuing evolved from hardwood to charcoal to electric cookers and gas grills, cooks could get a crisp sear on the meat from the grill, but they relied on barbecue sauce for much of the flavor. The addition of "liquid smoke" flavoring to sauces completed the debasement.

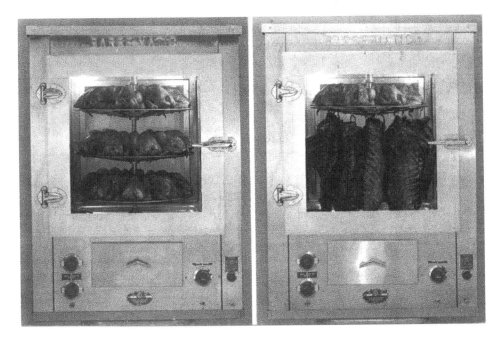

Promotional postcard for the rotisserie oven from Dallas-based Barbe-Matic, Inc., which promised, "Barbe-Matic's Lazy Susan Does it the Easy Way." (Author's collection)

Originally, barbecue was defined by the way it was cooked: anything roasted slowly over an open fire could be said to be "barbecued." By the middle of the twentieth century, many Americans' definitions had shifted to the sauce. Cookbooks from the 1950s and 1960s are filled with recipes for "barbecued chicken" that make no mention of a fire and involve a pan of chicken parts covered in a tangy sauce and baked in an oven. During the 1970s, "barbecue on bun" (oven-roasted pork that was shredded, covered with barbecue sauce, and served on a hamburger bun) became a staple of grade-school cafeterias. In 1981—three decades after founders Richard and Maurice McDonald removed the barbecue pits from their San Bernardino drive-in—barbecue returned to the McDonald's menu. Sort of. That year, the fast-food chain introduced the "McRib Sandwich," a pressed pork patty with rib-like marks seared into the meat, which was topped with sweet barbecue sauce, pickles, and onions and served on a long hoagie-style bun. Barbecue had strayed a long way from the pit.

10

THE REBIRTH OF AMERICAN BARBECUE

Traditional American barbecue, of course, was never really gone. In much of the country, old classic joints continued right along cooking and selling barbecue as they always had. Though their numbers were fewer than in prior decades, a new generation of restaurateurs continued to open businesses that followed the styles of their mentors, too. Barbecue had fallen back to a core set of specialized restaurants and had faded from the forefront of the public's awareness, but it was still there, dormant, waiting to spring back into full flower once America was ready for it again.

In 1977, Max Brantley, then a reporter for the *Arkansas Gazette*, published a short article about his favorite local barbecue spots. When he wrote the piece, he figured he was one of only a few "barbecue zealots" left in Arkansas. Once the paper hit the streets, he discovered he was far from alone and had, in fact, tapped into a simmering passion for the subject. "You think crime, pollution, bigotry, and official abuse of power are raging concerns of the day?" he wrote in a follow-up column. "Think again. Judging from the response to my articles, the next presidential candidate better have a barbecue plank in the platform." Brantley's barbecue piece generated more phone calls and letters than anything he'd previously written, many of them angrily taking issue with him for slighting or ignoring a favorite local spot.[1]

Other journalists joined Brantley in celebrating old-school barbecue joints. In July 1977, Vic Gold published an article in the *Washington Post's Potomac Magazine* that profiled the barbecue preferences of various members of Congress, noting, "The subject of barbecue evokes the worst in parochial elitism, even beyond that of specialized judges of continental haut cuisine or snobbish wine tasters." Gold, who hailed from Alabama by way of New Orleans, declared his allegiance to "real barbecue," which he defined as the stuff being served by either Ollie's or the Golden Rule in Birmingham.[2]

North Carolina native Jerry Bledsoe took offense at Gold's notion of "real barbecue" and responded with a five-part series for the *Charlotte Observer* profiling the legendary barbecue joints in the Tar Heel State. (In the process, he labeled Gold an "oyster sucker from Louisiana whose taste buds obviously are so Tabasco-seared he couldn't tell barbecue from baloney.") In the final installment of the series, which addressed barbecue in Lexington, North Carolina, Bledsoe noted that the town's barbecue places were not widely known, and he encouraged them to do something about it. "If Lexington had any ambition about it," he declared, "it would take immediate steps to protect, preserve, and promote this local treasure. It would proclaim itself the Barbecue Center of the World . . . and throw up the tents and have a big annual barbecue festival with music and dancing and other festivities to celebrate this regional delicacy that is becoming so rare." Just a few years later, in 1984, the town did just that, staging the first annual Lexington Barbecue Festival, an event that today draws more than 150,000 visitors to sample the area's famous Piedmont North Carolina–style barbecue.[3]

The rediscovery of barbecue was under way, and it was part of a more general cultural shift away from cosmopolitan aspirations and a renewed interest in local and regional traditions. For fifteen years, starting in 1967, Calvin Trillin wrote a series for the *New Yorker* called "U.S. Journal" for which he traveled around the country and wrote about topics that were intentionally unrelated to government or politics, including an occasional light article about eating in America. At first, he had difficulty tracking down local culinary specialties. People in the cities and towns he visited invariably pointed him to insipid upscale restaurants that tried to ape European cooking (Trillin took to calling these "La Maison de la Casa House, Continental Cuisine") rather than to a great local crab shack or fried-chicken joint. But that started to change. "At some point in the late seventies," Trillin later recalled, "a lot of Americans came to the realization that their local customs—playing bluegrass music, say, or growing corn or eating enchiladas—were not as shameful as they had once been led to believe."[4]

Trillin captured these local food customs in a wide-ranging series of reports that sampled everything from Cajun boudin to the Buffalo chicken wing, and he devoted particular attention to classic pit-cooked barbecue, for which he was an unapologetic champion. In a 1972 article for *Playboy* magazine, he asserted, "It has long been acknowledged that the single best restaurant in the world is Arthur Bryant's Barbecue at Eighteenth and Brooklyn in Kansas City." In "Stalking the Barbecued Mutton," Trillin explored the unique barbecue culture of western Kentucky, a style he feared was rapidly losing out to the competition of Kentucky Fried Chicken and similar fast-food chains. "With the franchisers and décor-mongers closing in," he wrote, "any authentic local specialty obviously needs celebrating. . . . 'Kentucky is the Barbecued-Mutton Capital of the World,' I would tell the first eater of influence I could find, 'Spread the word.'"[5]

A new breed of guidebook writers did exactly that, bringing to market for the first time books meant to help curious eaters find and explore America's legendary barbecue restaurants. Dozens of barbecue books had been published during the 1950s and 1960s, but they were all aimed at the backyard chef, providing recipes and grilling tips and making virtually no mention of traditional pit-barbecue restaurants. In 1979, Allie Patricia Wall and Ron L. Layne published *Hog Heaven: A Guide to South Carolina Barbecue*, which appears to be the first barbecue guidebook. Wall and Layne toured the Palmetto State, eating at over a hundred barbecue places and documenting not only the location and hours of operation but also the barbecue style, cooking technique, and a description of the business.

Hog Heaven was restricted in scope to a single state. In 1988, Vince Staten and Greg Johnson published *Real Barbecue*, a guidebook to the top one hundred barbecue restaurants in the nation. "At that time," Staten remembers, "there were hundreds of handbooks for those seeking out the great French restaurants of America but no glove-box guide to great barbecue." The book didn't sell particularly well—Staten estimates that the first edition sold fewer than eight thousand copies—but it helped establish a genre that flourished. Today, dozens of barbecue guidebooks—including a revised and expanded version of *Real Barbecue* that was published in 2007—help new generations of barbecue lovers explore the many regional variations of this inherently American food. In 1996, when Lolis Eric Elie set off with photographer Frank Stewart on the culinary tour that he chronicled in *Smokestack Lightning: Adventures in the Heart of Barbecue Country*, he hypothesized that "this art, so vital to our national identity, was dying or at least endangered." When he revisited the subject in his preface to the 2005 revised edition, Elie admitted that his original assumption had not been completely accurate. A lot of old-time places had since closed up and many of the older generation of pitmasters had passed away, but he had not anticipated "the strongly

Cover of Greg Johnson and Vince Staten's *Real Barbecue* (1988), the first national barbecue guidebook. (Photograph by author)

nostalgic trend in the country these days, a longing for the old ways. A longing so strong it has brought real barbecue to relative prominence in places where it was previously little more than a novelty."[6]

Barbecue Competitions

The Memphis in May World Championship Barbecue Cooking Contest, the country's largest barbecue competition, was first held in 1978 on a vacant lot just north of the Orpheum Theatre. It was just the second year of the Memphis in May festival, a two-day Memorial Day weekend celebration, and Rodney Barber, chair of the events committee, and Jack Powell, a chili cook-off champion, thought it would be ideal to have a barbecue contest to show off Memphis's most beloved food. Bessie Louise Cathey, who cooked ribs on a ramshackle backyard barrel cooker, beat out twenty-seven other contestants for the $500 grand champion prize. The next year, the contest moved to Tom Lee Park along the Mississippi River, where it is still held today, and within a few years more than two hundred teams were competing, and the competition had to move to an invitational format.[7]

Other contests emerged to rival Memphis in May. The Taylor International Barbecue Cookoff in Taylor, Texas, was started in 1978, and the first American Royal Barbecue was held in 1980 as part of the century-old American Royal Livestock Show. (The inaugural contest was won by Rich Davis, a Kansas City physician and child psychiatrist who would later leave his medical practice and turn his "KC Masterpiece" barbecue sauce into a national brand.) By 1985 Calvin Trillin observed, "There are so many barbecue cooking contests in the summertime a competitive barbecuer can haul his rig from fairgrounds to fairgrounds, like a man with a string of quarterhorses." But things were just getting started.[8]

In the mid-1980s, the Memphis in May organizers started sanctioning contests throughout the region, and the Memphis Barbecue Network was born. Sanctioned events used the same rules as the Memphis in May contest, and winners were guaranteed a spot at the World Championship in May. A rival sanctioning body, the Kansas City Barbeque Society (KCBS), got its start in 1985, when twenty die-hard barbecuers came together to stage a "spring training" cook-off. At the time, there were only three barbecue competitions in the Kansas City area—all of them in the summer and fall—so the KCBS created its own event so barbecuers could keep their skills sharp during the off-season. Before long, it was receiving calls from organizers of other barbecue competitions who wanted the KCBS to provide rules for their events, and the society became a sanctioning body, too.

According to Carolyn Wells, KCBS's executive director, the competition circuit grew at a steady 10 to 20 percent through the 1980s and 1990s. In 1996, Robb Walsh counted more than one hundred competitions in Texas alone. But things really took off after the September 11 terrorist attacks, as Americans looked inward and sought ways to spend more recreational time with family and friends. The rise of the Food Network and its around-the-clock barbecue specials added more converts. Today the KCBS is the country's largest competition barbecue sanctioning body, with over twenty thousand members and some five hundred sanctioned events each year.[9]

In the early days, barbecue contests were pretty bare-bones. Contestants slept in pup tents and cooked on Weber kettles and homemade contraptions. Now they travel the country in RVs and cook on professionally manufactured, high-tech barbecue rigs. Today's high-tech smokers have draft induction fans, electric thermostats, and augers that deliver a precisely calibrated stream of wood pellets to the firebox. Such innovations have caused a bit of controversy between the barbecue purists, who maintain that burning logs and tending the fire all night is essential to the art, and the pragmatists, who like getting a good night's sleep. But, as the KCBS's Wells says, "Everything in barbecue is controversial."

The pits aren't the only things that have changed. In the early days, competitive barbecuing was a fairly transparent excuse for boozing it up all night with the boys. (Calvin Trillin called the contests "a big attraction for the people I think of as the party-as-a-verb crowd.") Today's competitors are still a fun-loving lot, but they've toned it down a good bit and made the weekends more suitable for the entire family. For many participants, in fact, the family-friendly atmosphere is a big part of the appeal. It's common these days for entire families—including grandparents and small children—to travel together from one weekend competition to another, and they establish strong friendships with members of other teams. The result is a close-knit community whose members share stories, swap tips on recipes and technique, and cheer on one another's victories in the competitions.[10]

While competitions have contributed to the ever-growing popularity of barbecue, some critics have complained that they are blurring traditional regional differences and making barbecue more homogeneous. They point to standardized competition rules like those of the Kansas City Barbeque Society, which call for judging four categories of meat (chicken, pork ribs, pork, and beef brisket), and the fact that contestants from all over the country are competing side by side without much concern for the local barbecue style. Others claim that expensive customized barbecue rigs and meticulous techniques like using syringes to inject the meat with flavorings have taken barbecue far from its original roots. "It was once the province of lower-middle-class and working-class people," author John T. Edge has said, "and now it's the equivalent of the bass boat for the middle classes."[11]

Despite traditionalists' concerns, a few things about barbecue competitions are clear. First, they have helped introduce barbecue not only to a new segment of eaters but also to a new population of cooks, who have become the next generation of

The rig for the Blackjack Barbecue team at the 2008 Southern National Barbecue Championship and Bluegrass Festival, Mount Pleasant, South Carolina. As competition barbecue has increased in popularity, the contestants' gear has become more elaborate and high-tech. (Photograph by author)

pitmasters dedicated to the practice of slow-smoking meats. Many cooks who honed their skills on the competition circuit have gone on to open their own barbecue restaurants, launch lines of commercial sauces, and lead cooking classes to teach the craft to other aspiring cooks. The contests also show that barbecue's power to bring people together still endures. That is certainly the case for the members of competition circuit teams and the tight bonds they form with their fellow competitors. It is also the case for the communities where the contests are held. Barbecue competitions are usually paired with some other event, such as a music festival or a local community celebration, and the proceeds raised are generally donated to a charitable cause. The gleaming stainless-steel custom pits and the Winnebagos and the corporate sponsorships may be new, but the phenomenon of thousands of people coming together to eat barbecue outdoors is as old as the country itself.

Barbecue Sauce

Around the same time that barbecue competitions were becoming popular across the country, a new category of "premium" barbecue sauces entered the market. The first of these was KC Masterpiece, a brand created by Rich Davis, the Kansas City physician and child psychiatrist who won the inaugural American Royal Barbecue in 1980. Davis got into the condiment business by marketing a product called Muschup, a combination of mustard and ketchup in a single bottle. Not surprisingly, Muschup was a commercial failure, but fortunately Davis had decided to sell "KC Soul Style Barbecue Sauce" alongside his flagship product. The barbecue sauce sold three thousand cases in the first year. Davis changed the name to "KC Masterpiece," and in 1986 he sold the brand to the Kingsford Division of the Clorox Company (makers of Kingsford charcoal), which took it nationwide. KC Masterpiece remains the top-selling barbecue sauce in the premium category.

Other manufacturers soon launched their own premium brands. In 1987 Kraft brought out its Bulls-Eye line, creating two tiers of brands—the original Kraft Barbecue Sauce selling at around $1.50 per bottle, and Bulls-Eye selling in the two- to three-dollar range. Kraft launched Bulls-Eye with a half-million-dollar promotional campaign that featured sponsorship of professional rodeo events along with extensive print, radio, and television ads. The efforts paid off, and by the early 1990s Bulls-Eye was competing head-on with KC Masterpiece at the top of the premium barbecue sauce category. It took Heinz a little longer to get into the game, but in 2001 it licensed the brand of bourbon maker Jack Daniels to use on its own premium barbecue sauce. By 2008, one could still buy the original orange-tinted Kraft and Open Pit barbecue sauces, but as the market matured, variety became the order of the day and each major manufacturer started offering an array of flavors, such as honey and garlic, mesquite smoke, and hot and spicy. Over $350 million in bottled barbecue sauce was sold that year, and that amount more than doubled to $800 million in 2018.[12]

Clorox, Kraft, and Heinz remained the major players in the market, but there was plenty of room left for the smaller guys. Many barbecue restaurateurs started supplementing their regular business by bottling and selling their signature sauces. Arthur Bryant's and Gates's (from Kansas City), Big Bob Gibson (from Alabama), Corky's (from Memphis), Scott's (from North Carolina), McClard's (from Arkansas), and

Stubb's (from Texas) were just a few of the historic barbecue restaurants whose sauces could be purchased at grocery stores across the country. Celebrities started jumping on the bandwagon, too. Comedian Jeff Foxworthy launched his Redneck Barbecue Sauce, syndicated radio hosts John Isley and Billy James created "JohnBoy and Billy's Grillin' Sauce," and TV chef Emeril Lagasse marketed four flavors of "BAM! B-Q" sauce.[13]

Amid this explosion of variety, the famed regional distinctions in barbecue sauce started to blur. On the shelves of a typical South Carolina grocery store, one could find dozens of different brands of barbecue sauce, only a handful of which were the region's traditional mustard-based style. Most of the big barbecue restaurant chains— and even some of the smaller independents—started putting upward of six different types of sauce on their tables, to better serve the individual tastes of their patrons. Fewer and fewer youngsters were likely to have grown up knowing only one type of sauce, so fewer and fewer had a single type that became permanently emblazoned in their minds as the only "true" barbecue sauce.

Barbecue Chains and Franchises

In the 1960s and 1970s, the many entrepreneurs who tried to establish barbecue restaurant chains met with only limited success (see page 221). Regionalism has frequently been pointed to as the main barrier. Because barbecue styles and preferences differ so greatly from one state to another, the theory goes, it is hard to create a single barbecue product that appeals to customers in multiple regions. Other explanations include the inefficient, manually intensive nature of operating a barbecue restaurant— tending open wood pits is a skilled job and it is not easy to train new workers—and the corresponding difficulty of maintaining a consistent, repeatable product.

But something changed around the same time that Americans were rediscovering the joys of cooking and eating barbecue, and barbecue restaurant chains began to find success not only in maintaining a large number of profitable units but also in spanning wide geographical areas. The most successful of these barbecue entrepreneurs, Floyd "Sonny" Tillman, opened his first barbecue restaurant in Gainesville, Florida, in 1968. He later changed the name from "Fat Boys" to "Sonny's Real Pit BBQ," and the restaurant became a popular haunt for University of Florida students, particularly the football players. After opening 3 locations in Gainesville, Sonny began franchising in 1977. By 1988, when Tillman sold the company to outside investors and retired, the restaurant had 77 locations in six states. By 2008, with more than 130 restaurants in operation, Sonny's was the nation's largest barbecue chain.[14]

At that point, all of Sonny's restaurants were in the South, but their territory still cut across nine states with very divergent barbecue styles, including the Carolinas, Georgia, Kentucky, and Tennessee. And Sonny's wasn't the only chain spanning regional boundaries. In 2005, Marc Chastain, vice president of franchising for RibCrib Barbecue, told a reporter, "I think that the chain approach to barbecue is going to undress that regional preference theory a little bit." Four years later, the Oklahoma-based chain had 41 restaurants in a region extending from Mason City, Iowa, down to Lubbock, Texas, and had opened its first East Coast franchise in Lakeland, Florida. Orlando-based Smokey Bones BBQ grew to over 70 restaurants by 2007, while Minnesota-based Famous Dave's, with 118 outlets in twenty-nine states, had perhaps the widest geographic reach, stretching from Manchester, New Hampshire, to Tacoma, Washington.[15]

The offering at many of these chains blurred regional distinctions with abandon. Famous Dave's restaurants were designed to look like Minnesota fishing camps, with rough-hewn wood walls adorned with camping gear and fishing posters. The menu, though, featured styles ranging from "Georgia Chopped Pork" to "Texas Brisket." Bandana's Bar-B-Q, a twenty-seven-store chain based in St. Louis, Missouri, advertised a "Southern style" barbecue that founder David Seitz had learned as a boy in Jacksonville, Florida, but the Bandana's name as well as the restaurant's heavy cowboy-theme dripped Texas. Charleston, South Carolina–based Sticky Fingers featured Memphis-style dry-rubbed ribs and promoted "a flavor so good you'll think you're walking down Beale Street with B. B. King!" The walls of the restaurants were covered with photographs of bluesmen, and Delta-style electric blues was piped over the sound system. But the chain's fifteen restaurants were found mostly in the Carolinas, and the only two outlets in Tennessee were in Chattanooga, some three hundred miles east of Memphis.

The success of barbecue chains in the early twenty-first century was due to more than just a blurring of old regional tastes. It was also the result of changes within the industry itself. One important factor was equipment. The Little Pigs of America chain, which folded in the mid-1960s after a few brief years of rapid growth, helped its franchisees build their own wood-burning brick pits. At his first barbecue restaurant in

Gainesville, Sonny Tillman cooked over an open pit with blackjack oak. As he started to expand his operation, though, he switched to the combination gas and wood cookers manufactured by Southern Pride, whose equipment (along with that of its main rival, Old Hickory) was soon adopted by most of the country's top-grossing barbecue chains. These new high-tech, self-contained smokers included electric rotisserie racks, automatic time and temperature controls, and gas-fired wood boxes in which entire hickory logs could be burned to impart smoky flavor. They were a significant improvement over the rudimentary gas cookers installed by restaurateurs switching over from all wood in the 1970s and 1980s. With such equipment, restaurateurs could cook hundreds of pounds of meat overnight with the precision and control to ensure a consistent, repeatable product. Some chains even adopted pressure smokers, which sealed the smoke into a cooking chamber and cooked the meat under pressure. They could cook forty-five pounds of ribs in just an hour and a half, a boon for restaurateurs with high-volume operations.[16]

The growth in barbecue restaurants in the new millennium was not only through chains and franchises. "In Louisville," Vince Staten noted in 2004, "there has been a barbecue restaurant explosion in the last fifteen years. There was only one good place in town when we wrote [the restaurant guidebook] *Real Barbecue*. Now there are a half-dozen, all of them owned and operated by guys who do it for the love of 'cue." The competition barbecue phenomenon produced more than its fair share of restaurateurs, with hobbyists who mastered the art on the competition circuit deciding to set up shop and sell barbecue in a restaurant setting full-time. Increasingly, classically trained chefs with years of experience in fine dining restaurants started trading their white jackets and toques for overalls and opening their own barbecue restaurants complete with wood-fired pits. Though traditional pit-cooked barbecue was becoming harder to find and the boundaries of regional styles were becoming less and less distinct, there was no shortage of restaurants where diners could enjoy smoked pork, brisket, and ribs.[17]

The long, slow decline of barbecue in the late twentieth century had been successfully reversed, and by 2010 barbecue was available in more parts of the country and in a wider variety than ever before. The purists might grumble over the fading of regional variations and the steady replacement of hardwood pits by electric and gas cookers. Indeed, this new incarnation of barbecue was quite different than it had been back in the days when the proprietors of roadside stands cooked meat over hardwood coals

Curtis All American Bar-B-Q in Putney, Vermont, shows that traditional barbecue still appeals to diners in every corner of the nation. (Courtesy Mike Murphy)

and served it with a homemade sauce that could be found only in that particular region. Many of the classic styles from the Golden Age—whole hog barbecue, hash made with hog heads and livers, older cuts of meat like beef shoulder clod—were becoming harder to find with each passing year. Newer restaurants tended to cook an increasingly standardized selection of brisket, ribs, pulled pork, and chicken, and they served them with an array of sauces, most of them of the thick, sweet variety made popular by the commercial sauce brands. It may have been slicker and more commercialized than in previous incarnations, but American barbecue was back.

AFTERWORD

The Second Golden Age of American Barbecue

THE FIRST EDITION OF this book closed on a hopeful if somewhat ambivalent note. The American barbecue tradition had narrowly escaped the dustbin of history, but it seemed to be headed toward an increasingly homogenized and corporatized future. I put as positive a spin as I could on the blurring of regional lines and the fading of old methods like wood-fired open pits and whole hog cookery. "Looked at over the full sweep of barbecue's history," I wrote, "these recent changes are hardly surprising, for barbecue has always been a dynamic tradition." The widely celebrated regional barbecue styles, I reasoned, were themselves less than a century old, and they represented just one of the many phases in barbecue's long history. It only made sense that barbecue would continue to evolve, even if it offended the sensibilities of traditionalists like me. After all, when the first barbecue stands and roadside joints appeared back in the early twentieth century, that era's traditionalists grumbled about them, too.

I could never have predicted what happened next. Barbecue's resurgence not only continued but shifted into something new and different. It did so in part by looking back and embracing the older techniques and traditions that seemed so imperiled in 2010. The geographical footprint of barbecue expanded rapidly, too. When the first edition of this book was published, barbecue was considered largely a southern thing, found primarily in the so-called Barbecue Belt, running roughly from Texas eastward to the North Carolina coast. Elsewhere in the country—in New England, the Upper Midwest, and the Mid-Atlantic states—diners weren't totally unfamiliar with barbecue, but their experience with it was generally from watching food shows on cable television and eating at restaurant chains that imported a mishmash of styles from somewhere else.

That was certainly the case in New York City. Just after the year 2000, as barbecue was surging in popularity, restaurateurs had already started bringing barbecue "concepts" to Manhattan. Danny Meyer of the Union Square Hospitality Group opened Blue Smoke in 2002, and Adam Perry Lang, a graduate of the Culinary Institute of America, launched Daisy May's BBQ the following year. These early entrants were very much in the homogenizing, regionally blurring mode, and their food had plenty of fine dining twists. "The worst thing we could have done," Meyer told one interviewer, "was to pretend that we were a barbecue joint rather than a New York restaurant." Lang's menu at Daisy May's ranged from Oklahoma-style beef shortribs to Cajun-inspired dirty rice, and his haute cuisine pedigree was reflected in his array of flavorful sauces. "[Lang] ranges through all regional barbecue styles and heads beyond," Julia Moskin wrote in her *New York Times* review of the restaurant, "into pineapple, ginger and any other ingredient that helps him achieve the explosive blend of spicy, sweet, tart and salty that is barbecue's flavor signature.[1]

But as more cooks and eaters became enamored with barbecue, they started digging a little deeper into the food's long history and exploring America's diverse regional styles. The arrival of Texas-inspired joints in New York—most notably Hill Country, which opened in 2007 and re-created a Lockhart-style meat market in the heart of Manhattan—put the Lone Star style front and center in the country's media capital. "I've never fallen afoul of a Texas Ranger," Peter Meehan wrote in the opening to his *New York Times* review of Hill Country, "but my first bite of the fatty brisket at Hill Country hit me like a Chuck Norris roundhouse kick to the head. . . . Was I eating beef barbecue this ridiculously good in Chelsea?"[2]

Soon, food writers, chefs, and other aficionados began making pilgrimages to Texas, Memphis, and the Carolinas to seek out legendary joints and sing their praises. In a June 2009 article for the *New York Times* titled "Pig, Smoke, Pit: This Food Is Seriously Slow," John T. Edge profiled Rodney Scott, the thirty-seven-year-old pitmaster at Scott's Variety Store. It captured Scott and his crew at the family's takeout barbecue operation in Hemingway, South Carolina, using a gigantic steel burn barrel to render oak logs into coals and shovel them beneath whole hogs cooking on open cinder-block pits. "Cooking this way isn't done much any more," Edge noted.[3]

The growing fascination with old-school barbecue was part of a larger trend in the American culinary scene, as chefs, diners, and critics increasingly turned their backs on formal French-inspired cuisine and began exploring their country's own culinary roots. The so-called pre-Prohibition cocktail movement had bartenders digging up dusty nineteenth-century bar guides and reviving classic recipes that had fallen out of favor a century before. Cities across the country witnessed the emergence of a vibrant food truck scene, where cooks could create and sell ambitious, intensely flavored food even if they had no interest in—or lacked the capital to supply—formal restaurant trappings like white tablecloths and waitstaff in coats and ties. Barbecue fit perfectly into this new culinary mode. As roadside entrepreneurs had discovered a century before, it didn't take much up-front investment to set up a pit and sell slow-cooked barbecue. Diners were increasingly drawn to more primal, elemental approaches to food, and nothing could be more primal than cooking meat over a wood fire. Indeed, at the same time, many fine dining restaurant chefs were installing wood-fired ovens and giant wood-burning grills in their kitchens and cooking everything from pizza to whole fish on them.

The meteoric rise of Texas brisket master Aaron Franklin, who burst onto the national scene in 2010, marked the arrival of a full-on American barbecue boom. An aspiring musician, Franklin moved to Austin at the age of nineteen to immerse himself in the city's thriving music scene. In 2002 he bought a $99 New Braunfels smoker from an outdoor store and cooked his first brisket for a gathering of friends in the backyard of the small house he and his wife, Stacy, rented in East Austin. Aaron was playing drums in bands and working odd jobs while Stacy waited tables, and their periodic backyard barbecues grew bigger as he became more passionate about cooking brisket.

Franklin worked a stint for John Mueller, grandson of the legendary Louis Mueller from Taylor, who had brought his family's barbecue style to a short-lived restaurant in Austin. Franklin said he learned a lot about cutting meat and greeting customers while working for Mueller, but he was never trained on the pit, since Mueller did all the cooking. In 2006, though, after Mueller's restaurant had closed, Franklin used the proceeds from a house remodeling job to buy his former boss's smoker, which had been custom-made from a five-hundred-gallon propane tank, and he rehabbed it himself with hopes of one day installing it at his own barbecue place. The Franklins lacked the funds to open a brick-and-mortar restaurant, so in 2008 they bought a blue and white 1971 Aristocrat Lo Liner trailer for $300 off Craigslist and retrofitted it with scavenged restaurant equipment. In December 2009, Franklin Barbecue opened in a lot behind a friend's coffee roasting shop on the frontage road to Interstate 35.[4]

The timing could not have been better. It was the peak era of food blogs, and social media platforms like Facebook and Twitter were on the rise. Through these new digital networks, barbecue fans could instantly share information about restaurant openings and compile "bucket lists" of must-visit places. Less than two months after Franklin's trailer opened, Daniel Vaughn, who wrote a popular Texas barbecue blog called *Full Custom Gospel BBQ*, paid them a visit and penned a glowing review. "If I lived in Austin, I would come here every day," Vaughn wrote. Texas food writer Robb Walsh agreed, writing on his *Texas Eats* blog that Franklin's brisket was "some of the best I've ever eaten." Suddenly customers were showing up hours before the trailer opened, and a long line formed each morning along the chain-link fence at the edge of the lot. Aaron Franklin added a second smoker, and Stacy quit her waitressing job to join him full-time. In July, Alice Laussade of the *Dallas Observer* advised her city's residents to make a drive south to Austin, for "Three Hours from Now, You Could Be in Brisket Heaven." In its November dining guide the *Austin American-Statesman* declared Franklin "Newcomer of the Year" among the city's food trucks.[5]

Less than a year after opening, the Franklins knew they could never supply the demand with a trailer-based operation, so they started looking for a brick-and-mortar restaurant. They opened Franklin Barbecue on Eleventh Street in March 2011, on the first day of the South by Southwest festival. They sold out of meat on their opening day and continued to sell out each day after that. That June, Andrew Knowlton, restaurant editor of *Bon Appétit*, declared Franklin Barbecue the best barbecue restaurant in the country. Around the same time, Joe Nick Patoski of the *New York Times* declared "the start of Texas' newest barbecue war," observing that Aaron and Stacy Franklin "represent a new generation of barbecue cooks who are elevating a food tradition once thought to be timeless and at the same time fading away." The young turks in Austin were now competing head-to-head with the famous old meat markets in towns like Lockhart and Taylor. "Austin joints are becoming so storied," Patoski added, "that ravenous out-of-towners who formerly used the capital city as a point of departure are lingering there instead."[6]

Customers lining up early in the morning outside Austin's Franklin Barbecue. (Photograph by author)

The hype surrounding Texas barbecue only grew. Television celebrities like Anthony Bourdain of the Travel Channel's *No Reservations* paid visits to Austin and raved about the barbecue they found there. Overhead shots of brown butcher paper–lined trays piled high with brisket, ribs, and sausage blanketed social media feeds. In early 2013, *Texas Monthly* hired Daniel Vaughn as the country's first full-time barbecue editor, and shortly thereafter the magazine brashly declared brisket to be "The Mount Everest of Barbecue" and added that the top fifty barbecue joints in Texas were also, by definition, the "Top 50" in the world. Food trucks were popping up on street corners in cities across the country, their pitmasters churning out brisket and hot links on custom wood-fired smokers. Classically trained chefs hung up their saucepans to open barbecue joints, and they made road trips down to Texas to crib techniques and styles. They were introducing an entire new generation of diners to traditional wood-cooked barbecue, and their offering tended to be Texas's "Holy Trinity" of smoked brisket, sausage, and ribs.[7]

Texas barbecue was well on its way to taking over the nation, and the world seemed next. "New York City—especially Brooklyn," noted *Houston Chronicle* barbecue columnist J. C. Reid in 2015, "is such a hotbed of Texas barbecue that I've noted some European barbecue fanatics making the pilgrimage to America and never getting past the Hudson River." Texas-style barbecue joints had opened in European cities like London, Paris, Berlin, and Rome and were starting to pop up in Japan, too.[8]

For a while, it looked like the wave of central Texas–style barbecue washing over the country might sweep away all the other regional styles. In places like Tennessee and the Carolinas, where ribs and pulled pork had long been menu staples, customers started demanding brisket, and many restaurateurs caved to the demand and added it to their menus. New restaurants opening their doors in places like Charlotte and Atlanta served their barbecue on metal trays lined with Texas-style brown butcher paper, replicating the images that had appeared on the glossy covers of countless food magazines.

But then the tide shifted again. In January 2015, I found myself in the back of a seminar room in Murphysboro, Illinois, watching Sam Jones, who had come all the way from Skylight Inn in Ayden, North Carolina, as he straddled a whole hog on a stainless-steel table, using a hatchet and hammer to split the backbone of a carcass that he was prepping for the pit. Several dozen students—most of them barbecue restaurateurs, some of whom had come from as far away as Alaska—watched intently, asking detailed questions while making notes on small pads. It was the fourth annual Whole Hog Extravaganza, a three-day educational event staged by Mike and Amy Mills, the father-daughter team behind 17th Street Barbecue. In addition to their two restaurants and a competition team, they had launched a consulting business to advise other restaurateurs on how to succeed in the trade, and this popular seminar was geared around teaching the fundamentals of cooking whole hogs.

Later that fall, I was invited to speak at a different type of whole hog event at the Southern Food and Beverage Museum in New Orleans. Howard Conyers cooked a pig overnight and gave a talk the next day about the science of whole hog cookery, and I spoke about the history behind this centuries-old American tradition. The attendees got to enjoy their fill of Conyers's barbecue, and for many it was first time they'd tasted the whole hog variety. Conyers, who grew up on a farm near Manning, South Carolina, learned to cook barbecue from his father. By the time he was a teenager he was tending the pits all night for family reunions and gatherings of the local Future Farmers of America (FFA). But a love for science took him far away from the farm. He earned a doctorate in mechanical engineering and material science, and he now lives in New Orleans and tests rocket engines at NASA's Stennis Space Center on the Mississippi-Louisiana border—making him perhaps the country's only rocket scientist/pitmaster.

After arriving in Louisiana, though, Conyers started to miss his family's barbecue. "I realized I had left something back home that is unique and special," he told me. So he tracked down a whole pig, improvised a pit, and cooked barbecue for his friends for a Super Bowl party. He did it again at the Hogs for the Cause barbecue competition in 2014. That led to a side project called Carolina QNOLA, a pop-up that has served traditional South Carolina–style barbecue at various events and seminars in and around New Orleans.

During the question-and-answer session after our talks, an audience member asked us whether we thought whole hog cooking would rebound in the future. Despite his passion for the tradition, Conyers was pessimistic. "It's just so expensive," he said, noting the cost of the wood and of the pigs themselves as well as the time and labor required. But I was more sanguine about the prospects, for I had recently come across others who were starting to cook whole hogs the old burn-barrel way for special occasions like fundraisers and Memorial Day parties. I had even met a few enterprising restaurateurs who were opening brand-new whole hog barbecue restaurants.

One of these was Tyson Ho, a most unlikely person to bring back an old southern culinary tradition. Born into a Chinese American family in Flushing, Queens, he became enthralled by barbecue's many regional styles after eating at Hill Country BBQ in Manhattan. Ho traveled around the South sampling those styles and fell in love with the whole hog barbecue he tasted in North Carolina. In 2014, after spending time learning to cook pigs from noted Raleigh pitmaster Ed Mitchell, Ho left a career in finance to open Arrogant Swine, a North Carolina–style whole hog barbecue joint in Brooklyn's Bushwick neighborhood, complete with custom-made wood-burning pits—something previously unheard of in the nation's largest city.

Around the same time, Bryan and Nikki Furman launched B's Cracklin' BBQ in Savannah, Georgia. Like Howard Conyers, Bryan Furman had grown up cooking whole hogs on his grandparents' farm in rural South Carolina. He started a catering business in Savannah and met enough success that he and his wife, Nikki, took a gamble on a brick-and-mortar restaurant—and they went whole hog with it, cooking heritage-breed pigs over hickory and cherry wood and serving them with sides made using old recipes and fresh local produce.

A platter from Sam Jones BBQ in Winterville, North Carolina, where proprietor Sam Jones serves the same style of whole hog barbecue, cornbread, and slaw that his grandfather introduced at Skylight Inn in Ayden—plus ribs, mac 'n' cheese, and draft beer. (Photograph by author)

At first, ventures like Arrogant Swine and B's Cracklin' BBQ seemed to be outliers amid all the Texas-style beef that was blanketing the nation. In the summer of 2015, though, Elliot Moss, who had made a name for himself as a chef at the Admiral in Asheville, opened Buxton Hall, cooking whole hogs in two big metal pits right inside the restaurant's open kitchen. Three months later, Sam Jones of Ayden's Skylight Inn opened Sam Jones BBQ in nearby Winterville, complete with an enormous screen-sided pit room where he and his crew cook whole pigs over cinder-block pits the same way his grandfather did. The following year brought Picnic in Durham, North Carolina, where Wyatt Dickson's custom-built pit can cook three 225-pound hogs at a time. Up in Tennessee, Pat Martin, whose first Martin's Bar-B-Que Joint had opened a decade before in Nolensville, Tennessee, added his fifth and sixth locations, one in Louisville, Kentucky, and another in downtown Nashville, the latter in a two-story building with three whole-hog pits. Whole hog has even made inroads into Texas, where Todd David at Cattleack Barbeque in Dallas, one of the state's top brisket cooks, serves whole hog barbecue one Saturday a month.

Perhaps no city in the country is more emblematic of the latest trends in barbecue than Charleston, South Carolina—which, coincidentally, is where I live. In 2016, Jim Shahin of the *Washington Post* paid the city a visit and filed a story on the barbecue he found there. "With apologies to Bruce Springsteen," the piece began, "I've seen the future of barbecue, and it is Charleston, S.C." Shahin highlighted the classically trained chefs who were "rejecting the mimicry common in other barbecue hot spots and are experimenting based on the regional low-country cuisine. Upscale barbecue is a nationwide trend, but nowhere else have I seen as much of it as I have here."[9]

Charleston had long had an international reputation for its acclaimed fine dining restaurants, but the fare focused on upscale versions of Lowcountry classics like shrimp and grits as well as fresh local fish and heirloom produce. For years there had been only two barbecue restaurants in downtown Charleston—the area Charlestonians know as the Peninsula—and both were part of regional chains.

But suddenly things changed. Aaron Siegel, who had cooked in some of the city's most prestigious fine dining kitchens before opening a barbecue restaurant west of town, announced that he was opening a new location in the heart of downtown and that he would be cooking his barbecue on wood-fired Lang and Oyler pits. Next, John Lewis, who had apprenticed with Aaron Franklin before becoming the pitmaster at Austin's celebrated La Barbecue food trailer, announced that he was moving east to Charleston to open a brisket joint—and he was building his restaurant literally around the corner from where Siegel had just broken ground on the new Home Team BBQ. The capper came when Rodney Scott, who in the wake of his profile in the *New York Times* had achieved international acclaim for his old-school whole hog, announced that he was coming to Charleston, too.

And they weren't the only ones. By the time Rodney Scott's Barbecue opened for business, the Charleston Peninsula was home to eleven barbecue joints, and nine were independent operations that had opened since 2010. Even more barbecue could be found outside downtown at places like Swig & Swine in West Ashley, where owner Anthony DiBernardo started cooking a whole hog once a week on wood-fired pits and later opened a second location in nearby Summerville with enough wood-fired pit capacity to cook three or more whole hogs every day. Such traditional Carolina fare mingled with more chef-inspired creations—like smoked chicken confit at Smoke BBQ or Poogan's Smokehouse's pork belly sliders with "redneck kimchee" on sweet Hawaiian rolls.

The Charleston area, of course, hadn't exactly been devoid of barbecue restaurants before this new crop of pitmasters showed up. For decades the Lowcountry had been an extension of the Midlands South Carolina barbecue region, with restaurants featuring pulled pork shoulder dressed in bright yellow mustard-based barbecue sauce and served with hash and rice on the side. Much of that style could be traced back to two families, the Bessingers and the Dukes. The patriarch of the former, Joe Bessinger, sold barbecue at the Holly Hill Cafe in Orangeburg County—an example of the type of roadside cafés that were popping up all over the country just before World War II. Seven of Bessinger's ten children ended up in the barbecue business, bringing their father's Orangeburg-style yellow mustard sauce down to Charleston in the 1950s and also up to Columbia. (That was the controversial Maurice Bessinger; see chapter 8.) The family's original Piggie Park drive-in was downtown on Rutledge Avenue, but as growth pushed outward from the Peninsula into the newly built suburbs, the Bessinger brothers followed—Melvin to Mount Pleasant and James Island, Thomas out to Savannah Highway in West Ashley, Robert up to Ashley Phosphate in North Charleston. All of these restaurants started out cooking on wood-fired brick pits, but—as was the pattern all over the country—they had switched over to gas-assist cookers by the 1980s.[10]

With all the attention the new restaurants were getting on the Peninsula, David Bessinger, Melvin Bessinger's son and owner of the two remaining Melvin's Barbecue restaurants, recognized that the bar was being raised, and he decided not to rest on his laurels. In 2014, he headed west to check out the operations at famous central Texas barbecue joints like Kreuz's and Smitty's in Lockhart and got tips from Ronnie Killen at Killen's Barbecue outside Houston. After he returned, he added brisket and beef ribs to the menu at Melvin's—items unheard of in the Carolinas just a decade before. Not long after, he made an even bigger change: he returned his restaurants to cooking on all-wood pits. Bessinger first installed a Lang 108-inch offset cooker at each Melvin's location, which they used to cook all of their brisket, turkey, and chickens. The arrival of a big Oyler 700 from J&R Manufacturing in Texas gave them the capacity to cook all their pork shoulders, too, making the Mount Pleasant restaurant once again a 100 percent all-wood-cooked restaurant. By 2016, it seemed, all-wood cooking—once an endangered species—had become mere table stakes for a serious barbecue restaurant.

David Bessinger, though, resisted one of the new elements of his city's evolving barbecue mode: alcohol. For decades, sweet tea and lemonade had been the traditional beverages in South Carolina barbecue joints, and you could count on one hand the number of places in the state that sold beer. But the newer, more upscale restaurants like Home Team and Lewis Barbecue not only have local beers on tap but also full bars with sophisticated cocktail menus. The original Hemingway location of Scott's Barbecue sells only iced tea and bottled sodas; for his new outpost in Charleston, Rodney Scott got a beer license. "Beer and barbecue just go together in Charleston," he told me.

But when we leave the flourishing dining scene in cities like Charleston and head out into the small towns and rural areas, the barbecue landscape isn't quite so verdant. Indeed, a sharp divide has opened between what we might call city 'cue and country 'cue, and that divide seems to reflect—as barbecue always has—larger societal and economic trends. Much of it has to do with capital. To meet fire codes and health department regulations, new restaurants that want to do all-wood cooking require significant investments. Those startup costs are compounded by customers' growing expectations of having "chef-driven" sides to enjoy along with their meal, and washing it down with craft beers or handmade cocktails. To open a successful barbecue restaurant these days, entrepreneurs have to go big, and that means they need financial backers with deep pockets. And they need to do it in a market that can support an average meal check of twenty dollars or more.

The market is quite different in the small towns that were once home to so many traditional barbecue restaurants. These have long tended to be smaller mom-and-pop places, and today they compete with global fast-food chains with paper-thin margins. Their customer base tends to approach barbecue not as a bucket-list culinary experience but as a regular meal, and most can't afford to pay more than seven or eight dollars for it. In 2015, Steve Grady—owner and pitmaster of Grady's Barbecue in Dudley, North Carolina lamented to the *Washington Post* that there were very few restaurants like his left. "Used to be a lot of barbecue places around here," he said. "Griffin's, Scott's, Holloway. About all of them are gone now." Grady himself was in his eighties, and he figured his restaurant would soon be gone, too, since none of his four sons had an interest in the business. That's proved to be the case with many barbecue families, as children seek less demanding and more lucrative careers and aren't inclined to take over family-run barbecue restaurants.[11]

The divergence has been particularly stark when it comes to race. The media frenzy that elevated pitmasters like Aaron Franklin to national fame largely ignored people of color. "The national press would have you believe barbecue is dominated by white hipster males," Texas food writer Robb Walsh groused in 2015, "but believe it or not, blacks, Latinos, and women are involved in the barbecue biz too." From Henry Perry and Matt Garner to Leon Finney and Ollie Gates, African American entrepreneurs were pioneers in the industry in the twentieth century, launching widely celebrated restaurants and helping establish the styles and conventions of their particular cities. In the twenty-first century, Rodney Scott and Bryan Furman are rare exceptions of African American barbecue restaurateurs who have managed to gain media attention in what is an increasingly PR-driven and capital-intensive business. In 2018, Furman told *Bon Appétit* that he was planning to change the logo of B's Cracklin' BBQ from a pig to a picture of his face. "I get tired of people coming here, thinking it's a white-owned business," he said. "You would not believe how many times I've been out there [on the restaurant patio], and they thought I'm the dishwasher or the cook."[12]

But there's reason to hope. In the past few years, there has been renewed interest in the less-celebrated restaurants and, in particular, in recognizing the full contributions of people of color to America's great barbecue traditions. Writers like Michael Twitty, author of *The Cooking Gene* (2017), have called out the mainstream food media for excluding African Americans from the cultural narrative of barbecue. Culinary historian Adrian Miller is at work on a book, tentatively titled *Black Smoke*, about the history of African American barbecue culture. In 2016, Jim Shahin of the *Washington Post* set out to visit as many under-the-radar African American–owned restaurants as he could and answer the question of whether black-owned barbecue joints are dying. "My travels have persuaded me," he wrote, "that there are more second- and third-generation black-owned barbecue restaurants than the world probably realizes. Just as the world doesn't fully realize the breadth of a largely invisible legacy." That legacy, we can hope, will be far less invisible in the future.[13]

And it's an important legacy, for barbecue is one of the most American of foods, and it's the one most intimately linked to the contours of the nation's history. It excites the passions of contemporary eaters, and it remains strong in Americans' memories, evoking nostalgia for "old-fashioned barbecue" eaten in years past. Barbecue's power to bring people together and establish community bonds has made it highly enduring. Yes, the tradition will continue to evolve over time, but for now, at least, its future seems secure.

NOTES

Chapter 1

1. Edward Ward, *The Barbacue Feast: or, the Three Pigs of Peckham, Broiled under an Apple-Tree* (London: 1707), 7–9. In the first edition of this book, I mistakenly concluded that Ward was describing a barbecue on the island of Jamaica. After all, Ward had visited Port Royal, Jamaica, in 1697 and recorded his experiences in *A Trip to Jamaica* (1698), and there is a community named Peckham in Jamaica. I have since obtained a complete and more legible copy of the book's text, and various details make clear that this was indeed an American-style barbecue staged in Peckham, England. "The Company now began to tumble in apace," Ward writes, "from the Dukedom of Bermondsey, the Broomary of Kent-street, the Merry-Banks of Rotherhithe, and the drunken little town of Deptford." Bermondsey, Rotherhithe, and Deptford were at the time separate towns and are now districts of South London. In my defense, Ward's convoluted prose is almost indecipherable to modern readers. The larger point—that the details of American-style barbecue were something new and very different to the English colonists—remains the same.

2. In *A History of South Carolina Barbeque* (2013), Lake High insists that barbecue was invented in what would eventually become South Carolina. He characterizes it as "the gift of two civilizations," one European and one Native American. He identifies the Spanish colony of Santa Elena (on the land now known as Parris Island, South Carolina) as the birthplace. Citing the drawings of Jacques le Moyne de Morgues, High notes that the local Cusabo peoples used an apparatus of green sticks to cook meats. He also notes that the Spanish brought pigs with them to Santa Elena and concludes that the two must have come together there in the short-lived colony to create barbecue.

In his book, High refers to the Civil War as the War for Southern Independence, and he adamantly denies what he terms "The Blacks Invented Barbeque Myth." Plantation workers, he asserts, "learned to cook barbeque the same way they learned to become cabinetmakers and blacksmiths: somebody needed the job done and showed them how to do it."

High's denial is probably the most extreme example of a writer excluding African Americans from the barbecue origin story. Most accounts simply omit African Americans without explicitly denying they played a role.

Michael Twitty, an African American food writer and culinary historian, has advanced a counternarrative that foregrounds the African influence. "Barbecue," he declared in the *Guardian* in 2015, "is as African as it is Native American and European." Twitty asserts that the word "barbecue" is itself West African in origin, noting that the Hausa "used the term 'babbake' to describe a complex of words referring to grilling, toasting, building a large fire, singeing hair or feathers and cooking food over a long period of time over an extravagant fire." Like High, he cites a Spanish colony, but an even earlier one: San Miguel de Guadalupe, which was founded somewhere on the Carolina coast by Lucas Vázquez de Ayllón in 1526 and lasted only three months. Twitty points out that enslaved Africans were among the six hundred settlers and that the Spanish brought pigs with them. "It was in that context," he concludes, "that barbecue made its debut on what is now American soil."

Both High's and Twitty's arguments are long on assertion and short on documentation. Neither cites any evidence that pigs were actually cooked barbecue style in these early Spanish colonies, and neither explains how the cooking technique might have spread from those short-lived, isolated settlements to the rest of the American mainland. Twitty's claim that barbecue descends from the Hausa word "babbake" sounds compelling (and is now routinely cited as fact in many internet accounts), but his case appears to be based solely on the similarity of the sounds of the words. He does not address the many centuries of written accounts linking "barbecue" and "barbacoa" to the Native American term for the hurdle of green sticks they used for cooking and drying food.

When I interviewed Lake High in 2014, he admitted that his Santa Elena argument was based on supposition instead of hard facts. "Writing history," he told me, "you either read what someone else wrote and pray that it's accurate, or you analyze the things yourself, draw your own conclusions, and pray that it's accurate." Instead of making definitive assertions and praying we are right, it seems a better approach to lay out the evidence that's available and admit where things are still murky, which is what I've attempted to do here. See Lake High, *A History of South Carolina Barbeque* (Charleston, SC: History Press, 2013); Michael Twitty, "Barbecue Is an American Tradition—of Enslaved Africans and Native Americans," *Guardian*, July 4, 2015.

3. Gonzalo Fernando de Oviedo, *A Natural History of the West Indies*, trans. and ed. Sterling

A. Stoudemire (1526; repr., Chapel Hill: University of North Carolina Press, 1959), 29. The original Spanish text describes the pits "que ellos llama barbacoas."

4. Jean de Léry, *Histoire d'un voyage fait en la terre du Bresil*, ed. Paul Gaffarel (Paris: A. Lemerre, 1880). Quotations translated by the author.

5. Robert Beverley, *The History of Virginia in Four Parts* (1705; repr., Richmond, VA: J. W. Randolph, 1855), 138; John Brickell, *The Natural History of North-Carolina* (Dublin, 1737), 340, 362.

6. *Diaries of Benjamin Lynde and of Benjamin Lynde, Jr.* (Cambridge, MA: Riverside Press, 1880), 138; Wilson Waters, *History of Chelmsford, Middlesex County, Massachusetts* (Lowell, MA: Courier-Citizen, 1917), 784; *The Holyoke Diaries*, ed. George Francis Dow (Salem, MA: Essex Institute, 1911), 50, 56; William D. Williamson, *The History of the State of Maine* (Hallowell, ME: Glazier, Masters, 1832), 340.

7. *Post Boy* (Boston), August 17, 1767, 3; *Boston News-Letter and New-England Chronicle*, May 25, 1769, 2.

8. Cultural historian David Hackett Fischer has identified these differences in feasting habits as part of the four distinct "folkways" in colonial America, a term that encompasses a wide range of cultural characteristics such as dialect, architecture, and social customs. These folkways are associated with geographic regions—New England, the Tidewater South, the Delaware Valley, and the Southern Highlands—and their characteristics derive from the regions in Britain from which each group came—East Anglia, southern England, the North Midlands, and the Borderlands, respectively. See David Hackett Fischer, *Albion's Seed: Four British Folkways in America* (New York: Oxford University Press, 1989), 353.

9. Daniel W. Gade, "Hogs," in *Cambridge World History of Food*, ed. Kenneth F. Kiple and Kriemhild Coneè Ornelas (New York: Cambridge University Press, 2000), 536–41; Virginia DeJohn Anderson, *Creatures of Empire* (New York: Oxford University Press, 2004), 98.

10. Gade, "Hogs," 536–41.

11. Anderson, *Creatures of Empire*, 115, 121.

12. Social historian Rhys Isaac has noted that in Virginia "most of the dominant values of the culture were fused together in the display of hospitality, which was one of the supreme obligations that society laid upon heads of households." *The Transformation of Virginia, 1740–1790* (New York: Norton, 1982), 71.

13. John Kirkpatrick to George Washington, July 21, 1758, in *Letters to Washington and Accompanying Papers*, ed. Stanislaus Murray Hamilton (New York: Houghton, Mifflin, 1899), 3:379; Donald Jackson and Dorothy Twohig, eds., *The Diaries of George Washington*, vol. 3, *1771–75* (Charlottesville: University Press of Virginia, 1976), 204.

14. "Letters from Lawrence Butler, of Westmoreland County, Virginia, to Mrs. Anna F. Cradock, Cumley House, near Harborough, Leicestershire, England," *Virginia Magazine of History and Biography* 40, no. 3 (July 1932): 259–67. Joseph R. Haynes uncovered this letter and published it in *Virginia Barbecue: A History* (2016), and it offers the most detailed description known to date of an eighteenth-century Virginia barbecue.

15. For descriptions of early Virginia elections, see Charles S. Sydnor, *American Revolutionaries in the Making: Political Practices in Washington's Virginia* (1952; repr., New York: Free Press, 1965), 26–29; Isaac, *Transformation of Virginia*, 111.

16. Charles Sydnor notes, "Many of the candidates may have been perfectly circumspect in their pre-election behavior, but all of them, with hardly an exception, relied on the persuasive powers of food and drink dispensed to the voters with open-handed liberality." *American Revolutionaries*, 51.

17. Richard R. Beeman, "Deference, Republicanism, and the Emergence of Popular Politics in Eighteenth-Century America," *William and Mary Quarterly*, 3rd ser., 49 (July 1992): 414–18; Isaac, *Transformation of Virginia*, 112.

18. Washington to James Wood, July 28, 1758, quoted in Beeman, "Deference, Republicanism," 418. Richard Beeman and others have argued that although the hierarchical nature of the elections was predicated on the concept of voters' "deference" to their social superiors, practices such as treating marked the beginning of a trend of voters' using the ballot to advance their own interests. The Virginia gentry professed the classical Republican ideal of a disinterested elite governing for the public good with the deferential consent of the common citizens, but barbecues and other forms of treating were early signs that voters were exerting a certain amount of power and that their will would have to be respected. This changing tide was noticeable in Tidewater Virginia, where the social structure was relatively stable and well defined, but it would be even more evident on the frontier, where the social order was less certain and ordinary citizens were much more likely to demand that their representatives cater to their personal interests. In these environments, public gatherings such as barbecues would take on increased importance as venues where ambitious men could establish themselves in politics.

19. C. W., "HO'R B. I. Ode iv, Imitated," *Gentleman's Magazine, and Historical Chronicle*, no. 23, 240–41. "C. W." is likely Charles Woodmason, a clergyman who arrived in Charles Town in 1752, bought land and became a planter, and then fell into disrepute after applying to become a stamp distributor in the wake of the 1765 Stamp Act. He spent the next eight years as an itinerant Anglican minister in the Carolina backcountry.

20. William John Grayson, "Autobiography of William John Grayson," ed. Samuel Gaillard Stoney, *South Carolina Historical and Genealogical Magazine* 49 (1948): 25–26.

21. "On the Fall of the Barbacue-House at Beaufort, S.C. during the Late Tremendous Storm," *Charleston Courier*, November 1, 1804, 2; John Hammond Moore, *The Confederate Housewife* (Columbia, SC: Summerhouse Press, 1997), 15; Grayson, "Autobiography," 37. Moore's two-page discussion of barbecue in antebellum South Carolina was one of the first scholarly treatments of the subject, and I am indebted to it for helping me find the trail of early newspaper accounts of barbecues.

22. William Henry Foote, *Sketches of North Carolina, Historical and Biographical, Illustrative of the Principles of a Portion of Her Early Settlers* (New York: 1846), 49.

23. Charles Woodmason, *The Carolina Backcountry on the Eve of the Revolution*, ed. Richard S. Hooker (Chapel Hill: University of North Carolina Press, 1953), 55; Spartanburg Unit of the Writers' Program of the WPA, *A History of Spartanburg County* (Spartanburg, SC: Band & White, 1940), 21.

Chapter 2

1. "Occoney Station, July 4th," *Miller's Weekly Messenger* (Pendleton, SC), July 9, 1808, 3.

2. John James Audubon, *Delineations of American Scenery and Character* (New York: G. A. Baker, 1926), 241. The exact date of the barbecue attended by Audubon is uncertain. The description, which was one of a set of essays originally published interspersed among the bird articles and illustrations in *Ornithological Biography*, was composed sometime during the 1830s, and in it Audubon comments that "although more than twenty years have elapsed since I joined a Kentucky Barbecue, my spirit is refreshed every 4th of July by the recollection of that day's merriment." This suggests the event occurred sometime during the 1810s.

3. This advertisement was quoted in full in the *Salem (MA) Gazette* on June 30, 1815. The northern editor took great delight in mocking the prospect of such an event: "Now, reader, suffer your fancy for one moment to revel on this picture of felicity—a hot July day—mercury at 94°—the earth parched and thirsty—every breeze like the breath of a furnace, wafting dust into your throat, nose, and eyes—around the festal board a thick clutter of ladies who had been liberally 'furnished with foreign liquors' & gentlemen who had 'free access to the use of domestic liquors'—before you on the groaning table, mountain high, an entire Swine broiled and roasted, its skin crisp and brown—making you perspire at the very thought of the flames by which it had been scorched—why, it is enough to make the 'solid flesh to melt' and dissolve into a thin dew!"

4. *Camden (SC) Journal*, July 2, 1831, 3.

5. *Jackson (TN) Gazette*, July 10, 1824, 3; *Greenville (SC) Mountaineer*, July 13, 1834, 1.

6. Manuscript from the Folklore Project of the WPA Federal Writers' Project. "American

Life Histories: Manuscripts from the Federal Writers' Project, 1936 to 1940," accessed October 10, 2008, www.loc.gov.

7. *Greenville (SC) Mountaineer*, July 12, 1834.

8. *North-Carolina Gazette*, July 10, 1778, quoted in Alan D. Watson, ed., *Society in Early North Carolina: A Documentary History* (Raleigh, NC: Division of Archives and History, 2000), 314. *Camden Journal*, July 8, 1826.

9. *Jackson (TN) Gazette*, June 5, 1824, 12; *Camden (SC) Journal*, July 2, 1831, 3. Committees of Arrangements were common practice not only for July Fourth celebrations but for a variety of civic and social events such as banquets and dances.

10. Willie Lee Nichols Rose, *A Documentary History of Slavery in North America* (Athens: University of Georgia Press, 1999), 107–10.

11. Robert B. McAfee, *The Life and Times of Robert B. McAfee and His Family and Connetions. Written by Himself* (1845), transcribed by Jenny Tenlen, accessed July 18, 2018, jtenlen. drizzlehosting.com.

12. David Crockett, *A Narrative of the Life of David Crockett of the State of Tennessee* (Philadelphia: Carey and Hart, 1834), 137.

13. Quoted by Daniel S. Dupre, *Transforming the Cotton Frontier: Madison County, Alabama, 1800–1840* (Baton Rouge: Louisiana State University Press, 1997), 172, 179–80. In his study of early politics in Madison County, Dupre found that "each year newspaper notices of several barbecues a week enticed people away from their labors with the promise of food, drink, excitement, and sociability."

14. Library of Congress Printed Ephemera Collection, Portfolio 29, Folder 13, American Memory, accessed March 8, 2008, hdl.loc.gov; "Improved Mode of Electioneering," *Norwich (CT) Courier*, October 12, 1825, 2.

15. "Barbecuensis," letter to the editor, *Southern Advocate*, July 13, 1827, quoted in Dupre, *Transforming the Cotton Frontier*, 182. Gander pulling was a particularly cruel form of frontier entertainment in which a large gander was tied to a fence post or similar platform so that participants could charge past on horseback, competing to be the first to grab the bird's neck and wrench it from its body.

16. *Southern Advocate*, April 28, 1828, and *Huntsville Democrat*, March 14, 1828, both quoted in Dupre, *Transforming the Cotton Frontier*, 184.

17. Dupre, *Transforming the Cotton Frontier*, 188.

18. *National Party Conventions, 1831–1988* (Washington, DC: Congressional Quarterly, 1991), 5.

19. It would be a mistake to assume, as Barbecuensis and his fellow Alabama antipopulists

did, that just because new campaign practices appealed to a broad audience they necessarily required politicians to stoop to base demagoguery. Yes, there was plenty of guzzling and gorging going on at the typical campaign barbecue, but the gatherings were more than just a craven exchange of food and drink for votes. As they became more formalized, barbecues began to contribute to, not diminish, the process of informed democracy. At the same time that politicians were slapping backs and cracking jokes at these gatherings, they were also getting to meet their constituents in person and hearing their wants and opinions. Some stump speeches were little more than florid oratory, but many turned into sophisticated debates on vital issues. Newspapers began printing the full text of speeches delivered at barbecues, sometimes taken directly from the orator's prepared text but more often transcribed word for word by a correspondent on the scene.

20. *Pendleton (SC) Messenger*, September 7, 1838, 3.

21. Philip Hone, *The Diary of Philip Hone*, ed. Alan Nevins (New York: Dodd, Mead, 1927), 264; Floyd C. Shoemaker, *Missouri—Day by Day* (Columbia: State Historical Society of Missouri, 1942), 399.

22. Clyde N. Wilson, ed., *The Papers of John C. Calhoun*, vol. 10, *1837–1839* (Columbia: University of South Carolina Press, 1981), 406. During the Jackson administration, Calhoun had defended the Bank of the United States against the assaults by the president, who was determined to dissolve the institution and place its deposits in selected state banks. In 1838, however, Calhoun changed his position and supported Martin Van Buren's plan to keep in place federal currency not in a national bank but in government-owned vaults, or "subtreasuries." Calhoun did not consider his shift to be inconsistent, since he viewed the deposit of federal funds in any bank—whether a national one or multiple state banks—to be a source of political corruption. But his sudden switch to the administration's subtreasury system created confusion and turmoil among South Carolina's political leaders, who had previously been stalwart defenders of the Bank. Some—most notably US senator William Preston and Representative Waddy Thompson Jr.—began negotiations with national Whig leaders such as Henry Clay over the possibility of creating a Whig party in South Carolina. The prospect of such party developments appalled Calhoun, who feared it would undermine the state's unity on issues of states' rights and defending slavery.

Two days after the Sandy Spring Church barbecue, Calhoun accepted an invitation "in the name of many of the citizens of Anderson District, who approve of my course on the great and agitating question of the day" to attend a barbecue dinner in Anderson. Though initially planned as a partisan gathering, the barbecue was merged with a similar event being organized for Waddy Thompson Jr., and the two men began to again debate the subtreasury issue head-to-head. Even when Calhoun was not able to attend barbecues in person, he used them to advance his arguments in the debate over the Bank. In late August 1838, he received an invitation from "the Republican and States Rights citizens of Richland district" on September 8. In a long letter to the Committee of Arrangements, Calhoun declined the invitation, citing "the season of the year, the great distance, and other causes not necessary to state," and then began a two-thousand-word discourse attacking the philosophy behind a National Bank and defending states' rights. The letter was intended as a public statement, and it was presumably read to the crowd at the barbecue. It was also printed in at least eleven newspapers, including local organs such as the *Columbia (SC) Telescope* and the *Charleston (SC) Courier* as well as out-of-state newspapers such as the *Richmond (VA) Enquirer* and the *Daily National Intelligencer* of Washington, DC. Calhoun wrote similar letters declining barbecues in Columbia, South Carolina, in July 1838 and Yanceyville, North Carolina, in September, on both occasions writing long public statements on the subtreasury and states' rights issues. In this manner, he was able to make his arguments reach far beyond the attendees of the barbecues to newspaper readers throughout the country. See Wilson, *Papers of John C. Calhoun*, 10:410.

23. "Mr. Kincaid's Address," *Burlington (VT) Weekly Free Press*, August 21, 1829, 1; Frederick Law Olmsted, "Historical Notes of the Capitol Ground," *Papers of Frederick Law Olmsted*, vol. 3, *The Early Boston Years* (Baltimore: Johns Hopkins University Press, 2013): 114–15; Haynes, *Virginia Barbecue*, 194–96. The barbecue groves fell into disuse after the Civil War, and by the time Olmsted wrote his historical sketch in 1883, the trees that remained were "feeble, top heavy, and ill grown." A few of the "barbecue trees" survived on the Capitol Grounds through the 1920s. The story of the Capitol's barbecue groves was rediscovered by Virginia barbecue historian Joe Haynes.

24. Samuel Eliot Morison, *The Oxford History of the American People* (New York: Oxford University Press, 1965), 456; Elizabeth R. Varon, "Tippecanoe and the Ladies, Too: White Women and Party Politics in Antebellum Virginia," *Journal of American History* 82 (September 1995): 498.

25. Morison, *Oxford History*, 458; Franklin Gorin, *The Times of Long Ago* (Louisville, KY: John P. Morton, 1929), 102; Edmund L. Starling, *History of Henderson County, Kentucky* (Henderson, KY, 1887), 172; David F. Wilcox, ed., *Quincy and Adams County: History and Representative Men* (Chicago: Lewis, 1919), 613.

26. James Edmonds Saunders, *Early Settlers of Alabama* (New Orleans: L. Graham & Son, 1899), 311.

Chapter 3

1. Quoted in Varon, "Tippecanoe and the Ladies, Too," 509.

2. "Hon. Preston S. Brooks at Home," *Charleston (SC) Daily Courier*, October 7, 1856, 1.

3. Lewis W. McKee and Lydia K. Bond, *A History of Anderson County, KY* (Baltimore: Regional Publishing, 1975), 141; *Cheraw (SC) Gazette*, July 12, 1837, 43; Frederic Richard Lees, *An Argument for the Legislative Prohibition of the Liquor Traffic* (London: William Tweedie, 1857), 287. These early reform efforts did not make their way into actual legislation, though in 1833 the Tennessee legislature passed an act dictating that any person preparing a barbecue within one mile of a worshipping church assembly "shall be dealt with as rioters at common law, and shall be fined in a sum not less than five dollars." *American Annual Register for the Year 1832–33* (New York: William Jackson, 1835), 310.

4. Ian R. Tyrell, "Drink and Temperance in the Antebellum South: An Overview and Interpretation," *Journal of Southern History* 48 (November 1982): 489. Temperance advocates frequently repeated the story of Paul Denton, an itinerant Methodist preacher, as a reformer who could give as good as he got. Denton reportedly held a camp meeting in one of the roughest, most disreputable districts in Texas, and he issued handbills announcing a grand barbecue where "the best drink in the world will be furnished, free." Predictably, a huge crowd turned out. When the rougher element demanded the liquor, Denton gestured to a spring near the grove and said, "There is the drink I promised! Not in simmering stills, over smoky fires, choked with poisonous gasses, and surrounded with the stench of sickening odors and rank corruptions, doth your Father in heaven prepare the precious essence of life, the pure cold water, but in the green glade and grassy dell, where the red deer wanders and the child loves to play, there God brews it." The crowd's reaction to Denton's trick is not recorded in any of the accounts, but the anecdote is most likely apocryphal. For example, see John W. Berry, *Uniac: His Life, Struggle, and Fall* (A. Mudge & Sons, 1871), 88–89; and Peter Turner Winskill, *The Temperance Movement and Its Workers: A Record of Social, Moral, Religious, and Political Progress* (London: Blackie & Sons, 1892), 52–53.

5. *South Carolina Temperance Advocate*, July 23, 1846.

6. Lee L. Willis III, "The Road to Prohibition: Religion and Political Culture in Middle Florida, 1821–1920" (PhD diss., Florida State University, 2006). Temperance barbecues were not limited to the South. On July 4, 1843, attendees from local churches assembled in Norwich Township near Columbus, Ohio, for an event that paralleled the traditional Independence Day barbecue format. "Temperance melodies" were substituted for some of the patriotic songs on the procession to the barbecue grove. The speaker was one Mr. Moseley, "the distinguished Washingtonian and efficient temperance advocate," whose oration addressed "the history of our institutions, their nature, and the tendency of the mighty temperance reformation to the perpetuity." "Temperance Barbecue of July Fourth in Norwich Township," *Weekly Ohio State Journal*, July 19, 1843, 2.

7. Mary E. Moragné, *The Neglected Thread: A Journal from the Calhoun Community, 1836–1842*, ed. Delle Mullen Craven (Columbia: University of South Carolina Press, 1951), 42; *Greenville (SC) Mountaineer*, July 14, 1843, 1, and July 12, 1844, 1.

8. *Savannah (GA) Daily Advertiser*, July 1, 1871, 2, and August 18, 1871, 2.

9. "Barbecue at Huguenot Springs," *Richmond (VA) Commercial Compiler*, June 4, 1846, 2; "An 'Old Virginia' Barbecue," *Alexandria (VA) Gazette*, September 14, 1849, 2.

10. "A Brunswick Stew," *Petersburg (VA) Intelligencer*, repr., *Alexandria (VA) Gazette*, June 26, 1855, 4.

11. "Brunswick Stew," *Exchange*, repr., *Pickens County Herald and West Alabamian*, September 26, 1977, 1; "'Brunswick Stew': The Origin of One of Our Most Delicious Stews," *Petersburg (VA) Index-Appeal*, repr., *Macon (GA) Telegraph*, August 19, 1886; *Brunswick County, Virginia: Information for the Homeseeker and Investor* (Richmond, VA: Williams Printing, 1907), 22. The last item, compiled by attorney Marvin Smithey under the supervision of I. E. Spatig, the commissioner of Brunswick County, Virginia, was a promotional pamphlet that included a capsule history of the county and solicited letters from residents of the Red Oak District to trace the history of the county's famous stew. The responses largely confirm and elaborate the story from the *Petersburg Index-Appeal*, and the pamphlet has been the source for most historical accounts of the stew's origins.

All of these accounts were written decades after the stew had become a popular Virginia dish, and the details vary considerably among them. The 1877 *Exchange* account, for instance, claimed that "Mr. John Haskins, of the famous 'Red Oak' neighborhood, was the originator of it," and he did so in the 1840s during the time of the Harrison and Tyler presidential campaign. The letter from "Tar Heel" in the *Index-Appeal* identified James Matthews as the originator and claimed he started making the stew in 1816; one of the correspondents in Smithey and Spatig's pamphlet recalled that Matthews earned his reputation "about 1828." Taken together, though, the evidence points clearly to the Red Oak neighborhood of Brunswick County as the place of origin, with James Matthews being the first to earn a reputation for cooking Brunswick stew.

Later accounts have taken these details and tried to pin down the creation to a very specific time and place. One often-repeated story claims that the stew was invented at a squirrel hunt in 1828 by James "Uncle Jimmy" Matthews. The stew is frequently described as an improvisation, with Matthews concocting the stew from squirrels, butter, onions, and bread after the venison or other meat the hunting party planned to eat spoiled. Various versions identify Matthews as the "family cook," "retainer," or "manservant" for Dr. Creed Haskins of Brunswick County, and later writers have assumed from those descriptions that "Uncle Jimmy" was a black man, most likely a slave owned by Haskins. The earlier accounts, like that of "Tar Heel" in the *Index-Appeal*, however, clearly portray Matthews as a white "man of refinement" from the Red Oak neighborhood and that "it was his way of cooking the squirrels which gained him such popularity and eclat with the ladies."

12. Marion Harland, *Marion Harland's Autobiography: The Story of a Long Life* (New York: Harper & Brothers, 1910), 124–25.

13. *Warrenton (NC) Gazette*, June 10, 1873, 3; Marion Cabell Tyree, *Housekeeping in Old Virginia* (Louisville, KY: John P. Morton, 1878): 212–13.

14. The details of the Nat Turner barbecue can be found in Thomas Wentworth Higginson, "Nat Turner's Insurrection," *Atlantic Monthly*, August 1861, 173.

15. Louis Hughes, *Thirty Years a Slave: From Bondage to Freedom* (Milwaukee: South Side Printing, 1897), 50; "Mose Davis," *Slave Narratives: A Folk History of Slavery in the United States from Interviews with Former Slaves*, vol. 4, *Georgia Narratives*, Part 1 (Washington, DC: Library of Congress, 1941), 1.

16. Virginia Tunstall Clay-Clopton, *A Belle of the Fifties: Memoirs of Mrs. Clay of Alabama, Covering Social and Political Life in Washington and the South, 1853–66*, ed. Ada Sterling (New York: Doubleday, Page, 1904), 217.

17. "Mahala Jewel," *Slave Narratives: A Folk History of Slavery in the United States from Interviews with Former Slaves*, vol. 4, *Georgia Narratives*, Part 2 (Washington, DC: Library of Congress, 1941), 315.

18. Hughes, *Thirty Years*, 46–47; Walter L. Fleming, *Civil War and Reconstruction in Alabama* (New York: Columbia University Press, 1905), 243.

19. Frederick Douglass, *Narrative of the Life of Frederick Douglass* (1845; repr., New York: Penguin, 1982), 116.

20. "Estella Jones," *Slave Narratives: A Folk History of Slavery in the United States from Interviews with Former Slaves*, vol. 4, *Georgia Narratives*, Part 2 (Washington, DC: Library of Congress, 1941), 350.

21. See John F. Stover, *American Railroads*, 2nd ed. (Chicago: University of Chicago Press, 1997), 28–31.

22. *Charleston (SC) Courier*, July 16, 1847, 2.

23. Stover, *American Railroads*, 35; Robert T. Hubard to Edward W. Hubard, June 30, 1860, Hubard Family Papers, University of North Carolina Southern History Collection, Series 1.9–1.10, Reel 18.

24. *Charleston (SC) News & Courier*, June 21, 1842, and June 29, 1842.

25. Karl Jack Bauer, *The Mexican War, 1846–1848* (Lincoln: University of Nebraska Press, 1992), 69–70.

26. J. H. Wallace, "History of Kosciusko and Attala County," 1916, Attala County, accessed September 2, 2018, attala-county-history-genealogy.org.

27. Oran Perry, ed., *Indiana in the Mexican War* (Indianapolis: State of Indiana, 1909).

28. "Public Dinner to Col. Moore," *Austin (TX) City Gazette*, November 11, 1840, 3; Ernestine Sewell Linck and Joyce Gibson Roach, *Eats: A Folk History of Texas Foods* (Fort Worth: Texas Christian University Press, 1989), 146.

29. Advertisement, *Clarksville (TX) Northern Standard*, August 5, 1848, 3; "Barbecue on the Fourth of July," *Victoria (TX) Advocate*, June 7, 1850, 2.

30. "Fourth of July on the California Trail," *Philadelphia North American and United States Gazette*, October 3, 1849, 1.

31. "News from California," *Pittsfield (MA) Sun*, August 29, 1850, 2.

32. "Celebration of the Fourth in Suisun Valley," *San Francisco Daily Placer Times and Transcript*, July 11, 1853, 1.

33. "The Political Barbecue at San Jose," *San Francisco Alta California*, October 6, 1856, 7; *Lowell (MA) Daily Citizen and News*, November 25, 1856, 2.

34. Fanny G. Hazlet and Gertrude Hazlet Randall, "Historical Sketch and Reminiscences of Dayton, Nevada," in *Nevada Historical Society Papers, 1921–1922* (Reno: Nevada Historical Society, 1922), 16.

Chapter 4

1. Charles Sumner, "The Crime against Kansas," Wikisource, accessed September 2, 2018, en.wikisource.org.

2. "Hon. Preston S. Brooks at Home," *Charleston (SC) Daily Courier*, October 7, 1856, 1.

3. "Mr. Breckinridge Accepts an Invitation to Speak," *Washington (DC) Constitution*, August 28, 1860.

4. "The Breckinridge Barbecue," *New York Herald*, September 4, 1860, 1.

5. "The Great Kentucky Meeting," *Washington (DC) Constitution*, September 7, 1860, 2.

6. "The Douglas Barbecue," *New York Herald*, September 13, 1860, 3.

7. "From Our Own Correspondent," *Washington (DC) Constitution*, September 14, 1860, 2; background information on Bryan Lawrence is taken from genealogists' notes posted on the RootsWeb message board, accessed September 21, 2008, news.rootsweb.com.

8. "From Our Own Correspondent," 2.

9. H. M. Hamill, *The Old South: A Monograph* (Dallas: Smith & Lamar, 1904), 58–59.

10. Hamill, 59–60. A similar account appears in Mollie Hollifield, *Auburn: Loveliest Village of the Plain* (Auburn, AL: Auburn Bicentennial Committee, 1955), 10–14.

11. "From Port Sullivan," *Austin (TX) State Gazette*, March 9, 1861, 1; "Hurrah for San Augustine," *Austin (TX) State Gazette*, March 16, 1861, 1.

12. Robert E. Corlew, *Tennessee: A Short History* (Knoxville: University of Tennessee Press, 1981), 291–94.

13. B. G. Brazelton, *A History of Hardin County* (Nashville: Cumberland Presbyterian, 1885), 60–61. Tennessee's northern neighbor, Kentucky, staked out a position of neutrality, refusing to join the South in secession but also refusing to send troops to the federal army. In June 1861, "a grand Union barbecue" was given by the citizens of Oldham County, Kentucky, for their neighbors across the Ohio River in Clark County, Indiana. Over five thousand people attended, including one thousand women, and the *New York Herald* reported on June 17, 1861, "The Union sentiment was strong, and the feeling exhibited against rebels and traitors was very bitter." A few days later, the people of Woodford, Kentucky, held a large barbecue in honor of John J. Crittenden and the recent Union victory he helped lead, and Crittenden delivered a stirring speech in favor of neutrality and peace ("Crittenden Festival," *Philadelphia Inquirer*, July 4, 1861).

The secessionist forces in Kentucky were not silent. After losing the presidential race, John C. Breckinridge had returned to the US Senate and participated in a series of anti-Lincoln rallies in his home state. On September 5, the secessionists organized "a grand barbecue" in Owen County, about twelve miles from the state capital of Frankfort, where the legislature was about to convene to consider resolutions to more firmly bind Kentucky to the Union. The prosecession State Guard was invited, and some ten thousand people turned out in support of the cause. The Owen County meeting raised fears among the Unionists that an armed revolt was brewing, but the rallies were in fact the last gasp of the secession cause. After Confederate forces moved into the westernmost part of the state in early September, the legislature abandoned its neutrality and aligned itself with the federal government of the United States. At a barbecue in the woods owned by William Buford in Woodford County, Breckinridge and other secessionist leaders delivered farewell addresses to their supporters. On September 19, an armed federal force from Camp Dick Robinson began moving toward Lexington with orders to arrest Breckinridge. Warned of the movement, Breckinridge fled on horseback and made his way east to Richmond, Virginia, to cast his lot with the Confederacy. See Frank H. Heck, "John C. Breckinridge in the Crisis of 1860–1861," *Journal of Southern History* 21 (1955): 339–44; W. M. Railey, *History of Woodford County* (Frankfort, KY: Roberts, 1928), 91.

14. "Presentation to the Pennsylvania Twenty-Third," *Philadelphia Inquirer*, December 16, 1861.

15. "Mr. Cushing," *Houston Telegraph*, May 22, 1863, 4; "Barbecue and Fair," *Houston*

Telegraph, August 10, 1863, 2; "The Richmond Dinner," *Washington (AR) Telegraph*, August 19, 1863.

16. Thomas Wentworth Higginson, *Army Life in a Black Regiment* (1870; repr., New York: Penguin, 1997), 28.

17. Susie King Taylor, *A Black Woman's Civil War Memoirs*, ed. Patricia W. Romero and Willie Lee Rose (1902; repr., New York: L. Marcus Wiener, 1998), 49.

18. Eliza Frances Andrews, *The War-Time Journal of a Georgia Girl, 1864–1865* (New York: Appleton, 1908), 324.

19. Andrews, 324–30.

Chapter 5

1. Quoted in William H. Wiggins Jr., *O Freedom! Afro-American Emancipation Celebrations* (Knoxville: University of Tennessee Press, 1987), xvii.

2. Wiggins, *O Freedom*, xix.

3. Jones quoted in Robb Walsh, *Legends of Texas Barbecue Cookbook* (San Francisco: Chronicle Books, 2002), 114–15; see "Emancipation Park," Houston Parks and Recreation Department, accessed June 30, 2018, www.houstontx.gov.

4. "The Day Elsewhere," *Dallas Morning News*, June 20, 1893, 8; "Emancipation Day," *Dallas Morning News*, June 19, 1898, 4. The first appearance of the word "Juneteenth" in newspaper accounts of Emancipation Day celebrations is likely in the *Fort Worth Star Telegram*, June 16, 1903, which notes, "Prominent Negroes declare that the 'Juneteenth' celebration, which will be held here next Friday, will be the biggest thing that the colored people of Washington county have ever attempted."

5. "Mrs. Ella Boney," American Life Histories, manuscripts from the Federal Writers' Project, 1936–1940, Library of Congress, accessed June 30, 2018, www.loc.gov.

6. "Letter from Putnam," *Macon (GA) Telegraph*, July 19, 1866. The correspondent for the *Telegraph* highly approved of the theme of Turner's address and editorialized, "Other speakers should talk to the Negroes in the same way. The Southern people must have control of their education, and must win back, and hold the affection and esteem which were so nearly destroyed by Yankee emissaries."

7. "Mississippi. The Democratic Canvass," *Memphis Daily Avalanche*, June 17, 1868, 1.

8. The figure of forty-three votes is cited in "Grand Radical Barbecue," *Arkansas Gazette* (Little Rock), July 28, 1868, 1.

9. Keith S. Bohannon, "'These Few Grey-Haired, Battle-Scarred Veterans': Confederate Army Reunions in Georgia, 1885–1895," in *The Myth of the Lost Cause and Civil War History*,

ed. Gary W. Gallagher and Alan T. Nolan (Bloomington: Indiana University Press, 2000), 99.

10. Matthew J. Graham, *The Ninth Regiment New York Volunteers (Hawkins' Zouaves)* (New York: P. P. Cory, 1900), 466, 473; Mattie Thomas Thompson, *History of Barbour County, Alabama* (Eufaula, AL, 1939), 415.

11. *Perry (IA) Chief*, August 12, 1887, 12; *Mexia (TX) Evening News*, June 4, 1900, 1; "What a Real Barbecue Is," *Springfield (MA) Republican*, August 9, 1896, 8.

12. "'Big Sheriff' Callaway of Wilkes Returns after 25 Years of Service," *Atlanta Constitution*, April 8, 1906, 8.

13. "In the Barbecue County," *Atlanta Constitution*, August 26, 1889, 2.

14. "At Stone Mountain," *Atlanta Constitution*, June 12, 1890, 4.

15. "With Colonel Adair," *Atlanta Constitution*, September 22, 1893, 5; "A Real Georgia 'Cue," *Atlanta Constitution*, May 3, 1894, 5.

16. "Stone Mountain Barbecue," *Troy Times*, repr., *Sabetha (KS) Republican-Herald*, June 29, 1894, 7; Eliza Archard Conner, "Complimentary 'Q,'" *Akron (OH) Daily Democrat*, June 27, 1894, 2.

17. Conner, "Complimentary 'Q,'" 2.

18. "With Colonel Adair," *Atlanta Constitution*, September 22, 1893, 5.

19. Conner, "Complimentary 'Q,'" 2.

20. "'Big Sheriff' Callaway of Wilkes Returns after 25 Years of Service," *Atlanta Constitution*, April 8, 1906, 8; "The Passing Throng," *Atlanta Constitution*, July 2, 1894, 29.

21. Susan Foster Jones, *The Atlanta Exposition* (Charleston, SC: Arcadia, 2010): 7–8.

22. "Plans Coming In," *Atlanta Constitution*, September 1, 1894, 5.

23. "Guests of Southerners," *New York Times*, June 4, 1895; "Atlanta's Coming Show," *New York Times*, June 16, 1895, 28.

24. Maude Andrews, "The Georgia Barbecue," *Harper's Weekly*, November 9, 1895, 1072; "At a Barbecue," *Harper's Weekly*, October 24, 1896, 1051; John R. Watkins, "Barbecues," *Strand Magazine* 16 (1809): 463.

25. "'Big Sheriff' Callaway of Wilkes Returns after 25 Years of Service," *Atlanta Constitution*, April 8, 1906, 8.

26. "At Stone Mountain," *Atlanta Constitution*, June 12, 1890, 4.

27. "1870 United States Federal Census," Militia District 164, Wilkes, GA; roll M593_184, page 245A, image 90200, Family History Library Film 545683; "1860 U.S. Federal Census— Slave Schedules," accessed 2010, all at Ancestry.com.

28. "John W. Callaway Is Dead; Far-Famed as 'Cue Artist," *Atlanta Constitution*, February 11, 1915, 7.

29. Information about Wilkes's farm is taken from the the 1880 Agricultural Census, which is unfortunately the latest that survives (the 1890 records were destroyed by fire and later decades were ordered destroyed by Congress). "U.S., Selected Federal Census Non-Population Schedules, 1850–1880," Agricultural Schedule, 1880, Washington, Wilkes, GA; Archive Collection Number T1137, roll T1137:20, page 04, line 6, accessed 2010, Ancestry.com.

30. "South Carolina News," *Augusta Chronicle*, October 19, 1875, 1.

31. "What People Say," *Augusta (GA) Chronicle*, May 13, 1888, 2; "Royal Entertainers," *Augusta (GA) Chronicle*, June 6, 1899, 5.

32. "A Hen Barbecue," *Augusta (GA) Chronicle*, October 7, 1898, 5.

33. Advertisements, *Augusta (GA) Chronicle*, December 18, 1898, 11, 13; *Maloney's 1899 Augusta City Directory*, 674.

34. "Knights Templar Conclave Closed," *Augusta (GA) Chronicle*, May 5, 1899, 5.

35. "Had Enjoyable Time about Hundred Augustans Were the Guests of Mr. Charles S. Bohler," *Augusta (GA) Chronicle*, November 30, 1906, 9; "Glorious Fourth at Lakeview," *Augusta (GA) Chronicle*, June 28, 1908, 13. For Jones Wells & Co., see *Augusta City Directories, 1901–1903*.

36. "Will of John A. Bohler," *Will Books, 1777–1900, Georgia*. Court of Ordinary (Richmond County), 391. Accessed in 2010 via "Georgia, Wills and Probate Records, 1742–1992," Ancestry.com.

37. "Eats O'Possum and Talks Law: President-Elect Partakes of a Genuine Georgia Feast," *Macon (GA) Telegraph*, January 12, 1909, 1; "Barbecue Dinner by Mr. C. S. Bohler," *Augusta (GA) Chronicle*, January 12, 1909, 7.

38. "Pick, the Famous 'Cue Cook' Died Suddenly Yesterday," *Augusta (GA) Chronicle*, August 19, 1909, 3; "Famous 'Cue Cook Dies," *State* (Columbia, SC), August 19, 1909, 8; "Taft's Barbecue Cook Drops Dead," *New York Times*, August 19, 1909, 7.

39. "Boss of Burgoo and Barbecue," *New York Sun*, June 3, 1906, 7.

40. For a typical example, see *The WPA Guide to Kentucky*, ed. F. Kevin Simon (1939; repr., Lexington: University Press of Kentucky, 1996), 354.

41. R. Gerald Alvey, *Kentucky Bluegrass Country* (Jackson: University Press of Mississippi, 2000), 270. According to Confederate regiment rolls and enlistment records, two similarly named Jauberts served in the Confederate army. On July 1, 1862, a Gustavus Jaubert enlisted at Chattanooga, Tennessee, in Company B of John Hunt Morgan's Second Cavalry Regiment, Kentucky. A Gus Jaubert enlisted in the First Kentucky Infantry in Louisville, Kentucky, entering as a private on April 23, 1861, and being promoted to fourth corporal on April 30, 1862. A 1906 profile of Jaubert in the *New York Sun* reported that the burgoo maker served

four years in the First Kentucky Infantry. Since Gus Jaubert himself was interviewed for this profile, it seems likely that the *Sun's* account is correct.

42. "Boss of Burgoo and Barbecue," 7; *Lexington (KY) Central Record*, November 4, 1904, 1.

43. "Louisville Encampment," *Decatur (IL) Evening Bulletin*, September 13, 1895, 9; "Boss of Burgoo and Barbecue," 7. With credentials like this, it would seem hard for any cook to compete with Jaubert for the title of Kentucky's Burgoo King, but some tried. On July 2, 1904, the *Frankfort (KY) Roundabout* announced that David Kirkpatrick, manager of French's Restaurant, had been awarded the contract to make the burgoo for the local Fourth of July celebration, contending that "Dave is an experienced hand at the business and can make as good burgoo as Gus Jaubert, 'or any other man.'"

44. Ward, *Barbecue Feast*, 7–9.

45. Lettice Bryan, *The Kentucky Housewife* (Cincinnati: Shepard & Stearns, 1839), 95–96. Mrs. A. P. Hill, *Mrs. Hill's New Cook Book* (1872), repr. as *Mrs. Hill's Southern Practical Cookery and Receipt Book* (Columbia: University of South Carolina Press, 1995), 171.

46. *My Ride to the Barbecue: or, Revolutionary Reminiscences of the Old Dominion* (New York: S. A. Rollo, 1860), 58–59; "At a Barbecue," *Harper's Weekly*, October 24, 1896, 1051; Alex E. Sweet and J. Armoy Knox, *On a Mexican Mustang through Texas: From the Gulf to the Rio Grande* (Hartford, CT: S. S. Scranton, 1883), 437.

Chapter 6

1. US Census Bureau, "1990 Census of Population and Housing," 5, accessed July 1, 2018, www.census.gov. In 1920, 51.2 percent of the population lived in cities or suburbs, while 48.8 percent lived in rural areas.

2. Daniel Vaughn, "The First Barbecue Joint in Texas?," *Texas Monthly*, February 23, 2016; *Bastrop (TX) Advertiser*, August 28, 1886, 3; *Bastrop (TX) Advertiser*, October 2, 1886, 2.

3. "Local Briefs," *San Marcos (TX) Free Press*, July 19, 1888, 3; "Cheap Cash Market," *Waco (TX) Evening News*, September 24, 1888, 3.

4. *Los Angeles Times*, September 26, 1894, 6; *Maxwell's Los Angeles City Directory* (Los Angeles: Los Angeles Directory Company, 1895), 207; *Austin (TX) American-Statesman*, August 26, 1890, 6.

5. "Tragedy at Goldsboro," *Raleigh (NC) News and Observer*, July 14, 1888, 4; "Howard Anderson Hanged at Goldsboro," *Wilmington (NC) Messenger*, February 28, 1889, 1.

6. "Local News," *Goldsboro (NC) Headlight*, March 12, 1890, 5.

7. John Shelton Reed and Dale Volberg Reed, with William McKinney, *Holy Smoke: The Big Book of North Carolina Barbecue* (Chapel Hill: University of North Carolina Press), 60;

"Barbecue Stand," *Charlotte (NC) Observer*, March 30, 1899; "People's Column," *Charlotte (NC) Observer*, April 12, 1899.

8. Fire reports in *Dallas Morning News*, May 24, 1897, October 24, 1897, and November 4, 1898; *Faucett v. State*, 134 P. 839 10 Okla. Cr. 111 No. A-1207 (Criminal Court of Appeals of Oklahoma, 1913); *Kintz v. State*, 12 Okla. Cr. 95 152 P. 139 (1915); *Winterman v. State*, 179 S.W. 704 No. 3648 (Court of Criminal Appeals of Texas, 1915).

9. *Carolina Spartan* (Spartanburg, SC), August 13, 1868, quoted in Works Progress Administration, *A History of Spartanburg County* (Spartanburg: Band & White, 1940), 159. In some areas, such as the Midlands of South Carolina, it's still common for barbecue restaurants to be open only Thursday through Saturday.

10. Martha McCulloch-Williams, *Dishes and Beverages of the Old South* (New York: McBride, Nast, 1915), 275.

11. Quoted in Reed and Reed, *Holy Smoke*, 254.

12. See Bob Garner, *North Carolina Barbecue: Flavored by Time* (Winston-Salem, NC: John F. Blair, 1996), 7–8, 88; Jerry Bledsoe, "Even Yankees Know of Melton's Barbecue," *Charlotte (NC) Observer*, August 21, 1977, E1.

13. Bob Garner, "Six Generations of Barbecue," *Greenville (NC) Daily Reflector*, June 10, 2018, www.reflector.com.

14. Garner, *North Carolina Barbecue*, 8–13; Greg Johnson and Vince Staten, *Real Barbecue* (New York: Harper & Row, 1988), 74–76; Reed and Reed, *Holy Smoke*, 68–69.

15. *State* (Columbia, SC), July 4, 1923.

16. *State* (Columbia, SC), September 1, 1930, 8; *Columbia City Directories, 1912–1950*; "E. B. Lever Dies, Rites Tomorrow," *Columbia (SC) Record*, January 13, 1954, 23. In the first edition of this book, I noted that a man named Ray Lever kept the family style going with his restaurant near Blythewood, north of Columbia. Subsequent research shows that he was not related to E. B. Lever.

17. "Barbecue Stand Prey of Flames," *Virginian-Pilot* (Norfolk, VA), October 20, 1931, 16; "Refreshment Stand Destroyed by Fire," *Virginian-Pilot* (Norfolk, VA), September 2, 1932, 16.

18. *Virginian-Pilot* (Norfolk, VA), June 13, 1931, 12.

19. "Barbecue Dinner," *Atlanta Georgian*, July 30, 1906, 8; "A. M. Verner, Sr., 69, Cafe Owner, Passes," *Atlanta Constitution*, March 27, 1934, 18.

20. Robert F. Moss, "From Hooch to Haute Cuisine," *Charleston (SC) Post and Courier*, December 8, 2015.

21. Joe York, *BBGBBQ* (documentary film), Southern Foodways Alliance, accessed August 16, 2018, vimeo.com.

22. Pat Davis Sr., interview by Amy Evans, Southern Foodways Alliance oral history program, accessed August 16, 2018, www.southernfoodways.org

23. *Memphis City Directories, 1920–1958*; "Mills' on Vacation in Natchez," *Pittsburgh Courier*, July 25, 1936, 19; "Famous Foods: 'Barbecue King' Admits He Is Good, but Won't Give Any of His Secrets," *Rockford (IL) Register-Republic*, August 4, 1938, 12.

24. James Willis, interview by Brian Fisher, Southern Foodways Alliance oral history program, accessed August 17, 2018, www.southernfoodways.org.

25. Marcie Cohen Ferris, "We Didn't Know from Fatback," in *Cornbread Nation 2*, ed. Lolis Eric Elie (Chapel Hill: University of North Carolina Press, 2004), 97–103.

26. Rick Montgomery and Shirl Kasper, *Kansas City: An American Story* (Kansas City, MO: Kansas City Star Books, 1999), 102–13, 121.

27. Montgomery and Kasper, *Kansas City*, 169.

28. Montgomery and Kasper, 18; "Directory of the Negro League of Kansas City," *Kansas City (MO) Sun*, August 29, 1914, 2; "Henry Perry Has Cooked Good Barbecue for 50 Years," *Kansas City (MO) Call*, February 26, 1932, 1.

29. Doug Worgul and other chroniclers of Kansas City barbecue have recorded that Charlie Bryant became a business owner when he bought Perry's stand after the Barbecue King died in 1940. But Bryant's obituary in the *Kansas City Call* as well as city directories from the period show that Bryant was operating his own restaurant a few blocks away from Perry's throughout the 1930s. Obituary of Charlie Byant, *Kansas City (MO) Call*, November 10, 1952, 1; Doug Worgul, *The Grand Barbecue: A Celebration of the History, Places, Personalities, and Techniques of Kansas City Barbecue* (Kansas City, MO: Kansas City Star Books, 2001), 21–25.

30. Worgul, *Grand Barbecue*, 21.

31. Worgul, 37–38.

32. "Local Laconics," *Owensboro (KY) Messenger*, October 1, 1899, 12; "Owensboro Happenings," *Owensboro (KY) Messenger*, August 14, 1932, 4; "Miscellaneous," *Owensboro (KY) Messenger*, July 7, 1908, 6.

33. "Harry Green Has Passed Away," *Owensboro (KY) Messenger*, October 8, 1922, 2. In *Southern Food*, John Egerton wrote, "In 1890, a black man named Harry Green opened the first commercial barbecue stand in Owensboro," and that has caused many other commentators to state that Owensboro's first barbecue restaurant opened in 1890. Newspaper records, though, make it clear that although Green was cooking for events in the 1890s, he never owned a true restaurant and didn't start his commercial sales until around 1908. See John Egerton, *Southern Food: At Home, on the Road, in History* (New York: Knopf, 1987), 161–62.

34. John Foreman, interview by the author, September 30, 2015.

35. "Charles K. Forman," *Owensboro (KY) Messenger*, February 9, 1941, 8; advertisement, *Owensboro (KY) Messenger*, May 8, 1954, 5.

36. Walsh, *Legends of Texas Barbecue*, 16.

37. Daniel Vaughn, "Interview: Robert Patillo of Patillo's Bar-B-Q," *Texas Monthly*, April 8, 2015.

38. Vaughn, "Interview"; advertisement, *Beaumont (TX) Journal*, March 1, 1935, 12.

39. *Houston, Texas, City Directories, 1917–1936* (Houston: R. L. Polk).

40. Robb Walsh, "The Art of Smoke," *Houston Press*, August 24, 2000; Robb Walsh, "Barbecue in Black and White: Carving the Racism out of Texas Barbecue Mythology," *Houston Press*, May 5, 2003.

41. "Desire for Barbecue Burns in Lockhart Market," *Dallas Morning News*, October 8, 1878, 11.

42. Walsh, *Legends of Texas Barbecue*, 154.

43. Walsh, 154–57.

44. "Central Texas BBQ Dynasties," *Austin (TX) Chronicle*, November 9, 2001, food section.

45. A detailed treatment of the preparation of traditional Texas barbacoa can be found in Mario Montaño, "The History of Mexican Folk Foodways of South Texas: Street Vendors, Offal Foods, and Barbacoa de Cabeza" (PhD diss., University of Pennsylvania, 1992).

46. Quoted in Worgul, *Grand Barbecue*, 31.

47. Sadie B. Hornsby, "The Barbecue Stand," Federal Writers' Project Papers #3709, Southern Historical Collection, Manuscripts Department, Wilson Library, University of North Carolina at Chapel Hill.

48. John A. Jakle and Keith A. Scully, *Fast Food: Roadside Restaurants in the Automobile Age* (Baltimore: Johns Hopkins University Press, 1999), 40.

49. Rose Brown and Bob Brown, "A Good Roasting," *Collier's*, September 4, 1937, 28; Cecil Roberts quoted in Jakle and Scully, *Fast Food*, 43; "The Great American Roadside," *Fortune*, September 1934, 62.

50. *Burlington (NC) Daily Times*, April 12, 1930, 3, 6; July 30, 1930, 1; August 1, 1930, 5; November 21, 1930, 2; February 11, 1932, 6.

51. Michael Karl Witzel, *The American Drive-In* (Osceola, WI: Motorbooks International, 1994), 25–27; Dwayne Jones, "What's New with the Pig Stands—Not the Pig Sandwich!," *National Park Service Cultural Resource Management* 9 (1996).

52. Egerton, *Southern Food*, 150.

Chapter 7

1. Nell B. Nichols, "A Back Yard Barbecue," *Woman's Home Companion*, August 1924, 51.

2. Doris Hudson Moss, "Real Barbecues," *American Home*, August 1936, 29, 51; George A. Sanderson and Virginia Rich, *Sunset's Barbecue Book* (San Francisco: Sunset Magazine, 1939), 5.

3. Sanderson and Rich, *Sunset's Barbecue Book*, 5; Kevin Starr, *The Dream Endures: California Enters the 1940s* (New York: Oxford University Press, 2002), 7.

4. D. S. Graham Jr., "Outdoor Grills for the California Home," *Touring Topics*, November 1933, 28; Genevieve Callahan, "Here's the News in Barbecues," *Better Homes and Gardens*, May 1941, 50.

5. "Backyard Barbecue Solves War's Entertainment Problem," *Deming (NM) Headlight*, June 19, 1942, 4; "Outdoor Grills," repr., *Fitchburg (MA) Sentinel*, August 11, 1942, 6, 10; Sylvia Lovegren, *Fashionable Food: Seven Decades of Food Fads* (New York: Macmillan, 1995), 121.

6. Harold Coggins, "My Barbecue Pit," *Atlantic Monthly*, June 1947, 114.

7. Sanderson and Rich, *Sunset's Barbecue Book*, 55–58; Rufus Jarman, "Dixie's Most Disputed Dish," *Saturday Evening Post*, July 3, 1954. In a nod to barbecue's heritage, *Sunset's Barbecue Book* does include directions for old-fashioned "pit barbecue" that describes the typical large portions of meat cooked on iron spits over a hand-dug pit in the ground.

8. "The History of Weber," Weber-Stephen Products, accessed August 19, 2007, www.weber.com.

9. Robert L. Wolke, *What Einstein Told His Cook 2* (New York: W. W. Norton, 2004), 318–19; "Immense Revenue from By-Products for Ford's Plants," *Appleton (WI) Post-Crescent*, February 20, 1925, 26. During the 1920s Ford undertook an extensive effort to reclaim waste from automobile manufacturing and sell it for additional revenue. These products included Portland cement made from blast furnace slag, benzol and ammonium sulfate by-products from coke production, and—most important for America's backyard chefs—charcoal briquettes. By 1925, Ford was generating nearly $4 million in sales from recaptured by-products.

10. *Sheboygan (WI) Press*, July 1, 1930, 13, and June 2, 1931, 2.

11. In recent years there has been a return to lump charcoal by barbecue enthusiasts, who find that it provides better flavor and are skeptical of the various fillers and additives in briquettes. But lump charcoal's share of the market remains small.

12. "Gas Grills Find Favor with Chefs," *Dallas Morning News*, April 23, 1964, 6:2; "Arkla Air Conditioning Co. Moves into Air Cooled Equipment Field," *Dallas Morning News*, June 12, 1966, K13.

13. Alina Tugend, "Grilling Burgers on a Ferrari in the Backyard," *New York Times*, July 21, 2007, C5.

14. *Atlanta Constitution*, January 31, 1909, 11.

15. S. R. Dull, *Southern Cooking* (Atlanta: Ruralist, 1928); Dorothy Malone, *Cookbook for Brides* (New York: A. A. Wyn, 1947), 47.

Chapter 8

1. Nick Vergos, interview by Brian Fisher, October 16, 2002, Southern Foodways Alliance oral history program, accessed August 26, 2018, www.southernfoodways.org.

2. Vergos, interview; Steven Raichlen, *BBQ USA: 425 Recipes from All across America* (New York: Workman, 2003), 36.

3. "Greek Restaurateurs in Birmingham," March 13, 2005, Southern Foodways Alliance oral history program, accessed August 26, 2018, www.southernfoodways.org; Reed and Reed, *Holy Smoke*, 70.

4. "The NCBS Historic Barbecue Trail," North Carolina Barbecue Society, accessed March 8, 2009, www.ncbbqsociety.com.

5. Rufus Jarman, "Dixie's Most Disputed Dish," *Saturday Evening Post*, July 3, 1954, 89; David Cecelski, "E. R. Mitchell: Backyard Barbecue," *Raleigh News & Observer*, October 8, 2000.

6. Roy G. Taylor, *Sharecropper: The Way We Really Were* (Wilson, NC: J-Mark, 1984), 118–19.

7. August Kohn, *The Cotton Mills of South Carolina, 1907* (Columbia: South Carolina Department of Agriculture, 1907), 164; Reed and Reed, *Holy Smoke*, 52; "Thousand Textile Union Members at Barbecue," *Charlotte (NC) Observer*, June 7, 1919, 3.

8. Samuel Mitrani, "Labor Day," in *Encyclopedia of U.S. Labor and Working-Class History*, ed. Eric Arnesen (New York: Taylor & Francis, 2007), 760–61.

9. "Sam Rayburn to Address Labor Day Rally," *Dallas Morning News*, August 12, 1955, 13; "Gala Labor Day Celebrators to Close Busy Summer Season," *Dallas Morning News*, August 1956, 2:1.

10. Reed and Reed, *Holy Smoke*, 53.

11. "A History: 1929 to 1979 Plus . . .," *Mallard Creek Barbecue* (blog), accessed August 26, 2018, mallardcreekbbq.com.

12. Kathleen Purvis, "Pressing the Flesh, Dishing the Pork," *Charlotte (NC) Observer*, October 27, 2004, 1, 8.

13. Jarman, "Dixie's Most Disputed Dish," 90.

14. Quoted in Garner, *North Carolina Barbecue*, xiv.

15. "His Inaugural to Be Old-Fashioned," *Danville (VA) Bee*, December 30, 1922, 8; "Governor Asks Provisions for 200,000 Guests," *Duluth (MN) News-Tribune*, December 24, 1922.

16. "50,000 Already Present for Walton Ceremonies," *Dallas Morning News*, January 9, 1923, 4; Amy Dee Stephens, "It Started with a Deer," *Outdoor Oklahoma* 61 (January–February 2005): 12.

17. "22,000 Gallons of Soup, Made from Barbecue Leftovers," *San Antonio Express*, January 11, 1923.

18. "50,000 Already Present for Walton Ceremonies," *Dallas Morning News*, January 9, 1923, 4.

19. "Mammoth Barbecue to Mark Louisiana's Inauguration," *St. Petersburg (FL) Times*, May 13, 1940, 5; "Barbecue in Austin," *Time*, February 3, 1941. Huey Long was assassinated in 1935, but his machine remained in power in the state through the administrations of Richard W. Leche, who was elected to fill Long's seat, and Earl Long, Huey's brother, who was appointed to fill Leche's seat when Leche became the first Louisiana governor to be sentenced to prison.

20. William Anderson, *The Wild Man from Sugar Creek* (Baton Rouge: Louisiana State University Press, 1975), 64.

21. Quoted in Anderson, *Wild Man*, 69.

22. Jarman, "Dixie's Most Disputed Dish," 37.

23. James N. Gregory, *The Southern Diaspora: How the Great Migrations of Black and White Southerners Transformed America* (Chapel Hill: University of North Carolina Press, 2006), 12–19. The out-migration of white southerners was even greater during this period (over 2.5 million whites left the South during the 1940s alone), though they were moving to regions whose populations were already predominantly white and the shift in demographics was not as readily apparent. As Gregory argues, "the fate of white and black southerners outside their home region was often intertwined," and the southern diaspora in general was a transforming force for popular music and reshaped northern and West Coast political and religious life.

24. "Gives South Side a Thriving Zoo, $15,000 Hobby," *Chicago Tribune*, August 21, 1932, 47; "'Widow's Mite' Turns Out to Be a Check for $50," *Chicago Tribune*, June 24, 1928, 12. In the April 29, 1935, issue of the *Chicago Tribune*, the classified ads list five barbecue stands for sale outside the city proper.

25. James Lemons, interview by Amy Evans, March 26, 2008, Southern Foodways Alliance oral history program, accessed September 2, 2018, www.southernfoodways.org.

26. "Black Business Scores in Barbecue Sauce Trade," *Chicago Tribune*, November 14, 2017, 205; Brad Webber, "Restaurateur Created Mumbo Barbecue Sauce," *Chicago Tribune*, February 6, 2003, 2–10; Tracy Mack, "Adding Sizzle to the Grill," *Chicago Tribune*, May 22, 2007, 4.

27. Mike Espy, interview, Nash and Taggart Collection, University of Mississippi Libraries, accessed October 4, 2018, clio.lib.olemiss.edu.

28. "Barons of Barbecue," *Chicago Tribune*, June 28, 1995, 267.

29. "Founded Leon's Bar-B-Q," *Chicago Tribune*, April 6, 2008, 5; Espy, interview.

30. Hal K. Rothman, *LBJ's Texas White House: "Our Heart's Home"* (College Station: Texas A&M University Press, 2001), 166–69; Walsh, *Legends of Texas Barbecue*, 33; "Fort Worth Rites Set for 'Barbecue King,'" *Dallas Morning News*, January 30, 1968, 5; "Washington Texans Whoop It Up at Maryland Barbecue," *Dallas Morning News*, October 7, 1951, 2; "Annual Barbecue Set on June 14 by Texans in Capital," *Dallas Morning News*, May 31, 1952, 3.

31. Walter Jetton, with Arthur Whitman, *Walter Jetton's LBJ Barbecue Cook Book* (New York: Pocket, 1965), 9.

32. Brendan Gill, "Barbecue," *New Yorker*, August 29, 1964, 22; "Fort Worth Rites Set for 'Barbecue King,'" 5.

33. "Civil Rights Act of 1964," transcript, Our Documents, accessed August 27, 2018, www.ourdocuments.gov.

34. Richard C. Courtner, *Civil Rights and Public Accommodations: The Heart of Atlanta Motel and McClung Cases* (Lawrence: University Press of Kansas, 2001), 64–65.

35. *Katzenbach v. McClung*, FindLaw.com, accessed August 27, 2008, caselaw.findlaw.com; "Beyond a Doubt," *Time*, December 25, 1964.

36. "Bessinger Case Heard in Aiken," *Florence (SC) Morning News*, April 6, 1966, 3.

37. John Monk, "Barbecue Eatery Owner, Segregationist Maurice Bessinger Dies at 83," *State* (Columbia, SC), February 24, 2014.

38. Jim Shahin, "They Fed the Civil Rights Movement. Now Are Black-Owned Barbecue Joints Dying?," *Washington Post*, February 22, 2016.

39. "Young Remembers King in 'Heaven,'" *Atlanta Constitution*, December 11, 1985, 1-B; Jim Shahin, "MLK's Booth at His Go-To Barbecue Joint Became a Memorial. Then It Disappeared," *Washington Post*, September 19, 2016; John Kelso, "Georgia Split on Barbecue," *Austin (TX) American-Statesman*, September 19, 1985, 17. By the time Ernest Alexander died in 1986, Aleck's Barbecue Heaven was the last of his six restaurants still in business. It closed for good in the late 1990s, when the city seized the property through eminent domain and allowed a supermarket to be built on the site.

Chapter 9

1. R. David Thomas, *Dave's Way: A New Approach to Old-Fashioned Success* (New York: Putnam, 1991), 70.

2. Thomas, *Dave's Way*, 72. For the sake of accuracy, we should say that none of those Wendy's locations served barbecue until 2014, when the corporation's "Innovation Center" concocted a pulled pork barbecue sandwich on a brioche bun and rolled it out to six thousand locations across the United States. It lasted about a year.

3. Witzel, *American Drive-In*, 106–16.

4. Philip Langdon, *Orange Roofs, Golden Arches: The Architecture of American Chain Restaurants* (New York: Knopf, 1986), 74–75.

5. Reed and Reed, *Holy Smoke*, 245. Willie Bob Melton quoted in Jerry Bledsoe, "Even Yankees Know of Melton's Barbecue," *Charlotte (NC) Observer*, 1977.

6. Kathleen Zobel, "Hog Heaven: Barbecue in the South," *Southern Exposure* 5 (Summer and Fall 1977): 61; Alton Beck quoted in Jerry Bledsoe, "Lexington: The Last Bastion of Real Barbecue," *Charlotte (NC) Observer*, August 23, 1977, 8A; wood vs. gas statistics compiled by the author from restaurant surveys in Allie Patricia Wall and Ron L. Layne, *Hog Heaven: A Guide to South Carolina Barbecue* (Lexington, SC: Sandlapper Store, 1979).

7. South Carolina Department of Health and Environmental Control, *Regulation 61–25: Retail Food Establishments*, 148–49. DHEC's expansive definition of barbecue makes no mention of fuel source, calling it "a single process method of cooking by which meat, poultry or fish (either whole or in pieces) is covered and slow cooked in a pit or on a spit, using an indirect or direct heat source."

8. Scott Sexton, "Smoke from Barbecue Restaurants in Winston-Salem Sparks Burning Debate," *Winston-Salem (NC) Journal*, July 25, 2017. Kudos to the editor for packing not one but three smoke/fire references into the headline.

9. For a detailed description of the various types of pits used by barbecue restaurants in the 1970s, see Wall and Layne, *Hog Heaven*, 5–10.

10. Walsh, *Legends of Texas Barbecue*, 210; US Department of Agriculture, Economic Research Service, 2004; Daniel Vaughn, "The History of Smoked Brisket," *Texas Monthly*, January 24, 2014.

Chapter 10

1. Max Brantley, "The Ribs Hit the Fan," *Arkansas Gazette*, July 21, 1977, repr., *Cornbread Nation 2*, ed. Lolis Eric Elie (Chapel Hill: University of North Carolina Press, 2004), 108–10.

2. Vic Gold, "Beyond Grits," *Washington Post Potomac Magazine*, July 17, 1977.

3. Jerry Bledsoe, "Lexington: The Last Bastion of Real Barbecue," *Charlotte (NC) Observer*, August 23, 1977, 8A.

4. Calvin Trillin, preface to *The Tummy Trilogy* (New York: Farrar, Straus and Giroux, 1994), xi.

5. Trillin, *Tummy Trilogy*, 17; Calvin Trillin, "Stalking the Barbecued Mutton," *New Yorker*, February 7, 1977, 76.

6. Vince Staten, "Real Barbecue Revisited," in *Cornbread Nation 2*, ed. Lolis Eric Elie (Chapel Hill, University of North Carolina Press, 2004), 138; Lolis Eric Elie, *Smokestack Lightning: Adventures in the Heart of Barbecue Country* (1996; repr., New York: Ten Speed Press, 2005), viii–ix.

7. "History of World Championship Barbecue Cooking Contest," *Memphis Commercial Appeal* (blog), accessed January 4, 2009, blog.commercialappeal.com (no longer available); Calvin Trillin, "Thoughts of an Eater with Smoke in His Eyes," *New Yorker*, August 12, 1985, 56.

8. Trillin, "Thoughts of an Eater," 58–59.

9. Robb Walsh, "Summer and Smoke," *Natural History*, August 1996, 68; Carolyn Wells, interview by the author, September 2, 2008.

10. Calvin Trillin, "Barbecue and Home," in *Feeding a Yen: Local Specialties, from Kansas City to Cuzco* (New York: Random House, 2004), 181.

11. Quoted in Matt Guarente, "Griller Warfare," *Independent*, June 15, 2003.

12. "Forecasted Retail Sales Value of Barbecue Sauces in the United States from 2017 and 2021," Statista, accessed October 6, 2018, www.statista.com.

13. As the varieties expanded, the lines became blurred between processed mass-market sauces and homemade originals. Most restaurants simply placed bottles of Heinz ketchup and French's mustard on their tables and made no pretense of creating their own versions. Barbecue sauce was different. A study by *Restaurants & Institutions* magazine showed that it was the condiment that operators most frequently "customized." French's Cattlemen's Barbecue Sauce, the top-selling food service brand, was marketed directly to restaurants as being "extendable," with advertisements promising restaurateurs, "You can add on-hand ingredients to Cattlemen's Barbecue Sauces to increase servings or create signature sauces without sacrificing depth of flavor." "Private label" sauces, produced by large manufacturers and repackaged by restaurants and other retailers, became a big business, too. That tasty "secret-recipe" sauce down at the local barbecue joint might not have been quite as local as some diners thought.

14. Anthony Clark, "Founder Reflects as Sonny's Turns 40," *Gainesville (FL) Sun*, September 7, 2008.

15. Allison Perlik, "Hot Spots: Taking Their 'Cue," *Restaurants & Institutions*, May 1, 2004.

16. Janice Matsumoto, "Pit Boss: Proper Equipment Can Turn Smoke into Sales," *Restaurants & Institutions*, May 15, 2002.

17. Staten, "Real Barbecue Revisited," 139.

Afterword

1. John T. Edge, *The Potlikker Papers: A Food History of the Modern South* (New York: Penguin, 2017), 259.

2. Peter Meehan, "The Brisket Speaks with a Texas Accent," *New York Times*, July 11, 2007, F10.

3. John T. Edge, "Pig, Smoke, Pit: This Food Is Seriously Slow," *New York Times*, June 9, 2009, D1.

4. Aaron Franklin and Jordan Mackay, *Franklin Barbecue: A Meat-Smoking Manifesto* (Berkeley, CA: Ten Speed Press, 2015), 10–35.

5. Alice Laussade, "Three Hours from Now, You Could Be in Brisket Heaven," *Dallas Observer*, July 15, 2010; "Inside the Dining Guide," *Austin (TX) American-Statesman*, November 5, 2010, S2.

6. Paula Forbes, "Bon Appetit Declares Franklin the Best Barbecue in America," *Eater Austin*, June 15, 2011; Joe Nick Patoski, "Barbecue's New Battle Breaks Out in Austin," *New York Times*, June 18, 2011. Knowlton's declaration came out in the July 2011 print edition of *Bon Appétit*, but in an indication of how fast barbecue buzz could spread in the new world of social media, by the time the issue was officially on newsstands the story was already being discussed and responded to by both bloggers and mainstream journalists like Forbes and Patoski. *Eater's* coverage was grouped under the breathless content tag "ZOMG BBQ."

7. Patricia Sharpe, "The Mount Everest of Barbecue," *Texas Monthly*, May 17, 2013.

8. J. C. Reid, "Have We Reached Peak Barbecue?," *Houston Chronicle*, April 3, 2015.

9. Jim Shahin, "Today's South Carolina Barbecue Is Chef-Inspired, Upscale—and the Future," *Washington Post*, August 2, 2016.

10. Another Orangeburg County family, the Dukes, brought their Midlands style of cooking to the Lowcountry, too. They long maintained an outpost in North Charleston, though the barbecue itself was cooked at the family's restaurant up in Orangeburg. That style can still be found at the Dukes out on James Island, where the buffet brims with hash and rice, yellow mustard sauce, and loaves of white bread.

11. Jim Shahin, "Why North Carolina's Barbecue Scene Is Still Smoldering," *Washington Post*, September 21, 2015.

12. Robb Walsh, "7 Dirty Truths about BBQ (That Nobody Wants to Talk About)," *First We Feast*, July 15, 2015; Hilary Cadigan, "The Unmistakable Bryan Furman, Georgia's New King of Barbecue," *Bon Appétit*, June 25, 2018.

13. Michael Twitty, "Barbecue Is an American Tradition—of Enslaved Africans and Native Americans," *Guardian*, July 4, 2015; Jim Shahin, "They Fed the Civil Rights Movement. Now Are Black-Owned Barbecue Joints Dying?," *Washington Post*, February 22, 2016.

REFERENCES

Books on Barbecue

Auchmutey, Jim. *Smoke Lore: A Short History of Barbecue in America*. Athens: University of Georgia Press, 2019.

Berry, Wes. *The Kentucky Barbecue Book*. Lexington: University Press of Kentucky, 2013.

Caldwell, Wilber W. *Searching for the Dixie Barbecue: Journeys into the Southern Psyche*. Sarasota, FL: Pineapple Press, 2005.

Elie, Lolis Eric, ed. *Cornbread Nation 2: The United States of Barbecue*. Chapel Hill: University of North Carolina Press, 2004.

———, ed. *Smokestack Lightning: Adventures in the Heart of Barbecue Country*. New York: Farrar, Strauss, and Giroux, 1996. Reprint, New York: Ten Speed Press, 2005.

Fertel, Rien. *One True Barbecue: Fire, Smoke, and the Pitmasters Who Cook the Whole Hog*. New York: Touchstone, 2016.

Franklin, Aaron, and Jordan Mackay. *Franklin Barbecue: A Meat-Smoking Manifesto*. Berkeley, CA: Ten Speed Press, 2015.

Garner, Bob. *North Carolina Barbecue: Flavored by Time*. Winston-Salem, NC: John F. Blair, 1996.

Haynes, Joseph R. *Virginia Barbecue: A History*. Charleston, SC: History Press, 2016.

Johnson, Greg, and Vince Staten. *Real Barbecue*. New York: Harper & Row, 1988.

Johnson, Mark A. *An Irresistible History of Alabama Barbecue: From Wood Pit to White Sauce*. Charleston, SC: History Press, 2017.

Jones, Sam, and Daniel Vaughn. *Whole Hog BBQ: The Gospel of Carolina Barbecue*. Berkeley, CA: Ten Speed Press, 2019.

McSpadden, Wyatt. *Texas BBQ*. Austin: University of Texas Press, 2009.

Meek, Craig David. *Memphis Barbecue: A Succulent History of Smoke, Sauce & Soul*. Charleston, SC: History Press, 2014.

Moss, Robert F. *Barbecue Lovers: The Carolinas.* Guilford, CT: Globe Pequot, 2015.

Reed, John Shelton. *Barbecue: A Savor the South Cookbook.* Chapel Hill: University of North Carolina Press, 2016.

Reed, John Shelton, and Dale Volberg Reed. With William McKinney. *Holy Smoke: The Big Book of North Carolina Barbecue.* Chapel Hill: University of North Carolina Press, 2008.

Vaughn, Daniel. *Prophets of Smoked Meat: A Journey through Texas Barbecue.* New York: Ecco, 2013.

Veteto, James R., and Edward M. Maclin, eds. *The Slaw and the Slow Cooked: Culture and Barbecue in the Mid-South.* Nashville: Vanderbilt University Press, 2011.

Wall, Allie Patricia, and Ron L. Hayne. *Hog Heaven: A Guide to South Carolina Barbecue.* Lexington, SC: Sandlapper Store, 1979.

Walsh, Robb. *Barbecue Crossroads: Notes & Recipes from a Southern Odyssey.* Austin: University of Texas Press, 2013.

———. *Legends of Texas Barbecue Cookbook.* San Francisco: Chronicle Books, 2002.

Warnes, Andrew. *Savage Barbecue: Race, Culture, and the Invention of America's First Food.* Athens: University of Georgia Press, 2008.

Worgul, Doug. *The Grand Barbecue: A Celebration of the History, Places, Personalities, and Techniques of Kansas City Barbecue.* Kansas City, MO: Kansas City Star Books, 2001.

Articles on Barbecue

Andrews, Maude. "The Georgia Barbecue." *Harper's Weekly,* November 9, 1895, 1072.

Bass, S. Jonathan. "'How 'Bout a Hand for the Hog': The Enduring Nature of the Swine as a Cultural Symbol of the South." *Southern Cultures* 21, no. 3 (Spring 1995): 301–20.

Hitt, Jack. "A Confederacy of Sauces." *New York Times Magazine,* August 26, 2001, 28–31.

Jarman, Rufus. "Dixie's Most Disputed Dish." *Saturday Evening Post,* March 7, 1954, 36–91.

Lovegren, Sylvia. "Barbecue." *American Heritage* 54, no. 3 (June 2003): 36–44.

Shahin, Jim. "They Fed the Civil Rights Movement. Now Are Black-Owned Barbecue Joints Dying?" *Washington Post,* February 22, 2016.

Walsh, Robb. "Barbecue in Black and White: Carving the Racism out of Texas Barbecue Mythology." *Houston Press,* May 5, 2003.

———. "Summer and Smoke." *Natural History* 105, no. 8 (August 1996): 68–72.

Zobel, Kathleen. "Hog Heaven: Barbecue in the South." *Southern Exposure* 5 (Summer and Fall 1977): 61.

Online Resource

Southern Foodways Alliance oral history program, www.southernfoodways.org

Historical Context

Brickell, John. *The Natural History of North Carolina*. Dublin, 1737.

Courtner, Richard C. *Civil Rights and Public Accommodations: The Heart of Atlanta Motel and McClung Cases*. Lawrence: University Press of Kansas, 2001.

Dupre, Daniel S. *Transforming the Cotton Frontier: Madison County, Alabama, 1800–1840*. Baton Rouge: Louisiana State University Press, 1997.

Edge, John T. *The Potlikker Papers: A Food History of the Modern South*. New York: Penguin, 2017.

Egerton, John. *Southern Food: At Home, on the Road, in History*. New York: Knopf, 1987.

Fischer, David Hackett. *Albion's Seed: Four British Folkways in America*. New York: Oxford University Press, 1989.

Foote, William Henry. *Sketches of North Carolina, Historical and Biographical, Illustrative of the Principles of a Portion of Her Early Settlers*. New York, 1846.

Gregory, James N. *The Southern Diaspora: How the Great Migrations of Black and White Southerners Transformed America*. Chapel Hill: University of North Carolina Press, 2006.

Hilliard, Sam Bowers. *Hog Meat and Hoecake: Food Supply in the Old South, 1840–1860*. Carbondale: Southern Illinois University Press, 1972.

Isaac, Rhys. *The Transformation of Virginia, 1740–1790*. New York: Norton, 1982.

Jakle, John A., and Keith A. Scully. *Fast Food: Roadside Restaurants in the Automobile Age*. Baltimore: Johns Hopkins University Press, 1999.

Lovegren, Sylvia. *Fashionable Food: Seven Decades of Food Fads*. New York: Macmillan, 1995.

Montaño, Mario. "The History of Mexican Folk Foodways of South Texas: Street Vendors, Offal Foods, and Barbacoa de Cabeza." PhD diss., University of Pennsylvania, 1992.

Moore, John Hammond. *The Confederate Housewife*. Columbia, SC: Summerhouse Press, 1997.

Root, Waverly, and Richard de Rochemont. *Eating in America: A History*. New York: Morrow, 1976.

Sydnor, Charles S. *American Revolutionaries in the Making: Political Practices in Washington's Virginia*. 1952. Reprint, New York: Free Press, 1965.

Witzel, Michael Karl. *The American Drive-In*. Osceola, WI: Motorbooks International, 1994.

Woodmason, Charles. *The Carolina Backcountry on the Eve of the Revolution*. Edited by Richard S. Hooker. Chapel Hill: University of North Carolina Press, 1953.

INDEX